Representation through Taxation

Social scientists teach that politicians favor groups that are organized over those that are not. *Representation through Taxation* challenges this conventional wisdom. Emphasizing that there are limits to what organized interests can credibly promise in return for favorable treatment, Gehlbach shows that politicians may instead give preference to groups – organized or not – that by their nature happen to take actions that are politically valuable. Gehlbach develops this argument in the context of the postcommunist experience, focusing on the incentive of politicians to promote sectors that are naturally more tax compliant, regardless of their organization. In the former Soviet Union, tax systems were structured around familiar revenue sources, magnifying this incentive and helping to prejudice policy against new private enterprise. In Eastern Europe, in contrast, tax systems were created to cast the revenue net more widely, encouraging politicians to provide the collective goods necessary for new firms to flourish.

Scott Gehlbach is Associate Professor of Political Science at the University of Wisconsin–Madison. He is also a research associate of CEFIR in Moscow, where he spent the 2007–2008 academic year as a Fulbright-Hays Faculty Research Abroad Fellow, and is a recent recipient of an SSRC Eurasia Program Postdoctoral Research Fellowship. His dissertation on the political economy of taxation in postcommunist states, upon which this book is based, won the Mancur Olson Award for the best dissertation in the field of political economy. Professor Gehlbach is the author of numerous articles in leading journals, including the *American Political Science Review*, the *American Journal of Political Science*, and the *Journal of Politics*. He received his Ph.D. in political science and economics from the University of California–Berkeley.

T0382619

Cambridge Studies in Comparative Politics

General Editor
Margaret Levi   *University of Washington, Seattle*

Assistant General Editor
Stephen Hanson   *University of Washington, Seattle*

Associate Editors
Robert H. Bates   *Harvard University*
Torben Iversen   *Harvard University*
Stathis Kalyvas   *Yale University*
Peter Lange   *Duke University*
Helen Milner   *Princeton University*
Frances Rosenbluth   *Yale University*
Susan Stokes   *Yale University*
Sidney Tarrow   *Cornell University*
Kathleen Thelen   *Northwestern University*
Erik Wibbels   *Duke University*

Other Books in the Series

(*Continues after the index*)

Representation through Taxation

REVENUE, POLITICS, AND DEVELOPMENT IN POSTCOMMUNIST STATES

SCOTT GEHLBACH

University of Wisconsin–Madison

CAMBRIDGE
UNIVERSITY PRESS

CAMBRIDGE UNIVERSITY PRESS
Cambridge, New York, Melbourne, Madrid, Cape Town,
Singapore, São Paulo, Delhi, Tokyo, Mexico City

Cambridge University Press
32 Avenue of the Americas, New York, NY 10013-2473, USA

www.cambridge.org
Information on this title: www.cambridge.org/9780521168809

First published 2008
First paperback edition 2010
Reprinted 2011

A catalog record for this publication is available from the British Library.

Library of Congress Cataloging in Publication Data

Gehlbach, Scott.
Representation through taxation : revenue, politics, and development in postcommunist
states / Scott Gehlbach.
    p. cm. – (Cambridge studies in comparative politics)
Includes bibliographical references and index.
ISBN 978-0-521-88733-5 (hardback)
1. Taxation – Political aspects – Former communist countries.   2. Taxation – Political
aspects – Europe, Eastern.   3. Taxation – Political aspects – Former Soviet republics.
I. Title. II. Series.
HJ2599.57.G44   2008
336.2009171´7–dc22   2008002442

ISBN 978-0-521-88733-5 Hardback
ISBN 978-0-521-16880-9 Paperback

*To my parents, who
showed me the world*

Fantastic grow the evening gowns;
Agents of the Fisc pursue
Absconding tax-defaulters through
The sewers of provincial towns.
                    W. H. Auden, "The Fall of Rome"

Contents

List of Tables

List of Figures

Acknowledgments

This book is the product of an outstanding intellectual environment at three institutions: the University of California at Berkeley, the Centre for Economic and Financial Research (CEFIR) in Moscow, and the University of Wisconsin at Madison. As a graduate student in political science and economics at UC Berkeley, I was taught the skills and mindset of a research scholar, and I wrote a dissertation with the support of faculty in two departments. I spent the last two years of graduate school as a visiting scholar at CEFIR, where I developed the ideas that became my dissertation. That work then matured into a book-length manuscript during my first years as a faculty member at UW Madison, during which I returned to Russia periodically. I put the finishing touches on the manuscript back at CEFIR, on leave from Madison during the 2007–2008 academic year.

At Berkeley, I benefited from the strong support of a dissertation committee under Henry Brady's generous leadership. Henry, George Akerlof, George Breslauer, Matthew Rabin, and Jim Robinson supplied a constant stream of suggestions, critiques, and advice, notwithstanding the physical distance between Berkeley and Moscow that prevented us from meeting in person. Not surprisingly, given the ecumenical approach these scholars employ in their own research, each provided encouragement as I worked to weave the perspectives of two disciplines into a coherent dissertation. I often think of, and try to live up to, their example in my own work with graduate students.

My friends and colleagues at CEFIR have provided a home and intellectual support during my periodic stays in Moscow. Academic seminars at CEFIR have been the first stop for several of my research projects, including this one, and I am grateful to those who have helped me to clarify concepts and arguments. Sergei Guriev, Konstantin Sonin, Alexandra

Vacroux, Ksenia Yudaeva, and Ekaterina Zhuravskaya in particular read and commented on multiple drafts of the work in this book, and a large portion of any credit for what follows rightly accrues to them.

At Madison, I found a community of scholars unusually generous toward junior faculty, and I have learned much from my colleagues that has enriched this and other projects. Most prominent among their contributions is the book colloquium initiated and organized by Melanie Menion, for which Graham Wilson as chair generously provided financial support from discretionary funds. Melanie, David Canon, Kathie Hendley, Jon Pevehouse, Aseema Sinha, and Dave Weimer contributed substantial time to reading the manuscript, preparing comments, and participating in the general discussion. Josh Tucker graciously agreed to be the outside discussant at this forum, taking on the task of commenting on the book *in toto*. Together, the many suggestions of the colloquium participants helped me to clarify and frame arguments, anticipate objections, smooth out rough edges, and generally produce a better product.

At various stages I benefited from the comments of seminar and conference participants. A few of these came at critical junctures in the development of this project, and I am grateful to those who helped me to choose the right path. At the October 2002 workshop of the Project on Honesty and Trust in Budapest, Janos Kornai told me I had used "three wrong words" in describing various concepts; I subsequently changed two of the three but rightly or wrongly have kept the third. The flat reception at a seminar at the Mershon Center at Ohio State encouraged me to rework the model that ultimately formed the core logic of "representation through taxation." The Duke Workshop on Post-Communist Political Economy and Democratic Politics, organized by Herbert Kitschelt and his graduate students, was an opportunity to make the transition from the article to book phase of the project. Finally, presentations of the nearly completed manuscript at Middlebury College and the Center for Russia, East Europe, and Central Asia at UW Madison gave me the opportunity to think through and receive feedback on issues that were still outstanding.

Many colleagues and friends provided helpful comments and discussions on the manuscript and its components. Beyond those mentioned previously, and those I will be embarrassed to have forgotten, I thank Marc Berenson, Erik Berglof, John Earle, Gerald Easter, Charles Franklin, Guido Friebel, Tim Frye, Pauline Jones-Luong, Cynthia Kaplan, Cathie Jo Martin, Monika Nalepa, Conor O'Dwyer, Will Pyle, Gerard Roland, Mark Schrad, Scott Straus, Dan Treisman, and Jason Wittenberg. Margaret Levi was especially generous in her feedback at multiple phases in the project's evolution, beginning with our discussion of my dissertation in Budapest and concluding with her role as series editor. I also thank Eric Crahan for his early and continual enthusiasm and for his role in shepherding the manuscript through the publishing process.

Others provided critical assistance in conducting the research in this project. Lev Shlosberg was instrumental in organizing interviews in Pskov, and Noah Buckley-Farlee and Anastasia Kokina spent days in the dusty newspaper archives at Khimki collecting newspaper articles as background research for that case study. Pradeep Mitra kindly shared the data on tax structure in postcommunist countries that I analyze in Chapter 2, and Francesca Pissarides, the SME data that I summarize in Chapter 5. Geraint Jones helpfully answered a number of questions about the BEEPS data. Finally, Galina Belokurova and Stéphane Lavertu provided invaluable help in editing the final manuscript.

A number of organizations graciously offered financial support in the form of research funding or teaching relief. I thank them for this support, which I received as a Fulbright-Hays Doctoral Dissertation Research Abroad Fellowship, an IREX Individual Advanced Research Opportunities Fellowship, an SSRC International Dissertation Research Fellowship, an SSRC Eurasia Program Postdoctoral Research Fellowship, a UW Madison Graduate School Fall Research Competition Award, and a Fulbright-Hays Faculty Research Abroad Fellowship.

Substantial portions of two of my journal articles appear here, with some modification. Chapters 3 and 4 build on "The Consequences of Collective Action: An Incomplete-Contracts Approach," *American Journal of Political Science*, 50(3):802–823. Chapter 5 is based on "Revenue Traps," *Economics and Politics*, 19(1):73–96. I thank Blackwell Publishing, publisher of both journals, for permission to reprint that material. I also thank the World Bank for permission to adapt Figure 5.3, which is taken from *Transition: The First Ten Years*, a 2002 publication of the World Bank.

I owe a special debt to John Earle, without whom I would not have become a social scientist; to Henry Brady, who made it his project to make me a political scientist; to my family, who understood intuitively that I should do what I loved as a child; and to Masha, for more than I can say without writing another book.

Note on Transliteration

I transliterate Russian-language material using the Library of Congress system, with a few exceptions:

- I use "ya" rather than "ia" and "yu" rather than "iu" when words begin with those letters.
- I use "y" at the end of names that would otherwise end in "ii."
- I use the typical spelling for words that appear commonly in English-language literature on Russia (e.g., "oblast," not "oblast'").
- I spell the names of Russian authors writing in English as they do.

1

Taxes, Representation, and Economic Development in the Russian Heartland

On November 10, 1997, Evgeny Mikhailov sat down with a handful of journalists to discuss his first year as governor of Pskov oblast, a beautiful but struggling region in northwestern Russia just over the border from Belarus and the Baltics. Mikhailov had received his share of attention the year before when he beat out the incumbent governor to become the only member of Vladimir Zhirinovsky's nationalist Liberal Democratic Party of Russia to be elected head of a Russian region. Given Zhirinovsky's often outrageous statements on questions of foreign policy – he once suggested building a giant fan to blow radioactive waste over the Baltic states – many expected Mikhailov's first year to be dominated by saber rattling and diplomatic disputes. However, Mikhailov's electoral platform had emphasized economics, not geopolitics, and in this year-end press conference the focus was on economic achievement.[1]

At the top of the governor's list of achievements during the previous year was the creation of a local vodka industry under government control. To an outsider, it might seem a strange accomplishment to trumpet. Vodka had not been produced in Pskov in recent memory, and consumers could already choose from among a wide range of vodkas produced within and outside of Russia. Any economics student would have suggested that the region focus instead on promoting those sectors in which it had some comparative advantage. In an interview three years later, the governor was explicit in naming those sectors: tourism (the region is a train ride from Moscow and St. Petersburg and boasts many early Orthodox churches and

---

[1] "Takoi korotkii dolgii god," *Pskovskaia Pravda*, November 11, 1997.

1

monasteries) and transit (Pskov oblast is a natural trade corridor between Russia and the West).[2] Vodka had no direct link to either.

Of course, nowhere is public policy governed solely by the prescriptions of an economics textbook. Whatever policy *should* be, social scientists are taught to anticipate that it *does* tend to favor those interests that are organized, that is, those that have overcome their "collective-action problems." However, in Pskov oblast there were no organized interests clamoring for local vodka production. Rather, the regional economy was organized around machine building, some light industry, food processing, and agriculture, all of which could stake a claim for government assistance and all of which suffered from the regional administration's laserlike focus on the vodka industry.[3]

Despite the lack of comparative advantage in vodka production and absence of organized interests calling for its promotion, vodka had one major advantage over other industries that the local administration might have chosen to promote: it is, by Russian standards, relatively easy to tax, a function both of the primary method of taxation (excise taxes that required that the government observe only output, not profits) and of centuries' experience in taxing alcohol.[4] And like most regions in Russia during the 1990s, Pskov oblast was starved for revenue. The collapse of the socialist economy and the Soviet state had left regional finances in tatters. The region subsisted in large part on transfers from Moscow, but this support was seen as unreliable.[5] During the electoral campaign Mikhailov had emphasized the absence of a regional financial base and the futility of counting on federal transfers,[6] and in interview after interview Pskov officials spoke of the

---

[2] "Idu na tretii srok," *Pskovskaia Pravda*, February 28, 2001. See also Centre of Social Projecting Vozrozhdeniye (2003).

[3] "Zhdem milosti u rynochnoi ekonomiki," *Pskovskaia Pravda*, July 4, 2001.

[4] On the history of vodka in Russian and Soviet politics, see, for example, White (1995) and Herlihy (2002). The relative ease of collecting unit excise taxes was stressed to me by Vadim Petrukhin, head of the oblast Committee for Economic Development and Property Relations, in an interview in Pskov on July 13, 2005. The comparatively low level of barter in the vodka sector may also have made it an attractive source of tax revenue, as in contrast to many other industries during the 1990s, taxes could be collected primarily in cash rather than in kind (Schrad, 2001; Gaddy and Ickes, 2002). Nonetheless, government support of the vodka industry in Pskov oblast continued long after barter began to disappear with the 1998 ruble devaluation. I return to the relationship between barter and taxation in Chapter 2.

[5] "Nam predlagaiut real'no smotret' pravde v glaza," *Pskovskaia Pravda*, August 6, 1998.

[6] Alexseev and Vagin (1999, p. 44).

2

need to increase local tax revenue.[7] (It is important to stress that excise tax *rates* were not under the direct control of the regional government – this is not the traditional argument that governments heavily tax goods such as alcohol for which demand is inelastic.[8])

In essence, Mikhailov opted to structure the tax base to his needs, using the instruments at his disposal to promote that economic activity that he knew he could tax. In its first year, Mikhailov proclaimed, newly established Pskovalko had contributed eight billion rubles (slightly more than one million dollars, big money in a small and impoverished region) to the regional budget, with room to grow.[9] Even after the local economy started to rebound (as did the Russian economy more generally) following the 1998 ruble devaluation, growth in the vodka sector still far outstripped that in the local economy as a whole: in the first nine months of 1999, alcohol production was up 160 percent on the year before versus 19 percent for industrial production overall.[10]

The Pskov experience was by no means unique. Throughout much of the postcommunist world, a politics characterized by "representation through taxation" took shape in the 1990s, with the representation of economic interests in the political arena determined by their anticipated tax compliance as well as by their organization. The winners – those who were best represented in the competition for resources – were not necessarily those who had overcome their collective-action problems. Rather, economic development was encouraged in sectors that were important sources of tax revenue at the expense of those that were not.[11] In other parts of the

---

[7] See, for example, "Pobeda razuma," *Pskovskaia Pravda*, June 1, 1999; "Biudzhetnye perspektivy u oblasti – est'!" *Pskovskaia Pravda*, January 11, 2000; "U nas vse voprosy vazhnye," *Pskovskaia Pravda*, December 19, 2001.

[8] If anything, inelasticity of demand would have worked against Mikhailov's strategy, as any attempt to shift the supply curve for vodka to the right would have little impact on the total quantity of vodka sold. One consequence, as I discuss later, is that sales of Pskov vodka came in considerable part at the expense of (less taxable) imports.

[9] "Takoi korotkii dolgii god," *Pskovskaia Pravda*, November 11, 1997. Mikhailov's statement predates the ruble redenomination of January 1, 1998. Official estimates of the contribution of regional alcohol policy to oblast revenues vary widely, though they are always substantial. See, for example, "U 'Skobaria' gosudarevo oko," *Pskovskaia Pravda*, June 19, 1997; "'Pskovalko' ne zhalko?" *Pskovskaia Pravda*, October 31, 1997; "A karavan idet...k situatsii na alkogol'nom rynke Pskovshchiny," *Pskovskaia Pravda*, December 11, 1997.

[10] "Na pod"eme," *Pskovskaia Pravda*, November 4, 1999.

[11] Although my argument extends far beyond the particular example of vodka politics, at least in Russia the vodka sector seems to have received particular attention in a number

postcommunist world, politics took the more familiar form of "representation through collective action," with the organization of interests the primary determinant of the provision of collective goods. Which of the two forms of politics predominated can be traced to decisions made in the early days of transition about what sort of tax systems to build following the collapse of the communist state.

In this book I tell this story. As it is a story that departs in important ways from what has become conventional wisdom in political economy, I begin by discussing the relationship of the book to what has come before. I do not aim here for an exhaustive overview of the literature: those interested in fuller contextualization will find it at the appropriate place in the chapters to follow. Rather, I place my argument in the tradition of three strands of literature, represented by three classic works of social science: Margaret Levi's *Of Rule and Revenue* (Levi, 1988), Mancur Olson's *The Logic of Collective Action* (Olson, 1965), and Robert Bates's *Markets and States in Tropical Africa* (Bates, 1981).

These three books, and the broader literatures of which they are a part, shape much of the way in which we think about revenue, politics, and development. Like all good social science, each of these perspectives is incomplete, abstracting from important features of empirical reality to focus on what is deemed most important. My aim is to show that some of what is absent or underemphasized is in fact a major part of the story, at least in that part of the world I know best. Because I suspect that similar logics may be at work in other political-economic environments, at various points in the succeeding chapters I lay out my argument in general form, hoping that experts in those environments will find my perspective instructive, if inevitably and consciously incomplete.

1.1 Structuring Tax Systems – and the Tax Base

"Rulers maximize revenue to the state, but not as they please," writes Margaret Levi in *Of Rule and Revenue*. For Levi, as for many other scholars, the desire of rulers to maximize revenue is axiomatic. Although there is the occasional exceptional case, in most places and at most times rulers value revenue for the ability it gives them to retain power, fight wars, pursue their

---

of regions beyond Pskov. See, for example, "New Rules on Alcohol Taxes Deal a Blow to Bootleggers," *Moscow Times*, January 13, 2003; "The Alcohol Issue in Russia and the Baltic Sea Region," Stockholm Centre on Health of Societies in Transition, Newsletter No. 13, June 26, 2000.

vision of the social good, and improve their own material standard of living. But because revenue to the state comes out of someone else's pocket, rulers cannot merely decree its collection. Rather, they must employ a range of carrots and sticks to encourage the transfer of wealth to the state. "The art of taxation," observed Jean Baptiste Colbert, finance minister to Louis XIV, "consists in so plucking the goose as to get the most feathers with the least hissing."

Of Rule and Revenue was one of the first systematic attempts to offer a general theory of the structure of tax systems. According to Levi, three factors influence the choice of revenue policy: the relative bargaining power of rulers vis-à-vis other actors, the transaction costs associated with negotiating and implementing a revenue policy, and the discount rates – the degree to which the present is valued relative to the future – of rulers. These three factors are in turn determined by the economic structure of society, the international context, and the form of government. Thus, for example, the gradual metamorphosis of the Roman Republic from a city-state based on subsistence agriculture into an empire dependent on grain from Sicily and Africa changed the transaction costs associated with taxation and led to the abandonment of the tribute in favor of tax farming (Levi, 1988, Ch. IV).

I begin my story by applying insights from Levi's and related work to the development of tax systems in Eastern Europe and the former Soviet Union. (Throughout the book, I follow the convention in the literature of referring to the states of Eastern Europe and the Baltics collectively as "Eastern Europe," and I use the phrase "former Soviet Union" to mean all post-Soviet states but those in the Baltics. As I will show, tax systems in the Baltic states of Estonia, Latvia, and Lithuania are indeed more East European than post-Soviet.) Taxation was largely an accounting matter under communism, and all postcommunist states faced the challenge of creating tax systems from scratch to extract revenue from private economic actors. Consistent with the framework suggested by *Of Rule and Revenue*, how these states responded to this challenge depended on incentives created by the international environment, on industrial structures inherited from communism, and on levels of economic development at the start of the postcommunist transition. Roughly speaking, the countries of Eastern Europe undertook the difficult task of learning how to tax individuals directly, in significant part to bring their tax systems in line with those of West European states ahead of the hoped-for accession to the European Union. In contrast, the countries of the former Soviet Union focused more on taxing enterprises and goods and services, the legacy of an industrial structure top-heavy with large, monopolistic enterprises, coupled with generally low levels of economic development and the absence of any realistic chance of joining the EU.

These are arguments that others have made, often based on extensive study of state institutions in particular countries, but I provide new evidence in Chapter 2 through the analysis of cross-national data on postcommunist tax structures. At the same time, I demonstrate that decisions made by state actors in structuring their tax systems had important consequences for patterns of tax compliance across the postcommunist world. In the former Soviet Union, officials focused on encouraging compliance by "old" forms of economic activity: the large, monopolistic enterprises that were the revenue base of the communist system. "New" sources of revenue, including small enterprises in competitive industries, were largely neglected. In contrast, in Eastern Europe there was a more balanced focus on new and old economic activity. The result was that "natural" differences in tax compliance were far greater in the former Soviet Union than in Eastern Europe: small firms were especially noncompliant relative to large firms, and firms in competitive industries were especially noncompliant relative to monopolies.

The consequence of these patterns of tax compliance takes me beyond the arguments in *Of Rule and Revenue* and related literature. Levi and others largely treat economic structure as given: governments form tax systems around existing economic activity rather than tampering with the economy itself. The postcommunist experience, however, suggests that governments may structure their tax *bases* to maximize revenue in the least costly way, promoting through various means those sectors that are relatively tax compliant at the expense of those that are not. In some cases, as with the creation of the vodka sector in Pskov oblast, such activity involves fundamentally *re*structuring the tax base, carving out sectors that did not previously exist for the sake of the tax revenue they will provide. In others, structuring the tax base implies maintenance of the status quo against other forces, with "old" economic activity favored over "new" because of its greater reliability as a source of revenue.

In the former Soviet Union in general, the incentive to structure the tax base to maximize revenue was especially large, given the degree to which familiar forms of economic activity remained important sources of tax revenue. In Russia in particular, federal arrangements that provided regional governments with a share of tax revenue extended the motive to regions such as Pskov. In principle, as stressed by the literature on "market-preserving federalism" (Weingast, 1995; Qian and Weingast, 1996; McKinnon, 1997), this incentive could have been blunted if regional governments anticipated that an increase in tax revenue would result in re-duced transfers from the federal government. However, in my discussions with regional officials I found little support for the notion that Pskov oblast would suffer reduced transfers to the extent that regional tax generation improved, and it is worth stressing that systematic evidence for such an effect in Russia relates only to revenue sharing between regional and local budgets, not federal and regional budgets.[12] On the contrary, as stressed above, developing the regional tax base was viewed as necessary given the unreliability of federal transfers.

Another characteristic of "market-preserving federalism" was, however, absent in Russia during the 1990s: the national constitution notwithstand-ing, regions often imposed barriers to trade with each other, thus prevent-ing the establishment of a common market across the Russian Federation. A particular example is Governor Mikhailov's creation of a state-owned distribution monopoly – the aforementioned Pskovalko – which was used to control the sale of vodka produced outside the oblast. Such "imports" – often from a neighboring region – posed two disadvantages from the per-spective of the regional budget, related to the fact that excise taxes were assessed on both the production and sale of vodka.[13] First, that portion of the excise tax collected from producers directly benefited only the region in which the vodka was produced. Second, the share of excise revenue from sales was particularly difficult to collect on imported vodka, as imports entered the distribution system through multiple channels and often with falsified documents.[14] The creation of Pskovalko gave the regional govern-ment control over price, which could be used to keep out imported vodka to the extent that such imports were routed through government distribution, while simultaneously making it easier to collect excises on that which was imported.[15] Pskovalko's monopoly status was critical to its success in ful-filling these tasks. As Mikhailov's successor Mikhail Kuznetsov would state

---

[12] See Zhuravskaya (2000). Blanchard and Shleifer (2001) suggest that poor economic perfor-mance in Russia, relative to that in China, can be linked to such fiscal disincentives. Way (2002) and Treisman (2006) provide alternative perspectives.

[13] The division between the two shifted from year to year, with consequences for the distribution of excise revenues among governments. I return to this point in Chap-ter 4.

[14] "U 'Skobaria' gosudarevo oko," *Pskovskaia Pravda*, June 19, 1997.

[15] "Otvoevannaia alkoNEzavisimost'," *Pskovskaia Lenta Novostei*, May 19, 2005.

years later in reference to the Pskovalko monopoly, it is "far more difficult to organize the control of five small enterprises than one large one."[16]

In and of itself, this local protectionism would have encouraged the production of vodka in Pskov oblast. But the Mikhailov administration did not stop there. Local vodka production was promoted both through old-fashioned (if legally contested) subsidization and through the application of what Russians euphemistically refer to as "administrative resources." With respect to the former, spirit – the basic component of vodka – was initially subsidized to reduce the production cost of vodka[17]; beginning in 1999 regional law mandated direct transfers to vodka producers.[18] The logic, delightfully expressed to me by a woman who heads a successful nonprofit organization in Pskov, is that of any investor: one takes a little money out of a bag ("meshok"), uses that money to make a profit, and then puts more money back into the bag. Of course, market institutions also provide capital for business development, but the whole point of Pskov policy was to encourage development of an industry that provided the state – not private investors – with an unusually high return.

As to the use of "administrative resources," private manufacturing assets were seized by the regional government in 1997 as payment of debt to the oblast government and used to establish Pskovpishcheprom, a vodka manufacturer majority owned by Pskovalko.[19] Over the next several years, according to an investigation by the Audit Chamber of the Russian Federation, Pskovpishcheprom would be the primary beneficiary of subsidies for vodka production[20] and eventually would displace those other local producers that had emerged after Mikhailov's election. Thus was the regional administration able to establish a state-controlled company with a dominant position on the local market on the cheap, a reminder that in

---

[16] "'U nas teper' rezhim otkrytykh dverei,'" *Ekspert Severo-Zapad*, May 30, 2005. Tarschys (1998) discusses the importance of trade monopolies for taxation.

[17] "'Goriuchee'... dlia Pskovskoi ekonomiki," *Pskovskaia Pravda*, January 16, 1997; "Brosok na Pskov," *Rossiiskaia Gazeta*, February 21, 1998.

[18] "Gospodderzhka alkogol'noi otrasli mozhet byt' otmenena," *Pskovskaia Pravda*, December 11, 2003. "Gospodderzhka proizvoditelei alkogolia zakonna, zakliuchila genprokuratura," *Pskovskaia Pravda*, May 14, 2004.

[19] "Komu prinadlezhit Pskovskaia oblast," *Pskovskaia Guberniia*, May 26, 2004; Kryshtanovskaya (2005, pp. 357–358). Readers familiar with Russian politics will recognize a strategy used at other times by regional and national authorities, most visibly in the dismantling of oil major Yukos, whose primary assets were subsequently transferred to state-owned Rosneft.

[20] The report is reprinted in "Izvineniia neumestny," *Pskovskaia Guberniia*, March 9, 2005.

contemporary Russia, as in many developing and transition countries, the state has many instruments with which to intervene in the economy.[21]

1.2 The Nature of Representation

Pskov governor Evgeny Mikhailov's strategy in building a local vodka sector was multifaceted, but the rationale behind the policy was simple, best expressed by the governor himself in an online forum in which he participated under the pseudonym "Specialist" after leaving office: "In all sensible regions the authorities fight fiercely for their producer, especially when the producer pays a lot of taxes."[22] In Pskov oblast this fight created many obvious losers: distributors who were forced out of business with the establishment of Pskovalko, owners of assets seized in the creation of Pskovpishcheprom, and producers and consumers of imported vodka. But the losses were not limited to these actors. The far greater impact may have been on those sectors that suffered from neglect as the regional administration's attention was directed elsewhere.

Mikhailov and his administration had scarce resources at their disposal. In an interview in 1997, Mikhailov spoke of "singling out one or two spheres" where he would "try to achieve success," a sentiment he echoed exactly four years later when he said that given resource constraints it was necessary to find the "most advantageous small projects."[23] In other words, Mikhailov could not be all things to all people. The question was which

---

[21] It is intuitive that state-owned enterprises are more tax compliant, though as I show in Chapter 2 there is only weak evidence in support of this point for firms in postcommunist states. In any event, with time the state position in Pskovpishcheprom deteriorated: beginning in 2000, a series of share dilutions transferred control of Pskovpishcheprom to other owners, and by 2004 Pskovalko held only a 36.3 percent stake. The circumstances surrounding these transactions are unclear, but as I discuss below, the change of ownership did not eliminate the importance of local vodka production to the Pskov tax base. See "Izvineniia neumestny," *Pskovskaia Guberniia*, March 9, 2005; "'Uvazheniia zasluzhivaiut tol'ko dobrosovestnye konkurenty,'" *Pskovskaia Pravda*, June 3, 2004; "Komu prinadlezhit Pskovskaia oblast," *Pskovskaia Guberniia*, May 26, 2004.

[22] "Otvoevannaia alkoNEzavisimost': Aktual'nyi kommentarii," *Pskovskaia Lenta Novostei*, September 19, 2005. The identity of the "Specialist" was confirmed to me by two individuals in Pskov oblast. At least one forum participant also apparently identifies the "Specialist" as Mikhailov, referring to him as "E.E."; the initials correspond to Mikhailov's first name and patronymic, Evgeny Eduardovich.

[23] "Gubernator Evgeny Mikhailov: 'Ya budu rabotat' po-svoemu, nesmotria na nachavshuiusia strel'bu,'" *Pskovskaia Pravda*, February 28, 1997; "Idu na tretii srok," *Pskovskaia Pravda*, February 28, 2001.

spheres would attract the attention of his administration, that is, which would be best represented.

Mancur Olson provided an answer to questions of this sort in *The Logic of Collective Action*. Taking issue with the pluralistic tradition then hegemonic within political science, Olson argued that "privileged and intermediate groups often triumph over the numerically superior forces in the latent or large groups because the former are generally organized and active while the latter are normally unorganized and inactive" (Olson, 1965, p. 128). In the competition for influence, in other words, the winners are those groups – often small – that have managed to overcome their organizational problems, not those with the largest collective stake in the outcome.

As we have already seen, however, there was no organized lobby asking for state assistance in establishing a vodka sector in Pskov oblast. Rather, the logic of collective action favored existing interests that had inherited Soviet-era networks of organization and influence.[24] These interests lost out not because of the greater organizational capacity of the (nonexistent) vodka sector but because the revenue potential of vodka helped Mikhailov and his administration to satisfy various political constraints. In Pskov as elsewhere in Russia, unpaid state wages and benefits were an enormous political problem that demanded government attention. Vodka revenues were seen as instrumental in addressing this problem.

In principle, other sectors might have competed for government attention by promising that their members would better comply with tax law in return for benefits of the sort received by the vodka industry. After all, if firms are willing to pay lobbyists to represent their interests, why not pay more taxes to achieve the same outcome? But such promises would not have been credible. First, greater tax compliance by any individual firm would have contributed to the collective good of beneficial treatment of that firm's sector by state officials, benefiting not only the tax-compliant firm but also its competitors. Second, any agreement among members of a sector to collectively pay more taxes would have been difficult to enforce, as the tax compliance of individual firms is often hard to gauge, even to other firms within the same industry. Given these two considerations, individual firms had an incentive to hide what they could get away with. As I spell out in detail in Chapter 3, the "taxability" of sectors – the degree to which firms in those sectors find it costly to hide revenues from tax authorities – determines

---

[24] See, for example, McFaul (1995) and Ledeneva (1998).

the division of gains between the state and private economic actors ex post, thus influencing the incentives of politicians to provide collective goods ex ante. (Throughout the book, I use the term *collective good* to refer to any good that if provided to some members of a group cannot be denied to others in the same group, and I use the term *sector* to refer to any group of firms that shares a common organization and technology.) When sectors differ little in their taxability, Olson's logic of collective action predominates, with organized sectors benefiting at the expense of unorganized ones. But when differences in taxability across sectors are large and tax revenue is politically important, collective goods are disproportionately provided to sectors that are relatively easy to tax.

In Pskov, it was the paradoxical good fortune of the nascent vodka industry that it could hide relatively little from tax authorities. In contrast, many other firms found it comparatively easy to evade taxes. Perhaps nowhere in Russia was this more true than in the small-business sector. When the Russian politician Irina Khakamada ran the Russian State Committee for the Support and Development of Small Enterprises, she was told by entrepreneurs that efforts to change the tax system were futile, as "We evade all taxes... The government won't get our money anyway."[25] In my own conversations with small-business owners in Russia, I have similarly found a surprising frankness about the frequency and ease with which taxes are evaded. Russian entrepreneurs are not immune to shakedowns by tax officials, of course, and some do wind up in court, but for at least the first decade of transition it was far easier for small firms to hide revenues from tax authorities than it was for large enterprises. (Tax *arrears* were more heavily concentrated in large enterprises, but this merely reflected the relative difficulty large firms had in keeping taxes from being assessed in the first place.) As discussed above, this was generally the case throughout the postcommunist world, though to a much greater degree in the former Soviet Union than in Eastern Europe.

The frustration of many government officials over tax evasion by small business was neatly articulated by Valentina Smirnova, deputy chair of the oblast finance committee in neighboring Novgorod region. In a newspaper interview, Smirnova complained about the difficulty of tapping entrepreneurs as a revenue source, even after the introduction in 2001 of a

---

[25] Interview on Radio Maiak, December 19, 1997, quoted in Gustafson (1999).

unified tax on imputed income that was based not on reported income but on the number of square meters of retail space:

> Having analyzed the situation with tax receipts from small business, we saw that at the start of 2001 the oblast had 12,627 entrepreneurs. Of these 7,016 gave tax inspectors declarations saying that they had no income. That is, 55.6 percent of small businessmen paid not a single kopek of taxes. And when the unified tax was instituted and it was necessary for small shopkeepers to pay 300 rubles [approximately 10 dollars] per month, they choked in indignation: "My taxes increased 300 times!" Yes, indeed, 300 times, but starting from zero ... True, our people, as always, are "wise and cunning" – they didn't sit on their hands, but looked for ways to evade the tax. And in the course of a year they managed to remove 98 thousand square meters of retail space from the tax rolls. The most impressive metamorphosis took place in the Rus' shopping center, where all of the space is rented out to entrepreneurs. I won't go into details, but of the 224 million rubles that we expected to flow into the budget, by our estimates only 157 million will be collected.[26]

Given this limited contribution by small business to tax revenue, it is perhaps no surprise that budgetary support of the small-business sector in Pskov dried up just as Mikhailov's economic advisor was declaring that "one working factory will provide more tax revenue than all small enterprises taken together."[27] (It is worth stressing that those small businesses that do manage to establish themselves are often quite profitable. The problem is, therefore, not an absence of profits to tax.) Mikhailov himself echoed this sentiment in an interview three years later when he noted with envy that a single large chemical plant in Novgorod provided that region's budget with half its tax receipts.[28] The Pskov government's limited resources were seemingly better spent promoting economic activity that could fill regional coffers.

Across the former Soviet Union, a similar pattern of representation through taxation took shape during the 1990s. The survey data I analyze in Chapter 4 suggest that in post-Soviet countries, a sector's anticipated tax compliance was one of the most important determinants of treatment received from various public agencies. In contrast, in Eastern Europe the taxability of economic activity was generally unimportant; only capacity for collective action mattered. The explanation for this sharp divergence

[26] "Biudzhetu vazhen kazhdyi rubl'," *Novgorodskie Vedomosti*, December 1, 2001.
[27] "Ekonomika na 'avtopilote' zhit' ne mozhet," *Pskovskaia Pravda*, April 23, 1997; "K malomu biznesu – cherez bol'shie pregrady," *Pskovskaia Pravda*, November 27, 1997; Slider (1999, pp. 762–763).
[28] "Evgeny Mikhailov: 'My v seredine puti,'" *Pskovskaia Pravda*, August 16, 2000.

lies in the nature of tax systems developed in the 1990s following the collapse of communism. With the focus in the former Soviet Union on a small number of key revenue sources, tax authorities never learned to extract revenues from other sorts of enterprises or from individuals. As a consequence, politicians like Pskov governor Evgeny Mikhailov were led to promote those sectors that they knew would produce tax revenue, at the expense of those that would not. In contrast, in Eastern Europe – where tax systems had been structured to cast the revenue net more widely – there were fewer such perverse incentives.

The nature of politics in the former Soviet Union – with the organization of interests not the only or primary determinant of policy choice – can be traced to the confluence of state needs and state incapacity. Not only was tax revenue politically important, but tax systems had been structured in a way that made it difficult to extract revenue from particular economic actors. This led to a systematic bias against economic activity that was less taxable. The lesson is general. When policy concerns are predominant, preference may be given to groups that, by their nature, happen to take actions that are politically valuable, whether they are organized or not. Such periods of "extraordinary" politics, to borrow a phrase from East European debates over the political economy of reform in the early 1990s (Balcerowicz, 1994), are perhaps most likely in developing countries, where state needs are consistently unmet and state capacity persistently uneven. However, even in developed countries, there may be moments when "normal" politics is suspended. I discuss one such moment in the concluding chapter.

1.3 Revenue Dependence and Economic Development

In *Markets and States in Tropical Africa*, Robert Bates vividly illustrates the brutal consequences of Olson's logic of collective action for economic development. Throughout Africa, groups that find it possible to overcome their collective-action problems benefit at the expense of those that do not. Industrial interests triumph over agricultural ones, and within agriculture large producers are treated more favorably than small farmers. The result is a set of perverse economic policies that impoverish the peasant majority while enriching a chosen few. Even policies designed with the best of intentions eventually acquire a life of their own, as the rents they generate empower special interests to lobby for their continuation regardless of their effectiveness.

Bates's book was notable for debunking what was then the conventional wisdom among many scholars: that the international environment was the primary cause of Third World underdevelopment. By showing that the origins of African states' agricultural policies lay in domestic politics, *Markets and States in Tropical Africa* initiated a new paradigm for understanding economic development. Policy is determined by the organization of interests, itself often the result of earlier policy initiatives.

This paradigm is useful in explaining variation in development outcomes to the extent that policy makers care primarily about whatever organized groups can credibly promise to provide or threaten to withhold. However, in much of the postcommunist world, another consideration – the revenue needs of state actors – loomed at least as large. In those countries, revenue considerations not only helped to determine economic policy but also may have resulted in those policies' locking in over time.

As in Africa, large industrial enterprises in postcommunist states often benefited at the expense of other economic sectors, and to some degree this seems to be a result of those firms' greater capacity for collective action. But this is only part of the story in the eastern half of the postcommunist world. To put a fine point on it, small businesses in the former Soviet Union had two strikes against them in the competition for resources. Not only did they find it difficult to organize in defense of their interests, but the relative ease with which they hid revenues from the state gave politicians little other reason to promote their development. In contrast, entrepreneurs in Eastern Europe generally suffered only the first disadvantage.

The consequence for economic development has been marked. There is now almost universal agreement among economists studying the region that development of the small-business sector is instrumental to success in the transition from state socialism. Yet the performance of postcommunist states in promoting such development has been sharply uneven. In Eastern Europe, governments have generally provided a supportive environment for entrepreneurship, and by the late 1990s the proportion of the labor force employed in small firms was approaching Organisation for Economic Co-operation and Development (OECD) levels. In contrast, small business in the former Soviet Union has been hampered by overregulation, corruption, and generally poor treatment by public officials, with the result that entry of new businesses has been much more limited.

The key question is whether such biases will persist or will fade as post-Soviet states gradually learn how to extract revenues from other sectors of the economy. In Pskov it was not (just) the increasing ability of the vodka industry to lobby for support that guaranteed its continued survival but the growing dependence of the region on vodka revenues. Evgeny Mikhailov was defeated for governor in 2004, and in taking office his successor, Mikhail Kuznetsov – a Pskov businessman – promised a new era in local governance. Gone were the days of preferential treatment for particular sectors; all industries, the vodka sector included, would have to compete on a level playing field.[29] Yet even as Kuznetsov proclaimed the end of the Mikhailov era, he acknowledged the need to proceed with caution: the vodka sector was now the major source of revenue for the regional budget.[30] Apparently insufficient caution was exercised, as imports of vodka on which the region earned no excise revenue soared in early 2005.[31] By summer the Kuznetsov administration was in full retreat, reestablishing Pskovalko's monopoly distribution rights and proposing that imported vodka be priced at a sufficient premium to support local production and compensate the regional budget for lost excise revenue.[32]

The timing of this move coincided with my visit to Pskov in July, and I soon found my interest in the region being used to justify the actions of the regional administration. Hours after my first meetings, a story was posted on an Internet news site claiming that the "famous [sic] American political scientist Scott Gehlbach" had met with Vladimir Afanas'ev, head of the oblast alcohol committee, to discuss the "necessity of resuming the government alcohol production and distribution monopoly."[33] The story didn't quite say that this was my position (it wasn't), and it didn't perfectly capture Kuznetsov's position (the administration wanted a distribution but not production monopoly), but it did suggest that a media campaign was underway to justify an especially visible reversal by the new governor.

Pskov oblast was caught in a "revenue trap," where the mutual dependence of politicians and owners of labor and capital on the status quo prevented change. Given the presence of the vodka industry as a major revenue source, the Pskov government had no choice but to support it. But

[29] "'Segodnia nuzhno zabyt' o lichnykh interesakh,'" *Pskovskaia Pravda*, December 23, 2004; "Novyi pskovskii gubernator prodaet staryi avtomobil'," *Kommersant*, December 23, 2004.
[30] "Mikhail Kuznetsov: 'Nachinat' pridetsia s nulia," *Delovoi Peterburg*, December 10, 2004.
[31] "Administratsiia Pskovskoi oblasti namerena dobit'sia kompensatsii nedopoluchennoi chasti aktsiza s importnogo alkogolia," *Pskovskaia Lenta Novostei*, June 7, 2005.
[32] "Trezvyi podkhod," *Pskovskaia Guberniia*, June 15, 2005; "Otvet neizvestnomu avtoru," *Pskovskaia Guberniia*, June 29, 2005.
[33] "Amerikanskii politolog napishet o Pskovskoi ekonomike," *Pskovskaia Lenta Novostei*, July 12, 2005.

the industry's existence depended in large part on the continued support of the regional administration. It was a familiar pattern.[34] As I discuss in Chapter 5, the general failure of privatization in the former Soviet Union to effect a shift to truly new private economic activity – largely synonymous with small enterprise in the postcommunist world – may have resulted from such a trap. Mass privatization, intended to change the incentives of future generations of policy makers and thus tip both political support and factor allocation toward a "private property regime" (Frydman and Rapaczynski, 1994, p. 169), was not massive enough in the former Soviet Union to compensate for contemporaneous decisions that limited the revenue importance of new enterprise. Post-Soviet politicians thus continued to provide collective goods to that which they knew how to tax, with the result that labor and capital did not migrate to the new private sector as expected. In contrast, in Eastern Europe – where the design of tax systems provided fewer incentives to promote familiar economic activity – privatization had the desired effect.

As in *Markets and States in Tropical Africa*, I thus tell a story about the development and perpetuation of inefficient economic policies. In contrast to Bates's study, however, the organization of interests is neither necessary nor sufficient to explain the development outcomes on which I focus. Rather, the incentives of politicians were structured by tax systems created in the early days of transition that had the effect of magnifying or diminishing the political importance of the "new" and "old" economies. It is the capacity of the state to extract revenues from different types of economic activity, not the ability of economic agents to overcome their collective-action problems, that is central to my story.

1.4 Looking Ahead

In the chapters ahead I present my argument in full. By the time I am finished I aim to have provided answers to three questions, each central to

---

[34] And not only in the postcommunist world, even with respect to the particular example of alcohol taxation. As the economic historian John Nye documents in a recent work, a symbiotic relationship existed between British authorities and the domestic brewing industry in the eighteenth and nineteenth centuries, with brewers benefiting from protection against imported French wine even as the government depended on taxation of beer for revenues (Nye, 2007).

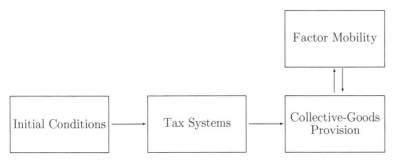

Figure 1.1 The argument in schematic form.

the political economy of postcommunism and each related to central issues in political economy more generally:

1. What explains variation in the tax systems that evolved after communism?
2. Who did postcommunist politicians favor in the provision of collective goods and why?
3. What are the consequences of variation in collective-goods provision for economic development in postcommunist states?

Figure 1.1 illustrates the general direction of the argument. Variation in initial conditions leads to variation in postcommunist tax systems, such that tax systems in the former Soviet Union are generally structured more around "old" revenue sources, whereas those in Eastern Europe draw more on "new" sources. These tax systems, in turn, determine the division of gains between politicians and firms from collective-goods provision and so structure the incentives of politicians to provide those goods. Politicians in the former Soviet Union respond to these incentives by promoting economic activity that they know how to tax, whereas their counterparts in Eastern Europe exhibit little bias of this sort. These initial outcomes then interact with factor mobility to determine long-run trajectories of economic development, with labor and capital responding to collective-goods provision and vice versa, until eventually politicians and factor owners settle into a relationship of mutual dependence.

I present the first step in this argument in Chapter 2. I begin by showing that the large variation in tax structures across postcommunist states is not random but rather related to a small number of initial conditions – the industrial structure inherited from communism, proximity to the West, and the level of economic development at the start of transition – that roughly divide the postcommunist world into two halves: countries in the former Soviet Union continued their Soviet-era reliance on enterprise taxation and taxes on goods and services, whereas those in Eastern Europe transitioned to new sources of revenue. I then illustrate the consequences of this difference for patterns of tax compliance among postcommunist firms. Generally speaking, officials in the former Soviet Union focused more on encouraging compliance by "old" enterprises, whereas those in Eastern Europe cast the revenue net more widely. The result was much larger systematic differences in the ability of firms to hide revenues from tax authorities in the former Soviet Union than in Eastern Europe.

In the next two chapters I demonstrate theoretically and empirically the consequences of this variation in tax systems for patterns of collective-goods provision. In Chapter 3, I build on the well-known lobbying model of Grossman and Helpman (1994, 2001), showing how the ex post division of gains between the state and private economic actors – determined by the taxability of firms in a sector and hence their anticipated tax compliance – influences the incentive of politicians to provide sector-specific collective goods ex ante. When tax revenue is politically important and differences in the taxability of sectors are large, politicians have an incentive to disproportionately provide collective goods to sectors that are easy to tax. In contrast, in the absence of either of these two conditions, collective-goods provision is determined primarily by the organization of sectors rather than their anticipated tax compliance.

I test the predictions of this model in Chapter 4 using data from the Business Environment and Enterprise Performance Survey (BEEPS), a survey of firms carried out in twenty-five postcommunist countries in 1999. Consistent with the geographic divide in tax systems documented in Chapter 2, data from the survey suggest two general patterns of collective-goods provision in the postcommunist world. In the former Soviet Union, the provision of collective goods – justice, police protection, and so on – is determined as much by anticipated tax compliance as it is by capacity for collective action, whereas in Eastern Europe only collective action seems to matter. Roughly speaking, politicians in the eastern half of the postcommunist world promoted that which they knew from experience how to tax, whereas those in the western half were driven primarily by the organization of interests.

I develop the final piece of the argument in Chapter 5. I show that the consequence of these patterns of collective-goods provision during the first decade of transition is that the economic activity necessary for sustainable development in postcommunist states – new private enterprise, exemplified by small firms in competitive industries – was crowded out in the former Soviet Union by government promotion of sectors that were important sources of revenue. The timing could not have been worse. Programs of mass privatization had been implemented throughout the postcommunist world in the early and mid-1990s with the hope that a sufficiently large shock to factor allocation would force state actors to shift support from the old economy to the new private sector; labor and capital would follow, reinforcing the political imperative to promote the new economy. In Eastern Europe things more or less turned out as planned, but in the former Soviet Union the shock was not large enough to compensate for the poor revenue potential of new private enterprise. Politicians and factor owners were caught in a "revenue trap," with politicians dependent on the old economy for revenue, even as labor and capital relied on continued government patronage of the old economy. With another shock like mass privatization not on the horizon, the status quo seemed likely to persist.

Finally, in Chapter 6, I revisit my answers to the three questions posed above and discuss the general lessons of the theoretical perspectives in this book.

2

The Creation of Tax Systems

Communism was the first truly totalitarian system, with the tentacles of the state stretching into corners of society hitherto reserved to private actors. Yet the communist state was structured for the society that it created, one organized around bureaucratic coordination and state ownership of the means of production. One of the paradoxes of postcommunism is that the withdrawal of the state from direct control and ownership of the economy therefore necessitated the creation of state structures unnecessary under communism. Nowhere was this more evident than with taxation, the very foundation of state authority. Laying claim to funds to run the state was largely an accounting matter when most productive assets were state owned. But with privatization and liberalization, bureaucracies had to be created to locate and encourage the transfer of what was now possessed by private actors.

Postcommunist states went about the task of creating tax systems in different ways during the 1990s. Roughly speaking, the non-Baltic states of the former Soviet Union (the countries of the Commonwealth of Independent States, or CIS) developed systems that continued to rely, as under communism, on enterprise taxation and taxes on goods and services. In contrast, the tax systems that emerged in Eastern Europe and the Baltics mirrored those of the European Union, with a greater emphasis on direct taxation of individuals.[1] I explore this development at some length, showing that various initial conditions – inherited industrial structure, proximity to the

---

[1] As discussed in the previous chapter, throughout the book I often favor convention over geographical accuracy by referring to the states of the CIS as the "former Soviet Union" and by including the Baltic states of Estonia, Latvia, and Lithuania in "Eastern Europe."

West, and level of economic development – all played a role in producing divergent patterns of revenue collection in the postcommunist world.

In the former Soviet Union, the accent on "old" revenue sources meant that officials focused especially on enterprises – large, monopolistic firms in particular industries – that they knew from experience how to tax, leaving other sectors comparatively free to hide revenues from the state. In Eastern Europe there was less bias of this sort. As I show in the following chapters, this difference had important implications for the political economies that emerged in the region. Dependent on a narrow slice of the economy for revenues, politicians in the former Soviet Union were inclined to favor those sectors in the provision of collective goods. Politicians in Eastern Europe, where tax systems cast a wider net, faced fewer such perverse incentives.

2.1 Taxation under Communism

"[T]he existence of *public* finance," write Vito Tanzi and George Tsibouris, "presupposes that of *private* finance" (Tanzi and Tsibouris, 2000, p. 3, italics in original). But in communist systems private finance was limited, with most productive assets owned and capital flows controlled by the state. Moreover, the benchmarks that guide taxation in market economies – prices and incomes – had little meaning under communism. Prices for goods and services were set by the plan, not equilibrated by supply and demand, as were workers' wages and the allowable profit of enterprises. Taxation was thus reduced to an accounting exercise, with state officials determining which capital flows within the giant enterprise that was the state should be designated as "taxes" and which should be given some other label.

The task of carrying out this accounting exercise was made easier by certain institutional features common to nearly all communist states. Economic activity was concentrated in large industrial enterprises, often local monopolies, thus facilitating the process of control through the plan (Brown, Ickes, and Ryterman, 1994; Roland, 2000, ch. 1). Moreover, all financial transactions were funneled through the state "monobank," so "taxation" of an enterprise amounted to debiting the enterprise's account and crediting some other account at the bank (Kornai, 1992, pp. 131–134).

The predominance of large, monopolistic enterprises and easy transfer of funds from enterprise accounts determined the shape of taxation under communism. Nearly all taxes were collected at the enterprise level. Direct taxation of individuals, a large share of total tax proceeds in advanced market economies, was comparatively small in communist economies. In the Soviet Union in the early 1980s, for example, individual income taxes of all types contributed approximately 8 percent of total revenue (Newcity, 1986, p. 38). Social insurance contributions (payroll taxes) typically made up a somewhat larger share (Newbery, 1995), but the lion's share of revenue came from taxes on enterprise profits and the turnover tax (a sales tax assessed on both commodities and manufactured goods). Other revenue sources depended on the local economic context. Trade taxes, for example, were relatively important in the Soviet Union due to its reliance on energy exports (Cheasty, 1996).

The system of communist taxation created two important legacies for the postcommunist politicians who found themselves at the helm of states ill suited to a market economy. First, the collection of taxes at the enterprise level meant that postcommunist citizens were generally unaware of the true cost of the generous safety net provided by the state (Appel, 2006). Consequently, politicians faced public pressure to maintain spending levels even in the face of precipitous declines in economic output (e.g., Barbone and Marchetti, Jr., 1995). Second, to the extent that state officials knew how to tax anything, it was that with which they were most familiar: profits of large, monopolistic enterprises in particular industries and sales of commodities and manufactured goods. The first legacy implied political pressure for public spending and thus for the rapid creation of tax systems capable of raising the necessary funds from private actors. The second suggested that there would be a temptation to structure these systems around economic activity similar to that which had formed the revenue base under communism. As I show in the next section, this temptation was resisted with greater success in some countries than in others.

2.2 Taxation after Communism

What form did postcommunist tax systems take? In this section I describe general patterns of taxation in Eastern Europe and the former Soviet Union, using panel data from the World Bank on taxation in twenty-four postcommunist countries between 1994 and 2000.[2] I give a birds-eye view

---

[2] The countries included in the data set are Albania, Armenia, Azerbaijan, Belarus, Bulgaria, Croatia, the Czech Republic, Estonia, Georgia, Hungary, Kazakhstan, Kyrgyzstan, Latvia,

of postcommunist tax systems, comparing the average East European experience with the average post-Soviet one. In the following section I take advantage of variation within these two regions to estimate the impact of various initial conditions on postcommunist tax structure.

Three stylized facts summarize much of the variation in postcommunist tax systems:

1. Tax collection overall has been lower in the CIS than in Eastern Europe and the Baltics.
2. Countries in the CIS have relied more on the "old" revenue sources of corporate taxation and taxes on goods and services, whereas those in Eastern Europe and the Baltics have relied more on the "new" revenue source of direct taxation of individuals.
3. Variation in tax structures over time has been greater in the CIS than in Eastern Europe and the Baltics, with partial replacement between 1994 and 2000 in the CIS of one "old" revenue source (corporate taxation) with another (taxes on goods and services).

Figure 2.1 illustrates the first of these three stylized facts, showing for the two halves of the postcommunist world the average proportion of gross domestic product (GDP) collected over the period 1994–2000 in four summary categories of taxation, as well as the average proportion of GDP untaxed.[3] The average level of taxation is substantially higher in the western half of the postcommunist world: an average of 34 percent of GDP is collected through some form of taxation in Eastern Europe versus 23 percent in the former Soviet Union. The revenue shortfall in the former Soviet Union comes in all areas of taxation but one: corporate taxation.[4] In the others – income, social security, and payroll taxes; taxes on goods and

Lithuania, Macedonia, Moldova, Poland, Romania, Russia, Slovakia, Slovenia, Tajikistan, Turkmenistan, Ukraine, and Uzbekistan. I exclude Kazakhstan from the analysis because corporate and individual income taxes are not broken out separately for that country. Data are for consolidated general government revenues but for the following exceptions: Croatia (consolidated central government revenues), Russia (enlarged government budget), Turkmenistan (state budget), and Uzbekistan (consolidated general government revenues excluding extrabudgetary funds). Further details can be found in Mitra and Stern (2003).

[3] More precisely, I average across years within countries and then take the unweighted mean across countries, so the proportions given represent means across country-years.

[4] My consideration of corporate taxes separately from other direct taxes differs from many other comparative studies of taxation (see, e.g., the review in Lieberman, 2002), reflecting my emphasis on "old" and "new" forms of taxation.

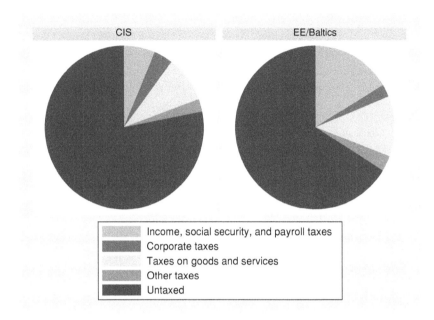

Figure 2.1 Tax revenue as proportion of GDP in CIS and Eastern Europe/Baltics, 1994–2000.

services, comprising mostly value-added tax (VAT) and excise taxes; and other taxes – East European states generally raised larger sums.[5]

The absolute consensus among observers is that this difference in aggregate tax collection reflects the lesser success of post-Soviet states in raising revenue, rather than any lesser desire on the part of post-Soviet citizens or politicians for an activist government (e.g., Cheasty, 1996). Nonetheless, post-Soviet states were more successful in raising corporate taxes than were East European states, despite the greater economic collapse in the CIS and concomitant loss of profits among state-owned and formerly state-owned enterprises.[6] Indeed, corporate taxation was most important for post-Soviet states in 1994, which is the year of greatest economic contraction for most countries in the CIS. (Figures 2.A.1–2.A.3 in the appendix to this

[5] Some authors have argued that social security contributions and payroll taxes should not be considered true taxes, as in principle they are provided in return for a promise of future benefits (e.g., Weyland, 1998). However, in the context of the postcommunist transition there is little reason to believe that these promises are more credible than any other. I thus include these payments as taxes.

[6] On variation in the "transition depression," see, for example, Svejnar (2002).

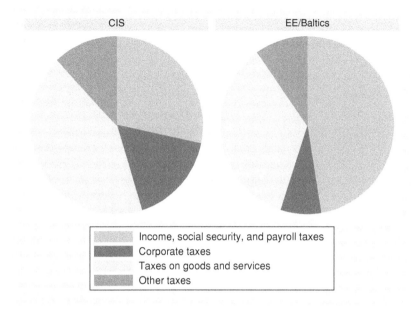

Figure 2.2 Tax structure in CIS and Eastern Europe/Baltics, 1994–2000.

chapter plot for each country the contribution over time of each of the major categories of taxation.)

The reality is that corporate taxation in many countries of the CIS was calculated from a profit base that disallowed deductions for advertising, interest, capital expenditures, and wages over a certain level (Martinez-Vazquez and McNab, 2000; Grafe and Richter, 2001). The aim in part was to maintain the tax base even in the face of declining profits (e.g., Lopez-Claros and Alexashenko, 1998).[7] This was part of a more general strategy among post-Soviet states to rely on revenue sources familiar from the communist era. Figure 2.2, which gives average tax structure between 1994 and 2000 for the two postcommunist regions, illustrates this second stylized fact of postcommunist taxation: the "old" revenue sources of corporation taxation and taxes on goods and services were relatively more important in post-Soviet countries, whereas the "new" revenue source of direct taxation of individuals was comparatively more important in Eastern Europe.

---

[7] Taxes on excess wages were also viewed as a way of moderating wage increases in an environment in which firms' budget constraints – typically "soft" under communism (Kornai, 1979, 1980) – had not yet hardened.

(Table 2.A.1, in the appendix to this chapter, reports mean tax structure for individual countries.)

Indeed, post-Soviet states were much quicker to implement a VAT – the market analogue to the communist turnover tax – than were those in Eastern Europe, with the change taking place just prior to the formal demise of the Soviet Union (Ebrill and Havrylyshyn, 1999).[8] Perhaps due to the haste in implementing a VAT regime, there were substantial problems with VAT collection throughout the former Soviet Union, including tax evasion that took advantage of rules governing trade within the CIS (Mertens and Tesche, 2002; Bird, 2006). Plugging these gaps was a major focus of post-Soviet tax policy and tax administration. The result, as shown in Figure 2.A.2 in the appendix to this chapter, was a general increase during the 1990s in the share of tax revenue contributed by taxes on goods and services for most countries in the CIS. In Eastern Europe taxes on goods and services also contributed an increasing share of tax revenue over this time period, though the change was smaller.

This evolution is the third stylized fact of postcommunist taxation. Variation in tax structure over time was greater in the former Soviet Union than it was in Eastern Europe, with a partial replacement of one "old" revenue source (corporate taxes) with another (taxes on goods and services) in the eastern half of the postcommunist world. Figure 2.3 illustrates the change, showing average tax structure in the two regions in 1994 and 2000, respectively. Within the CIS, taxes on goods and services account for an average of nearly half of all tax revenue by 2000, whereas corporate taxes decline from an average of 28 percent of total tax revenue in 1994 to only 12 percent in 2000. In Eastern Europe, in contrast, tax structures in 2000 look remarkably similar to those in 1994.

Thus, rather than converging to a common model of taxation, postcommunist states generally charted one of two different courses during the first decade of transition. In the former Soviet Union, states focused on familiar revenue sources: enterprise and indirect taxes, with the mix between the two shifting over time. In Eastern Europe, in contrast, tax systems emphasized the direct taxation of individuals. The degree to which states conformed to one of these two ideal types is remarkable. Nonetheless, there is variation in tax structure in both halves of the postcommunist world. In the following

---

[8] The countries of Eastern Europe generally waited some time to replace their turnover taxes with a VAT. When the change came, the VAT was typically modeled on that of the European Union. See, for example, Martinez-Vazquez and McNab (2000).

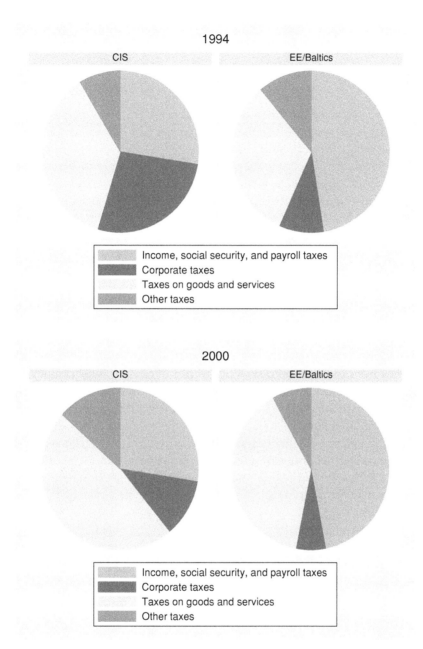

Figure 2.3 Tax structure in CIS and Eastern Europe/Baltics, 1994 (top) versus 2000 (bottom).

section I take advantage of this variation to identify the impact of initial conditions on the nature of the tax systems that emerged during the 1990s.

2.3 Initial Conditions and Postcommunist Tax Structure

What accounts for the different routes taken by states in designing postcommunist tax systems? In the spirit of Margaret Levi's *Of Rule and Revenue*, a small but growing literature has emphasized the role of domestic and international factors in shaping the incentives of revenue-seeking state actors in Eastern Europe and the former Soviet Union. Based on extensive study of state institutions in particular countries, this work has identified conditions at the beginning of transition that pushed tax systems in one direction or another. Here I broaden the scope of inquiry, using the data described above to show the impact of these initial conditions on tax systems across the postcommunist world.

I demonstrate in particular that much of the variation in postcommunist tax structure can be traced to three initial conditions that varied across countries in Eastern Europe and the former Soviet Union: the industrial structure inherited from communism, proximity to the West, and the level of economic development at the start of transition. This approach differs from many other comparative studies of taxation, which emphasize instead the influence of domestic political institutions on tax policy (e.g., Meltzer and Richard, 1983; Cheibub, 1998; Steinmo and Tolbert, 1998; Gould, 2001; Franzese, 2002; Boix, 2003; Persson and Tabellini, 2005). In the postcommunist context, political institutions are endogenous to the transition itself and thus possibly to the tax systems that emerged in the early 1990s. My strategy thus traces the development of tax systems, which are themselves institutional in character, to variables exogenous to the transition.[9]

As discussed above, the predominance of large, monopolistic enterprises characteristic of socialist economies encouraged a general reliance on enterprise taxation under communism. Similarly, the development of the energy sector in the Soviet Union fostered the growth of trade taxes. These

---

[9] Baturo and Gray (2006) and O'Dwyer and Kovalčík (2007) examine the impact of domestic politics on the probability of flat-tax adoption in postcommunist countries. However, the emphasis in both studies is on changes in tax policy that largely took place in the second decade of transition, well after the initial development of tax systems that is my focus. On the role of initial conditions in determining economic institutions, see, for example, Engerman and Sokoloff (1997, 2000); Acemoglu, Johnson, and Robinson (2001, 2002).

industrial structures were an important inheritance to postcommunist states, providing an incentive to build tax systems around familiar revenue sources. Nonetheless, not all postcommunist states were equally endowed – Slovakia was more heavily industrialized under communism than Slovenia, and Turkmenistan is richer in natural resources than Armenia – so this incentive was stronger in some countries than others. Gerald Easter provides a particularly compelling example, comparing the postcommunist experience of Russia and Poland. In Russia, the concentration of economic activity in a few large enterprises, many in natural resources, encouraged a reliance on corporate taxation and energy excises. (Trade taxes were cut at the behest of international financial institutions; see, e.g., Rutland, 2001.) In contrast, in resource-poor Poland political leaders were forced to seek out other forms of revenue; after a period of some contestation, they finally settled on a policy that stressed personal-income taxation (Easter, 2002*a*).

In addition to inherited industrial structure, the physical proximity of countries to the West played an important role in the development of postcommunist tax systems. The strong pull of the European Union (EU) clearly encouraged many countries to harmonize their tax systems with those of the EU as part of the accession process (Newbery, 1995; Martinez-Vazquez and McNab, 2000; Appel, 2006). With taxation in the European Union centered more on direct taxation of individuals than was the case in communist countries, this should have forced a shift away from "old" to "new" sources of tax revenue.[10] That said, many postcommunist countries are simply too far from Western Europe for the possibility of EU accession to have provided any real incentive, so the impact of potential EU membership should have been stronger for countries further west.

Beyond the lure of EU accession, proximity to the West may have provided a disproportionate incentive to reduce the corporate tax burden as a way of attracting Western capital. The Baltic states of Estonia, Latvia, and Lithuania provide a case in point. Early in the transition the three countries provided tax holidays and other incentives to foreign investors; eventually, low tax rates were applied to all corporate profits. By 2000, Estonia had a zero-percent rate on retained earnings (Stepanyan, 2003). The incentive to follow suit may have been less in many other post-Soviet states, more distant from the West and its markets.

---

[10] Mitra and Stern (2003) report that for the same time period as that examined here, the average proportion of taxes collected as income, social security, and payroll taxes among EU members was 0.51, close to the average for countries in Eastern Europe and the Baltics.

Finally, postcommunist countries differed at the beginning of transition in their levels of economic development. Consistent with arguments in the literature on state capacity in general (e.g., Fearon and Laitin, 2003) and tax administration in particular (e.g., Gordon and Li, 2005), Conor O'Dwyer has shown that those postcommunist countries that were richer typically developed more effective state administrations (O'Dwyer, 2006). Taxes differ, of course, in the level of administration required for their implementation – indirect taxes are less demanding of tax administrations than are direct taxes (e.g., Alt, 1983; Chaudhry, 1997) – so variation in economic development at the beginning of transition should be reflected in postcommunist tax structures. Moreover, to the extent that switching to "new" sources of tax revenue such as direct taxation of individuals requires bureaucratic restructuring and retraining of personnel, such changes should have been more successful in wealthy countries with generally greater administrative capacity. Both possibilities can be seen in the example of Bulgaria, among the poorer countries of Eastern Europe, where the institution of a personal income tax was undercut in part due to the inability of tax authorities to collect the tax from newly self-employed individuals (Bogetic and Hillman, 1994).

These initial conditions are familiar concepts to students of the postcommunist transition, and in identifying the relative role of each in determining postcommunist tax structures I use measures employed in previous studies. I present data for all measures in Table 2.A.2 in the appendix to this chapter.

- Industrial structure: Systematic data on industrial structures inherited from communism are generally unavailable, so I rely on two proxy measures.[11] The first, energy efficiency, follows Pop-Eleches (2007) in assuming that postcommunist countries are less energy efficient to the extent that they are endowed with large, Stalinist manufacturing enterprises. In particular, I use GDP per unit of energy use (defined as constant 2000 purchasing power parity (PPP) dollars per kilogram of oil equivalent) from the World Bank's 2005 World Development Indicators database. Data are from 1992, the first year generally available, but for Azerbaijan, for which the measure is from 1993. Unfortunately, no data are available for Macedonia, so that country is dropped from the subsequent analysis. As shown in Table 2.A.2, countries such as Hungary and Slovenia that escaped the worst of heavy industrialization under communism are in fact more

---

[11] Brown, Ickes, and Ryterman (1994) provide estimates for Russia based on industrial-census data. I am aware of no similar effort for other countries in the region.

energy efficient than their neighbors.[12] The second measure, natural resources, defines countries as being "poor," "moderate," or "rich" in natural resources, using the coding in de Melo, Denizer, Gelb, and Tenev (2001).

- Physical proximity to the West: As in Kopstein and Reilly (2000), I measure distance from the West as the distance in kilometers from a country's capital to Vienna or Berlin, whichever is closer. Defining distance in this way roughly captures cultural and historical commonality with the countries of the European Union, important for determining the incentive effect of EU membership, as well as proximity to the markets of Western Europe, which may influence the competition for Western capital. Below I discuss the extent to which these and other geographic explanations can be disentangled using this variable.

- Economic development: I use 1989 gross national product (GNP) per capita at PPP in dollars from de Melo et al. (2001).

As Table 2.A.3 in the appendix to this chapter shows, CIS membership is strongly correlated with all four measures: countries in the former Soviet Union, less the Baltics, are on average less energy efficient, richer in natural resources, farther from the West, and poorer.

Because the initial conditions that are determinants of tax structure are time invariant (e.g., distance from Berlin or Vienna in 1994 is the same as distance from Berlin or Vienna in 2000), it would be inappropriate to treat each observation of tax structure in a country as an independent draw. In particular, it would be impossible to control for any unobserved time-invariant characteristics through the inclusion of fixed effects and simultaneously identify the impact of initial conditions. I thus estimate a type of "between effects" model, exploring variation between but not within countries by averaging the proportion of each of the four categories of taxes discussed above across the entire period (1994–2000) for which I have data. This is a conservative strategy, as there are only twenty-three countries for which I have data on both tax structure and initial conditions. However, as I will show, there is sufficient variation in both

---

[12] Albania's very high energy efficiency may be due in part to the exceptionally rapid deindustrialization that took place in that country in the early 1990s (e.g., Barbone and Marchetti, Jr., 1995). All qualitative results reported below are robust to exclusion of Albania from the analysis.

to be able to precisely estimate the impact of initial conditions on tax structure.[13]

Analyzing the impact of initial conditions on tax structure poses two technical complications: the proportion of total revenue from any one tax is bounded between zero and 1, and all proportions must sum to 1. Formally, if p_{it} is the proportion of total revenue from tax t in country i, then $p_{it} \in [0, 1]$ for all i and t and $\sum_t p_{it} = 1$ for all i. This is a problem well known to students of multiparty elections – no party can receive a negative vote or more than the total vote, and the votes for each party must sum to the total vote – though to my knowledge no previous statistical analysis of the determinants of tax structure has taken this into account. A standard solution to dealing with such "compositional data" is to transform the data by choosing some base category T, and for all other categories $t \neq T$, calculating the natural log of the ratio of category t's share to category T's:

$$q_{it} \equiv \ln \left(\frac{p_{it}}{p_{iT}} \right). \tag{2.1}$$

I use the average proportion of all taxes collected as other taxes as the base category and define the other categories as in the discussion above: income, social security, and payroll taxes; corporate taxes; and taxes on goods and services.[14]

Transformed in this way, we may then specify the empirical model

$$q_{it} = \mathbf{x}_i \beta_t + \epsilon_{it},$$

where $\mathbf{x}_i$ is the vector of initial conditions discussed above for country i, β_t is a vector of parameters (specific to tax t) to be estimated, and ϵ_{it} is the unobserved residual. (Due to the small number of degrees of freedom, I include the trichotomous measure of natural resources in $\mathbf{x}_i$ rather than "dummying out" the variable. However, I obtain qualitatively similar results if I instead include two dummy variables. Further, the qualitative results are unchanged if I use the natural log of the other initial conditions.) I assume in particular that ϵ_{it} is multivariate normal, with the ϵ_{it} correlated across taxes t within countries i – a higher share of one tax implies a lower share for

---

[13] My approach differs, for example, from that in Martin (1991), Garrett (1998), and Swank and Steinmo (2002), where the focus is instead on the impact of time-varying characteristics on within-country variation in tax policy.

[14] Using log ratios and defining categories in this way requires that I recode a small number of cases in which the proportion of other taxes is zero to instead be positive but very small. The particular recoding is immaterial to the results.

all remaining taxes – but uncorrelated across countries and with a variance matrix for the system of equations that is homoskedastic across countries.[15]

Table 2.A.4 in the appendix to this chapter reports estimated coefficients and standard errors for this system of equations. However, the results reported in this table are not substantively informative, as the dependent variables in these equations are log ratios of proportions of total tax revenue, not the proportions of tax revenue that are of interest. In particular, the effect of an initial condition may be significantly different from zero even if the estimated coefficients on that condition are not. To derive more informative results, I derive expected values for each of the three log ratios, varying one initial condition at a time while setting the other initial conditions at their means. I then reverse the transformation in Equation (2.1) to produce expected values of the proportion of total tax revenue for each of the four categories of taxes, given values of the initial conditions. I illustrate results for all categories but the base category of other taxes in Figures 2.4–2.7.

The estimated impact of energy efficiency, the first of two proxies for industrial structure, is depicted in Figure 2.4. By far the strongest effect of energy efficiency is on corporate taxation. Holding other initial conditions at their means, the least energy-efficient economies, that is, those that are assumed to have industrial structures most oriented around large manufacturing enterprises, are estimated to have a share of corporate taxation nearly five times higher than that of the most energy-efficient economies. Postcommunist states with economies centered around a few large enterprises seem to have relied much more on corporate taxation than those with less concentrated industrial structures. In contrast, the estimated impact of energy efficiency on taxes on goods and services and on income, social security, and payroll taxes is insignificant, though the two categories

---

[15] This distributional assumption allows use of the STATA programs in the CLARIFY package (King, Tomz, and Wittenberg, 2000; Tomz, Wittenberg, and King, 2003) to estimate the effects I report below; see Tomz, Tucker, and Wittenberg (2002). A number of alternative approaches have been proposed, mostly dealing with issues specific to multiparty election data (nonparticipation of parties in some districts and heteroskedasticity arising from the random nature of the voting process) that do not concern me here; see, for example, Katz and King (1999); Honaker, Katz, and King (2002); Jackson (2002); and Mikhailov, Niemi, and Weimer (2002). Note that because the regressors are the same in each equation, generalized least squares (GLS) on Zellner's model of seemingly unrelated regressions is equivalent to equation-by-equation ordinary least squares (OLS; Zellner, 1962). I use feasible generalized least squares (FGLS) on the system of equations – the `sureg` command in STATA – for convenience.

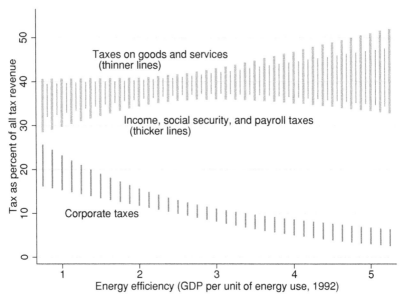

Figure 2.4 Inherited industrial structure (as proxied by energy efficiency of economy) and tax structure, 1994–2000. Vertical bars represent 95-percent confidence intervals.

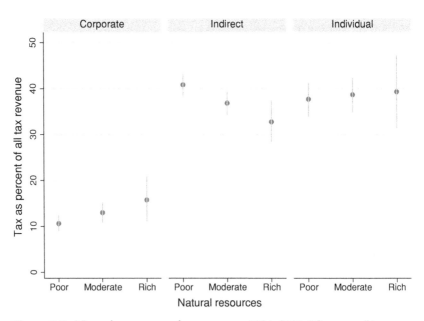

Figure 2.5 Natural resources and tax structure, 1994–2000. "Corporate" is corporate taxes; "individual" is income, social security, and payroll taxes; and "indirect" is taxes on goods and services. Dots represent point estimates, vertical bars 95-percent confidence intervals.

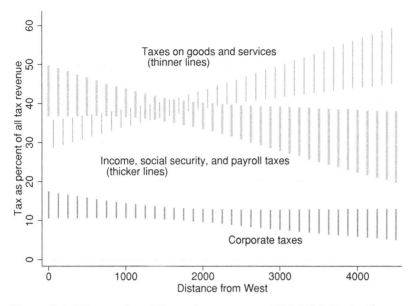

Figure 2.6 Distance from West and tax structure, 1994–2000. Vertical bars represent 95-percent confidence intervals.

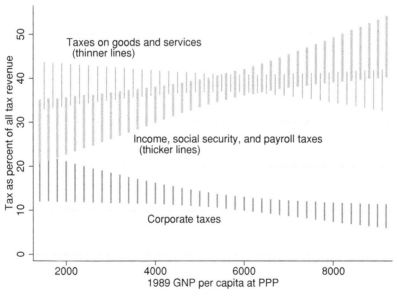

Figure 2.7 Economic development and tax structure, 1994–2000. Vertical bars represent 95-percent confidence intervals.

collectively account for a substantially larger share of tax revenue as energy efficiency increases.

Figure 2.5 reports the estimated effect of natural-resource wealth on tax structure, displaying the result separately for each of the three main tax categories. Greater resource wealth is associated with an increase in corporate taxes, coupled with a decrease in taxes on goods and services. However, the estimated impact is small and uncertain. Of the two measures of industrial structure, energy efficiency exhibits by far the larger effect.

Figure 2.6 shows the estimated impact of distance from the West on tax structure. Countries that are closer to the West are predicted to have very different tax structures than those that are more distant, holding other initial conditions at their means. In particular, the closer is a country to the West, the larger is the expected share of income, social security, and payroll taxes and the smaller is the expected share of taxes on goods and services. The evidence is thus consistent with the argument that the pull of the European Union encouraged countries to go about the difficult task of learning how to tax individuals (a "new" tax), the major source of revenue for countries in the EU, rather than relying on the administratively easier taxation of goods and services (an "old" tax).

One potential problem with this interpretation is that distance from the West not only reflects the pull of the European Union but also other factors that may have independently influenced the development of post-communist institutions: time spent under communism, cultural heritage, and so on. In Poland, for example, the structure of postcommunist tax agencies drew to some extent on that country's experience with taxation in the interwar period (Berenson, 2006*a*). Unfortunately, as scholars of post-communism know all too well, there is no econometric way to completely disentangle these effects: variables representing the location, history, and culture of postcommunist countries are very highly correlated with each other. However, as an additional check I reestimated the model, replacing distance from the West with a dummy variable equal to 1 if the country opened membership negotiations with the European Union by 2000.[16] The qualitative results are identical, though the model with the EU-negotiation variable explains substantially more variation in the use of individual versus other taxes. Of course, whether a country opened negotiations with the EU

---

[16] The following countries did so: Bulgaria, the Czech Republic, Estonia, Hungary, Latvia, Lithuania, Poland, Romania, Slovakia, and Slovenia. My empirical strategy mirrors Pacek, Pop-Eleches, and Tucker (2007), who use EU negotiations to measure the impact of prospective EU membership on electoral turnout.

is endogenous to the postcommunist transition, so these results should be treated with caution. Nonetheless, they provide some additional support for the argument that countries that aspired to EU membership oriented their tax systems more around direct taxation of individuals.

The related argument that competition for Western capital might have encouraged disproportionate reductions in the corporate-tax burden among East European countries finds less support. To the extent that such pressure existed, it appears to have been no greater for countries closer to Western markets: the estimated effect of distance from the West on the share of corporate taxes in total tax revenue is insignificant. Thus, to the extent that it is possible to disaggregate the impact of proximity to the West on postcommunist tax structure, the evidence here suggests that the EU-accession effect was primary.

Finally, Figure 2.7 displays the estimated impact of economic development, as measured by 1989 GNP per capita at PPP, on tax structure. The most evident effect is that higher economic development is associated with a large increase in the administratively difficult taxation of individuals. Interestingly, this increase comes partly at the expense of corporate taxation, which like other forms of direct taxation is generally difficult to administer but in the postcommunist context has the advantage of being a familiar revenue source. Thus, postcommunist countries that at the beginning of transition were wealthier, and thus presumably endowed with greater administrative capacity, were more likely to have replaced "old" forms of taxation with "new" ones.

Summarizing, the estimated impact of initial conditions on postcommunist tax structure is as follows:

- Countries that were less energy efficient, and therefore presumably had industrial structures oriented more around large manufacturing enterprises, relied far more on corporate taxes.
- Countries that are rich in natural resources depended somewhat more on corporate taxes and somewhat less on taxes on goods and services, though the estimated effects are weak and imprecise.
- Countries that are physically closer to the West oriented their tax systems more around income, social security, and payroll taxes and less around taxes on goods and services.
- Countries that started the postcommunist transition at a higher level of economic development shifted more to income, social security, and payroll taxes.

Taken together, these results demonstrate the overwhelming importance to postcommunist tax structure of two factors idiosyncratic to the transition: the institutional and economic legacy that favored corporate taxation in countries with Stalinist industrial structures, and the strong incentive effect of EU accession. At the same time, they provide only partial support for hypotheses that extend to countries not in the postsocialist region. Economic development is strongly correlated with postcommunist tax structure, perhaps in part because richer states have larger administrative capacity and so find it easier to tax individuals. But economic development has the opposite effect on corporate income taxation that might be expected more generally, and the estimated effect of resource wealth is small.

For scholars looking for generalizable results, this is a mixed bag. It would make little sense to relate tax structure across some broader set of countries to energy efficiency, much less distance from Vienna or Berlin. Nonetheless, this analysis does highlight the strong dependence of state capacity on history: it is the communist experience that drives both the relationship between industrial structure and taxation and the geopolitical imperative to unite Eastern and Western Europe. It also suggests avenues through which history may matter beyond those stressed in the literature, where Charles Tilly's (1992) argument about the relationship between interstate conflict and state capacity looms large.[17] Finally, it suggests that arguments by scholars of the "resource curse" may be extended by considering the effect on institutions of factor endowments more generally; in the transition context, it is capital invested by previous generations in large industrial enterprises that especially seems to matter.

Variation in postcommunist tax structures is thus systematically related to variation in initial conditions. But how exactly did postcommunist states generate the particular mix of revenues that these initial conditions imply? The evidence I present in the following section suggests that postcommunist tax structures were determined in significant part by decisions about which of the various taxes written into law to actually try to collect.

2.4 Tax Revenue and Tax Compliance

Largely neglected by scholars and many policy makers at the beginning of transition, the process of state building is now seen as central to the

---

[17] In recent work, Besley and Persson (2007) provide evidence that both fiscal and legal capacity are greater in countries with a long history of interstate conflict.

postcommunist experience. The "need to reconstruct public authority" is a "common denominator across Eastern Europe and the former Soviet Union" (Grzymala-Busse and Jones Luong, 2002, p. 530). Perhaps nowhere is this need felt more keenly than in the process of taxation: states starved of revenue are neither "grabbing" nor "captured" but merely "incapable" (Easter, 2002a).[18]

Postcommunist states satisfied this need by reconstructing public authority in different ways. As we have seen, countries in the former Soviet Union generally structured their tax systems more around the "old" revenue sources of corporate taxation and taxes on goods and services, whereas those in Eastern Europe concentrated more on direct taxation of individuals. This divergence was not merely the result of differences across countries in tax rates but of the extent to which tax systems were oriented to collect some taxes over others.

Figures 2.8 and 2.9 make the general point, illustrating the importance of tax collection in determining corporate income tax revenue in postcommunist countries using data from Schaffer and Turley (2002). Figure 2.8 shows, perhaps predictably, that corporate tax revenue is greater where corporate income tax rates are higher. However, there is substantial variation around the regression line, with four of the five largest outliers post-Soviet republics that collected more revenue than their tax rates suggest: Belarus, Uzbekistan, Ukraine, and Turkmenistan. (The fifth – Tajikistan – is a generally poor collector of all taxes, in part due to the long civil conflict that plagued that country during the 1990s; see, e.g., Kireyev, 2006.) In contrast, Figure 2.9 shows that corporate tax revenue is predicted quite well by the *effectiveness* of countries in collecting those taxes that are assessed, where effectiveness is measured as the ratio of the effective corporate tax rate (corporate tax revenue divided by income from capital) to the statutory rate.[19]

This is not a case of corporate tax collection being driven by good tax collection overall. Countries that are good at collecting corporate taxes are

[18] The picture of the postcommunist state as a "grabbing hand" is from Frye and Shleifer (1997), whereas in the postcommunist context the image of the "captured state" is most associated with Hellman (1998) and Hellman, Jones, and Kaufmann (2000). Other notable accounts of postcommunist state building include Herrera (2004, forthcoming), O'Dwyer (2004, 2006), and Colton and Holmes (2006).

[19] The correlation between the statutory corporate tax rate and the measure of effectiveness of tax collection is low: 0.12. In a regression of corporate tax revenue on both measures, the estimated impact of each is significantly different from zero at conventional levels, though the impact of effectiveness of tax collection is much more precisely estimated.

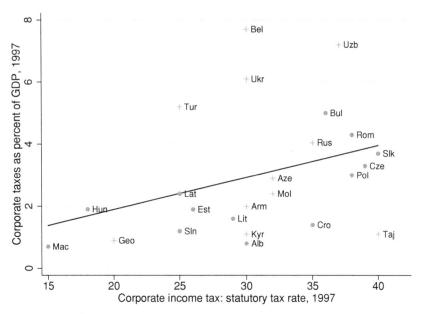

Figure 2.8 Corporate taxation: revenues versus statutory tax rate. Countries in CIS marked with crosses, countries in Eastern Europe and Baltics marked with circles.

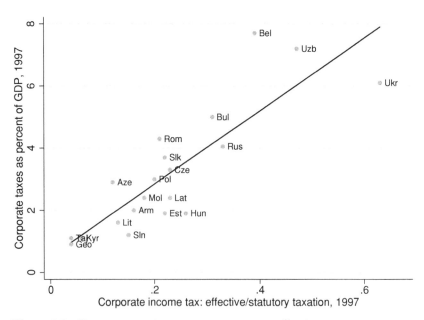

Figure 2.9 Corporate taxation: revenues versus tax collection.

not necessarily any better at collecting taxes on individuals, for example.[20] Rather, for reasons discussed above, certain countries chose to continue the communist-era focus on taxation of enterprises. Moreover, they did so unevenly. Throughout the former Soviet Union, officials concentrated their energies on encouraging compliance among familiar revenue sources, establishing "large taxpayer units" that employed a range of carrots and sticks to encourage compliance among communist-era enterprises (Ebrill and Havrylyshyn, 1999; Tanzi, 2001; Mitra and Stern, 2003; Berenson, 2006a), while expending less effort to extract revenues from historically underdeveloped sectors such as retail trade. In Russia, this tendency seemed to accelerate as the country lunged toward fiscal crisis in the mid- to late 1990s, with the tax police increasingly free to target even the most politically powerful companies (Easter, 2002b). Countries in Eastern Europe did not ignore large taxpayers, but in general the revenue net was cast more widely.

One particular manifestation of this difference in emphasis was that East European countries often seemed to work harder to figure out how to encourage tax compliance among small enterprises, which are hard to tax everywhere but especially so in transition countries given their novelty. Such efforts began early in Albania, for example, with the creation of a special tax regime for certain small enterprises in 1992. A more general system of small-business taxation was introduced in 1993, followed by a major overhaul in 1998, with the number of small businesses registered by tax authorities subsequently increasing by 28 percent in one year. In contrast, Ukraine did not get around to implementing a system of "presumptive" taxation (whereby to facilitate compliance, taxes are based on presumed rather than reported profits through the use of various indicators) for small businesses until 1998, when such a system was introduced by presidential decree. Attempts the following year to correct various inconsistencies in the system foundered in the Ukrainian parliament (Engelschalk, 2004).

The general result in many post-Soviet countries was that familiar forms of economic activity provided a disproportionate share of tax revenue. In Russia, for example, the fuel-and-pipeline sector in 1997 contributed approximately 12 percent of total gross domestic product (GDP), but more than a quarter of all tax revenue. In contrast, retail trade accounted for

---

[20] The correlation between the ratio of effective to statutory corporate taxation used in Figure 2.9 and the proportion of GDP collected as income, social security, and payroll taxes in 1997 is 0.19, versus a correlation between the ratio of effective to statutory corporate taxation and corporate tax revenue of 0.85.

a substantially larger 18 percent of GDP, but only 7 percent of all tax revenue (MacFarquhar, 1997). To some extent, this was the result of the inherently greater taxability of the fuel-and-pipeline sector (i.e., of the relative difficulty of hiding output that moves through pipelines and other government-controlled bottlenecks). However, this "natural" difference in taxability was exaggerated by the choices made by state officials in deciding which sectors to target. Quite simply, the enormous effort Russian officials devoted to extracting revenues from energy firms was not matched in most other sectors of the economy.

To further explore patterns of tax compliance, I turn to data from the 1999 Business Environment and Enterprise Performance Survey (BEEPS), a survey of firms conducted in twenty-five postcommunist countries by the World Bank and the European Bank for Reconstruction and Development. Through the BEEPS project, firms were surveyed on various aspects of business–state relations, including tax evasion.[21] In all, 4104 small and medium-sized enterprises were interviewed in twenty-five postcommunist countries and Turkey; in this book I exclude firms in Turkey from all analysis. Among postcommunist states in Eastern Europe and the former Soviet Union, only Tajikistan, Turkmenistan, and Yugoslavia were ultimately not included in the survey. Russian enterprises are somewhat more represented, with 552 of the 3954 firms in the subsample of firms in postcommunist countries.

Tax evasion is a crime, of course, so directly asking survey respondents if they evade taxes might yield uninformative responses or risk exposing respondents to legal action should confidentiality be compromised. As is conventional when questions touch on sensitive matters, respondents were instead asked about behavior by others who share similar characteristics: "What percentage of the sales of a typical firm in your area of activity would

---

[21] Sampling was done at the country level, with quotas established for industry, employment, location, ownership (foreign vs. domestic and private vs. state), and contribution of exports to total sales. Businesses were randomly sampled from business or telephone directories, with an initial screening interview by telephone to establish interest and conformity with quotas; unfortunately, no record seems to exist of the response rate at this initial screening stage. All follow-up interviews were carried out in person with a high-ranking officer of the firm. For purposes of consistency the survey was implemented in all countries by the local office of A. C. Nielsen. Further details on the survey and its implementation can be found in Hellman, Jones, Kaufmann and Schankerman (2000). Note that though Hellman et al. refer to a survey in 1999 of firms in twenty countries, six countries (Albania, Turkey, Latvia, Bosnia, the Serb Republic in Bosnia, and Macedonia) were added to the project later in the year.

you estimate is reported to the tax authorities, bearing in mind difficulties with complying with taxes and other regulations?"[22] For my purposes, this phrasing has the additional benefit of implying a sectoral characteristic, as the theoretical model presented in the following chapter suggests should be important to politicians providing sector-specific collective goods. Interviewers were instructed to assure respondents that their responses to this and other questions would remain anonymous. The response rate was quite high: 92.6 percent of all firms answered the question. Respondents were allowed to choose from eight predefined intervals (e.g., 70 to 79 percent). I code the responses as the midpoint of the intervals and treat the variable as continuous.[23] For consistency with the theoretical model presented in the following chapter, I recode this variable as the percentage of revenues *hidden* from tax authorities rather than the percentage reported. The mean level of revenue hiding is 21.5 percent, with 66.4 percent of firms stating that firms like theirs underreport sales to tax authorities. Variation is large, with a standard deviation of 25.9 percent.

Further, as I show below, this variation is systematic, with firms that are presumably more taxable (i.e., those that find it harder to hide revenues from tax authorities) reporting lower levels of revenue hiding. Thus, rather than refusing to answer the question or to admit that tax evasion takes place, respondents typically reported some level of revenue hiding, with the degree of hiding related to characteristics of the firm in an intuitive way. Although there are important differences in patterns of tax compliance across countries in the postcommunist world, the general empirical relationships are similar to those identified with the identical question in the much broader World Business Environment Survey (of which the BEEPS formed the initial stage) carried out by the World Bank in 1999 and 2000 in 80 countries (Batra, Kaufmann, and Stone, 2003; Tedds, 2007). Cross-country differences are also similar to those found with a similar question in a survey of firms in five postcommunist countries (Johnson, Kaufmann, McMillan, and Woodruff, 2000).

Table 2.1 presents the results of two OLS regressions – one for firms in the CIS and the other for firms in Eastern Europe and the Baltics – of revenue hiding on various firm characteristics plausibly associated with

---

[22] In three countries respondents were instead asked what percentage of sales is *hidden* from tax authorities. My results are robust to exclusion of firms in these countries from the sample.
[23] To check that this treatment does not drive the results, I reran the models discussed below as "interval regressions" (Stewart, 1983); the estimated coefficients are very similar.

Table 2.1. *Determinants of revenue hiding – CIS versus Eastern Europe and Baltics*

	CIS		Eastern Europe and Baltics	
	Estimated Coefficient	Standard Error	Estimated Coefficient	Standard Error
Log employment	−3.109**	−0.889	−1.601**	−0.430
Monopoly	−11.143**	−2.762	−6.464*	−2.608
1–3 competitors	−3.069	−1.361	−1.841	−1.730
State owned	−1.940	−1.983	−1.142	−1.154
De novo	−0.092	−2.261	−1.163	−1.603
Foreign ownership	−4.925	−3.229	−5.696*	−2.557
Exporter	−0.068	−1.930	−1.160	−1.605
Personal services	6.041	−5.419	2.014	−2.421
Wholesale trade	5.069*	−2.001	−0.764	−1.824
Transportation	4.562	−3.703	2.620	−2.334
Retail trade	1.614	−2.698	−0.500	−1.278
Construction	1.210	−2.082	−0.223	−2.528
Other	0.557	−5.974	−1.709	−2.320
Business services	−1.223	−3.572	−1.904	−2.463
Resource extraction	−3.245	−2.218	3.796	−2.901
Financial services	−8.616**	−1.564	−8.387*	−3.220
N	1758		1803	
R-squared	0.14		0.25	

Note. OLS regressions. Dependent variable is percentage of revenues hidden. Manufacturing is excluded industry dummy variable. Country and town-size dummies included. Standard errors corrected to allow for correlation of error terms across observations within countries. Significance levels: ** = 0.01, * = 0.05.

the ability to hide revenues from tax authorities.[24] As firm characteristics I include size (measured as the log of employment), degree of competition (two dummy variables indicating zero and one to three competitors, respectively), whether the firm is majority state owned or new ("de novo") or has any foreign ownership, whether the firm exports any goods directly, and a full set of industry dummy variables. Descriptive statistics and

[24] I obtain qualitatively similar results from a "fractional logit" model, which is appropriate when the dependent variable is a proportion (Papke and Wooldridge, 1996), and by regressing the log-odds ratio of the proportion of revenues hidden to that not hidden (with a small adjustment because some firms report zero revenue hiding and the log of zero is undefined) on firm characteristics. Further, as noted above, the OLS estimates are very similar to those from an "interval regression," where revenue hiding is treated as the underlying interval-coded variable. Note that the Tobit model is inappropriate here, despite the concentration of firms reporting zero revenue hiding, because revenue hiding cannot in principle take negative values (e.g., Sigelman and Zeng, 1999).

correlations for these firm characteristics (including membership in a business association, not used here but discussed in Chapter 4) are presented in Tables 2.A.5 and 2.A.6 in the appendix to this chapter. To control for variation across institutional environments in the average level of revenue hiding, I include both country and town-size dummies, the latter as a rough control for within-country variation in institutional environment as the precise location of firms within a country is not coded.[25] I report standard errors corrected to allow for correlation of error terms across observations within countries (i.e., I "cluster by country").

Two results stand out. First, for both subsamples, firms that are presumably more taxable do in fact report lower levels of revenue hiding. This is especially true of large firms and monopolies, both of which may be particularly visible to tax authorities and therefore relatively easy to tax. In addition, large firms may deal less in cash than do small firms – in Russia various schemes exist to facilitate cash transactions by large firms, but these are costly (Lopez-Claros and Alexashenko, 1998) – so the transactions of large enterprises are less easily hidden from state officials. Foreign ownership is negatively associated with revenue hiding – foreign firms may be constrained for reputational reasons to take fewer chances when deciding whether to hide revenues – though the coefficient on foreign ownership is precisely estimated only for the subsample of firms in Eastern Europe and the Baltics. Somewhat counterintuitively, state-owned enterprises are not significantly less likely to hide revenues, though it is likely that the revenues of state-owned firms are extracted by means other than formal taxation: the question in the BEEPS refers only to revenues reported to "tax authorities." Finally, controlling for other characteristics, new firms do not hide more than do old firms. However, as shown in Table 2.A.6 in the appendix to this chapter, new firms are overwhelmingly more likely to

---

[25] Note that country dummies alone would not control for variation across countries in the taxability of industries due to variation in those industries' ownership structures (see, e.g., Weinthal and Jones Luong, 2002, on variation in ownership of the natural-resource sector across post-Soviet states). I include ownership variables in part to pick up this cross-country effect. "Resource-extraction" firms in the sample are those engaged in either "farming/fishing/forestry" or "mining/quarrying." I treat state and foreign ownership asymmetrically because of the presumed mechanisms by which such ownership influences managerial behavior. State ownership is most likely to matter when the state has a controlling stake and thus has the ability to remove the manager if necessary (Shleifer and Vishny, 1994). In contrast, any level of foreign ownership may constrain managerial behavior, as foreign owners may choose to sell their stake or withhold further capital outlays if dissatisfied with their investment.

be small and somewhat less likely to be monopolies. Thus, even though there is no independent effect of de novo status, a typical new firm does hide more of its revenues than does a typical old enterprise. I take up this point further below.

Second, certain key characteristics – those that separate "new" from "old" economic activity – are much more highly correlated with revenue hiding among firms in the former Soviet Union than in Eastern Europe. For example, the estimated difference in revenue hiding between that reported by a very small firm with five employees and a large one with 1000 employees is 16 percentage points in the CIS but only 8 percentage points in Eastern Europe and the Baltics.[26] Monopolies report relatively greater tax compliance everywhere, but the size of this effect is nearly twice as large among firms in the CIS. Finally, the industry dummies line up in a somewhat more intuitive way for the subsample of firms in the CIS – for example, firms in personal service are more likely than manufacturing firms to hide, and manufacturing firms in turn are more likely than firms in resource extraction to hide – though the estimated coefficients are significantly different from each other only for industries on opposite ends of the spectrum. (Financial-service firms, often "new" in postcommunist countries, do report greater tax compliance, though this is consistent with the assertion of banking officials that their turnover is especially visible to tax authorities; see Hainsworth and Tompson, 2002.)

More generally, observable firm characteristics do much to explain variation in revenue hiding in the former Soviet Union but little in Eastern Europe, even though there is essentially no difference between the two halves of the postcommunist world in either the mean (21.3 in the CIS and 21.7 in Eastern Europe and the Baltics) or standard deviation (26.2 in the CIS and 25.6 in Eastern Europe and the Baltics) of the percentage of revenues hidden. The simplest way to see this is to observe that the R-squared statistic reported in Table 2.1 for the subsample of firms in the CIS is 0.14, versus 0.06 when only country dummies are included, whereas in Eastern Europe and the Baltics the difference is 0.25 versus 0.22. Roughly speaking, systematic variation in revenue hiding in the CIS is cross sectoral, whereas that in Eastern Europe and the Baltics is cross national.

The evidence is thus that the particular attention paid by officials in the former Soviet Union to "old" revenue sources has left a large gap

---

[26] To see this, recall that revenue hiding is regressed on the log of employment and observe that $\ln(1000) \approx 6.9$ and $\ln(5) \approx 1.6$.

between what firms that meet that definition and those that do not can get away with, whereas in Eastern Europe efforts to induce tax compliance have fallen on firms of various types more evenly. To further explore the new/old distinction, I calculate the predicted level of revenue hiding for new and old firms in each subsample by setting all covariates at their mean values for de novo and old enterprises, respectively. This approach takes into account the fact that new enterprises are more likely to be small, less likely to be monopolies, and so on, so the predicted level of revenue hiding for new and old enterprises may be quite different even though there is little or no independent effect of de novo status.[27] The same general pattern emerges. In both regions new firms are expected to have higher levels of revenue hiding, though the difference is substantially greater in the former Soviet Union: 25.8 percent for new firms versus 17.6 percent for old (a difference of 8.2 percent) in the CIS and 23.6 percent for new firms versus 18.9 percent for old (a difference of 4.7 percent) in Eastern Europe and the Baltics. New firms seem to find it especially easy to evade taxes, relative to old firms, in the former Soviet Union.

Finally, I perform the same exercise for individual countries, running regressions of the sort in Table 2.1 separately for each country and then for each country calculating the predicted level of revenue hiding for new and old firms according to the procedure outlined just above. These esti-mates are generally imprecise, as there is considerable noise in the revenue-hiding measure and, with the exception of Russia (and, to a lesser degree, Poland and Ukraine), the sample sizes for individual countries are not large. Nonetheless, a clear pattern of tax compliance across postcommunist coun-tries emerges from the data. As shown in Figure 2.10, where I use the ratio of revenues *reported* by old and new firms, old firms are relatively more tax compliant in countries that inherited from communism especially con-centrated industrial structures, as reflected in low energy efficiency. Ta-ble 2.A.7 in the appendix to this chapter presents a more formal test,

---

[27] The obvious drawback of this approach is that the BEEPS is not a true random sample of firms, so the sample means of the covariates for new and old firms may be poor estimates of the population means. An alternative approach would be to define a "typical" new and old firm (e.g., a typical new firm has five employees, has more than three competitors, is not state owned, etc.) and calculate predicted levels of revenue hiding for these ideal types. However, ignorance of population means for new and old firms implies that any such definition would be necessarily ad hoc. Moreover, what constitutes a "typical" new or old firm likely differs from country to country. Nonetheless, I calculated predicted values for various definitions of typical new and old firms, with qualitative results similar to those reported in this and the next paragraph.

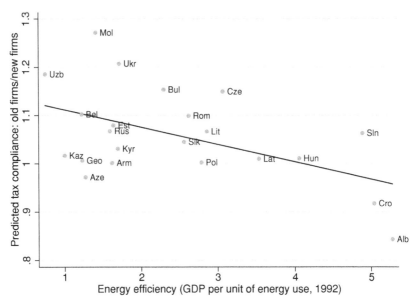

Figure 2.10 Inherited industrial structure (as proxied by energy efficiency of economy) and tax compliance. Predicted tax compliance is the predicted percentage of revenues reported to tax authorities with covariates set at mean values for old and new firms, respectively. The ratio of predicted tax compliance for old and new firms is depicted.

regressing the ratio of expected tax compliance of old and new firms on the four initial conditions discussed above. Only the estimated effect of industrial structure, as proxied by energy efficiency, is statistically significantly different from zero at the 5-percent level.[28] The implication is that countries with highly concentrated industrial structures, which as shown above are more inclined to favor corporate taxes in their tax structures, collected those taxes by encouraging compliance among Soviet-era enterprises.

The BEEPS data thus present the following picture, one complementary to that provided by cross-country data on tax structure: countries in the former Soviet Union, inclined for reasons exogenous to the transition to favor "old" over "new" taxes, constructed tax systems to most efficiently collect those taxes. The systems that emerged were not particularly

---

[28] In Table 2.A.7 I report results from a weighted least squares regression, where I weight observations by the number of firms in the regressions used to generate the tax-compliance ratios to reflect the generally greater precision of estimates in countries with more firms in the BEEPS sample. OLS regression produces very similar results.

good at inducing tax compliance among new firms but were somewhat better at collecting taxes from old ones (i.e., from large, monopolistic firms in certain industries). In contrast, the countries of Eastern Europe, turning more to "new" forms of taxation, built tax systems capable of collecting those taxes. Less reliant on old revenue sources, state officials devoted attention more equally to enterprises of all types. The consequence was relatively small differences in the tax compliance of old and new enterprises.

This picture is not without caveats, some of which are important when I use revenue hiding to capture the division of gains from collective-goods provision later in the book. First, hiding revenues is not the only way to evade taxes. The postcommunist experience has served up a rich menu of methods of tax evasion, not all of which require that revenues actually be hidden from tax authorities. One of these takes advantage of the growth of barter during the 1990s in many postcommunist economies. Firms receiving payment in goods rather than cash offer less for tax authorities to seize (Gaddy and Ickes, 1998, 2002; Hendley, Ickes, and Ryterman, 1998; Shleifer and Treisman, 2000; Aitken, 2001).[29] Credibly able to argue that they do not have the cash to make tax payments, firms may instead offer to "pay" taxes through write-offs of government debt for goods purchased from the enterprise, a procedure that may leave the government with less real tax revenue than appears on the books. In principle, then, revenue hiding and tax evasion through barter may be substitutes, so firms that are hiding more revenues may not necessarily be paying fewer taxes. The BEEPS questionnaire offers some limited assistance in dealing with this issue, including a question only for firms in Russia and Ukraine that asks whether the firm received tax offsets from any level of government. As it turns out, tax offsets and revenue hiding are *positively* correlated for these firms (the estimated coefficient on the tax-offsets variable when included in regressions of the sort in Table 2.1 is large and statistically significant), suggesting that revenue hiding and barter are complementary strategies of evading taxes and thus that revenue hiding may be a good measure of tax evasion more generally.

Similarly, politically powerful firms may report their revenues but then refuse to meet their tax obligations, appealing to political patrons for

[29] Barter may also provide other advantages, including the ability to price discriminate among consumers (Woodruff, 2000) and to protect working capital from outside creditors (Guriev, Makarov, and Maurel, 2002).

protection (Ponomareva and Zhuravskaya, 2004; Radaev, 2002). But in fact, after controlling for other firm characteristics, the measure of revenue hiding in the BEEPS is uncorrelated with responses to a question asking firms if they receive "subsidies (including tolerance of tax arrears) from local or national government." Firms that report that they – or more precisely, "typical" firms in their "area of activity" – hide revenues from tax authorities do in fact seem to be less tax compliant.

Finally, tax authorities may themselves do some of the hiding. Daniel Treisman, for example, has argued that Russian tax officials – dependent on regional governments for housing, wages, and other benefits not provided by Moscow – have often colluded with local firms and regional administrations to hide revenues from the federal center (Treisman, 1999*b*; Cai and Treisman, 2004; see also Berkowitz and Li, 2000; Gaddy and Ickes, 2002; Sonin, 2005; Easter, 2006*a*). This possibility creates obvious problems in interpreting the BEEPS question used to measure tax compliance: the question refers merely to "tax authorities" without specifying from which authorities taxes might be hidden. It also highlights that intergovernmental relations may complicate the theory of representation through taxation that I develop and test in the following two chapters. I deal with this issue in meat-axe fashion when exploring the empirical relationship between collective-goods provision and revenue hiding in Chapter 4, simply excluding firms in Russia, which has the most truly federal system in the postcommunist world and thus is likely most subject to problems of this sort, as a robustness check for the results I report there.

2.5 Summary

All postcommunist countries were gripped by revenue crisis in the early 1990s, as the institutions designed to finance the communist state proved ill suited to a market economy. Postcommunist officials were forced to rapidly create tax systems to extract revenues from private actors. The particular systems that they created depended on characteristics of the countries that they governed. Countries that were more endowed with highly concentrated industrial structures, farther from the West, and economically less developed created tax systems structured around enterprise taxation and taxation of goods and services, both important Soviet-era revenue sources. Countries that were less burdened by Stalinist industrial structures, closer to the West, and economically more advanced focused instead on direct taxation of individuals, a revenue source largely neglected by communist states. Roughly speaking, the countries of the former Soviet Union focused more on "old" revenue sources, whereas those of Eastern Europe emphasized "new" sources. Although the mix of revenues evolved somewhat over the 1990s, especially in the former Soviet Union, the basic divide was remarkably stable.

These differences in emphasis were reflected in patterns of tax collection across postcommunist countries. Officials in the former Soviet Union focused on extracting revenues from familiar sources: the large, monopolistic enterprises in particular industries that had formed the revenue base of the communist state. Natural differences in the taxability of economic activity, such as the relative ease with which small firms hide revenues from the state, were magnified by this policy. In contrast, tax systems in Eastern Europe were reformed to cast the revenue net more widely, with the consequence that systematic differences in what firms could hide from the state were generally much smaller.

The divide is particularly evident in the tax compliance of new and old enterprises. In both regions new firms hid more of their revenues from tax authorities than did old firms, but the difference was roughly twice as large in the former Soviet Union as in Eastern Europe. The degree to which new firms were relatively less compliant was especially sharp in countries endowed with highly concentrated industrial structures, implying that the emphasis on corporate taxation in those countries came about as authorities focused on encouraging compliance by Soviet-era enterprises.

The persistent divide between Eastern Europe and the former Soviet Union in the degree of reliance on novel or familiar revenue sources suggests that choices made during the early 1990s about how to build the postcommunist state had lasting consequences. Tax systems are institutions. Like other institutions, they are ultimately endogenous to the choices of social actors, with major change possible in the presence of some shock to the status quo. The collapse of communism was such a shock. However, in the short run tax systems serve to structure interactions between the state and private actors, determining (together with characteristics of economic actors) the division of gains between the two.

In the next chapter I demonstrate theoretically the process by which this division of gains determines the incentives of politicians to provide sector-specific collective goods. Analytically, I treat the taxability of economic activity as exogenous and show how differences in taxability across sectors may lead to bias in the provision of collective goods. I return to the results of this chapter when I examine patterns of collective-goods provision in Chapter 4. As will be seen, the taxability of economic activity exerts the strongest influence on provision of collective goods in those countries that least reformed their tax systems and thus possessed political economies especially dependent on familiar revenue sources.

2.A Appendix: Supplementary Tables and Figures

Table 2.A.1. *Mean tax structure, 1994–2000*

	Corporate Taxes	Taxes on Goods and Services	Income, Social Security, and Payroll Taxes	Other Taxes
EE and Baltics				
Albania	0.08	0.41	0.25	0.25
Bulgaria	0.13	0.35	0.43	0.09
Croatia	0.03	0.45	0.42	0.10
Czech Republic	0.11	0.30	0.53	0.06
Estonia	0.06	0.35	0.55	0.04
Hungary	0.06	0.37	0.48	0.10
Latvia	0.07	0.35	0.51	0.07
Lithuania	0.06	0.37	0.51	0.07
Macedonia	0.03	0.34	0.51	0.12
Poland	0.08	0.33	0.49	0.11
Romania	0.12	0.28	0.49	0.11
Slovakia	0.12	0.31	0.49	0.07
Slovenia	0.03	0.35	0.53	0.10
CIS				
Armenia	0.20	0.40	0.24	0.15
Azerbaijan	0.22	0.31	0.31	0.16
Belarus	0.22	0.43	0.26	0.09
Georgia	0.12	0.42	0.29	0.18
Kyrgyzstan	0.09	0.47	0.35	0.09
Moldova	0.12	0.42	0.36	0.10
Russia	0.18	0.30	0.37	0.15
Tajikistan	0.13	0.48	0.20	0.19
Turkmenistan	0.21	0.46	0.29	0.05
Ukraine	0.20	0.31	0.39	0.10
Uzbekistan	0.23	0.52	0.13	0.12

Table 2.A.2. *Initial conditions*

	Energy Efficiency	Natural Resources	Distance from West	1989 GNP per Capita at PPP
EE and Baltics				
Albania	5.28	Poor	811	1400
Bulgaria	2.29	Poor	818	5000
Croatia	5.04	Poor	268	6171
Czech Republic	3.06	Poor	251	8600
Estonia	1.64	Poor	1041	8900
Hungary	4.05	Poor	217	6810
Latvia	3.53	Poor	844	8590
Lithuania	2.86	Poor	822	6430
Poland	2.78	Moderate	516	5150
Romania	2.62	Moderate	856	3470
Slovakia	2.56	Poor	55	7600
Slovenia	4.88	Poor	276	9200
CIS				
Armenia	1.62	Poor	2399	5530
Azerbaijan	1.27	Rich	2780	4620
Belarus	1.22	Poor	955	7010
Georgia	1.23	Moderate	2338	5590
Kyrgyzstan	1.69	Poor	4467	3180
Moldova	1.41	Poor	945	4670
Russia	1.59	Rich	1608	7720
Tajikistan	0.89	Poor	4404	3010
Turkmenistan	1.62	Rich	3550	4230
Ukraine	1.71	Moderate	1054	5680
Uzbekistan	0.74	Moderate	4164	2740

Note. Data definitions and sources given in text.

Table 2.A.3. *Correlations: location and initial conditions*

	CIS	Energy Efficiency	Natural Resources	Distance from West	1989 GNP per Capita at PPP
CIS	1.0000				
Energy efficiency	−0.7674	1.0000			
Natural resources	0.4555	−0.3951	1.0000		
Distance from West	0.7356	−0.6399	0.3449	1.0000	
1989 GNP per capita at PPP	−0.3650	0.2106	−0.2034	−0.5793	1.0000

Table 2.A.4. *Initial conditions and tax structure*

	Estimated Coefficient	Standard Error
Equation 1: Log ratio of corporate taxes to other taxes		
Energy efficiency	−0.419	0.095
Natural resources	0.136	0.139
Distance from West (1000 km)	−0.117	0.105
1989 GNP per capita at PPP (1000 USD)	0.019	0.055
Constant	1.093	0.585
"*R*-squared"	0.576	
Equation 2: Log ratio of taxes on goods and services to other taxes		
Energy efficiency	−0.023	0.084
Natural resources	−0.171	0.123
Distance from West (1000 km)	0.110	0.093
1989 GNP per capita at PPP (1000 USD)	0.107	0.048
Constant	0.682	0.517
"*R*-squared"	0.249	
Equation 3: Log ratio of income, social security, and payroll taxes to other taxes		
Energy efficiency	−0.007	0.111
Natural resources	−0.037	0.161
Distance from West (1000 km)	−0.104	0.122
1989 GNP per capita at PPP (1000 USD)	0.183	0.063
Constant	0.450	0.678
"*R*-squared"	0.485	

Note. Seemingly unrelated regression. $N = 23$.

Table 2.A.5. *BEEPS data – summary statistics*

	Full Sample			CIS			Eastern Europe and Baltics		
	Mean	Std. Dev.	N	Mean	Std. Dev.	N	Mean	Std. Dev.	N
Revenue hiding	21.5	25.9	3662	21.3	26.2	1785	21.7	25.6	1877
Association member	0.240		3953	0.145		1866	0.326		2087
Log employment	3.97	1.59	3952	4.19	1.47	1866	3.78	1.67	2086
Monopoly	0.096		3949	0.096		1866	0.097		2083
1–3 competitors	0.129		3949	0.123		1866	0.135		2083
State owned	0.141		3870	0.132		1853	0.148		2017
De novo	0.528		3937	0.465		1855	0.583		2082
Foreign ownership	0.127		3947	0.102		1865	0.148		2082
Exporter	0.237		3945	0.138		1864	0.325		2081
Personal services	0.054		3951	0.036		1866	0.070		2085
Transportation	0.059		3951	0.056		1866	0.061		2085
Wholesale trade	0.137		3951	0.130		1866	0.143		2085
Retail trade	0.145		3951	0.141		1866	0.147		2085
Construction	0.087		3951	0.106		1866	0.070		2085
Other	0.015		3951	0.011		1866	0.019		2085
Resource extraction	0.123		3951	0.203		1866	0.051		2085
Business services	0.062		3951	0.042		1866	0.080		2085
Financial services	0.017		3951	0.006		1866	0.027		2085
Manufacturing	0.301		3951	0.267		1866	0.332		2085

Table 2.A.6. *Correlations in BEEPS data*

	Revenue Hiding	Association Member	Log Employment	Monopoly	1–3 Competitors	State Owned	De novo	Foreign Ownership	Exporter
				Full Sample					
Revenue hiding	1.0000								
Association member	-0.0685	1.0000							
Log employment	-0.1975	0.1675	1.0000						
Monopoly	-0.1043	-0.0174	0.1233	1.0000					
1–3 competitors	-0.0217	0.0403	0.0970	-0.1207	1.0000				
State owned	-0.0549	0.0496	0.3367	0.2322	0.0540	1.0000			
De novo	0.1229	-0.1012	-0.5796	-0.1454	-0.0361	-0.4350	1.0000		
Foreign ownership	-0.1016	0.1150	0.0873	0.0023	0.0587	-0.1123	-0.0104	1.0000	
Exporter	-0.0727	0.1975	0.2545	0.0525	0.1146	0.0566	-0.1378	0.1862	1.0000
				CIS					
Revenue hiding	1.0000								
Association member	-0.0201	1.0000							
Log employment	-0.2424	0.1266	1.0000						
Monopoly	-0.1239	0.0061	0.0867	1.0000					
1–3 competitors	-0.0278	0.0121	0.0795	-0.1213	1.0000				
State owned	-0.1075	0.0226	0.2689	0.2486	0.0224	1.0000			
De novo	0.1560	-0.0267	-0.5376	-0.1167	-0.0102	-0.3651	1.0000		
Foreign ownership	-0.0571	0.0676	-0.0278	0.0121	0.0351	-0.0987	0.0332	1.0000	
Exporter	-0.0574	0.1085	0.1816	0.0567	0.0791	0.0344	-0.0848	0.2003	1.0000
				Eastern Europe and Baltics					
Revenue hiding	1.0000								
Association member	-0.1116	1.0000							
Log employment	-0.1607	0.2588	1.0000						
Monopoly	-0.0833	-0.0279	0.1542	1.0000					
1–3 competitors	-0.0162	0.0538	0.1194	-0.1195	1.0000				
State owned	-0.0049	0.0639	0.4054	0.2176	0.0815	1.0000			
De novo	0.0896	-0.2221	-0.6022	-0.1724	-0.0677	-0.5169	1.0000		
Foreign ownership	-0.1415	0.1227	0.1924	-0.0031	0.0748	-0.1267	-0.0676	1.0000	
Exporter	-0.0920	0.1827	0.3736	0.0628	0.1369	0.0678	-0.2474	0.1596	1.0000

Table 2.A.7. *Initial conditions and tax compliance*

	Estimated Coefficient	Standard Error
Energy efficiency	−0.068**	0.018
Natural resources	−0.031	0.023
Distance from West (1000 km)	−0.036	0.019
1989 GNP per capita at PPP (1000 USD)	−0.001	0.010
Constant	1.302**	0.099
N	22	
R-squared	0.47	

Note. Weighted least squares regression; see text for details. Dependent variable is ratio of predicted tax compliance for old and new firms. Significance levels: ** $= 0.01$, * $= 0.05$.

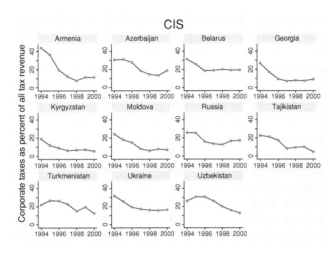

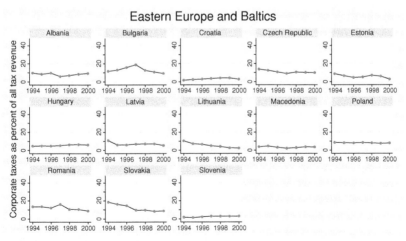

Figure 2.A.1 Corporate taxation over time.

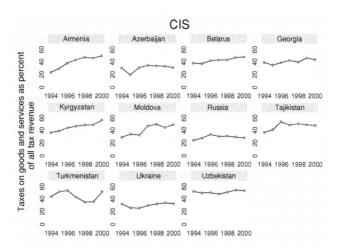

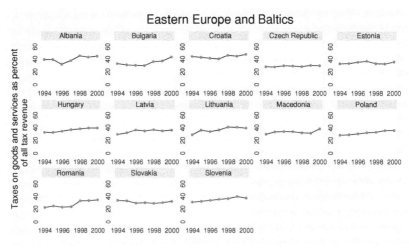

Figure 2.A.2 Taxation of goods and services over time.

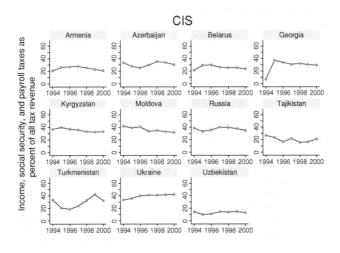

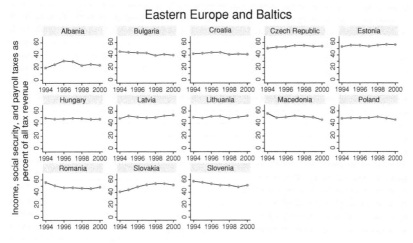

Figure 2.A.3 Taxation of individuals over time.

3

The Logic of Representation through Taxation

Politics, writes Harold Lasswell, is the question of "who gets what, when, how" (Lasswell, 1936). Since Mancur Olson's classic study of *The Logic of Collective Action* (Olson, 1965), students have been taught that the first and best answer to this question is that organized groups get what they want, at least most of the time, by coordinating contributions of time and money to influence the political process. Others may have a larger collective stake in political outcomes, but because of the free-rider problem their voices are heard more faintly and their desires attended to less assiduously.

Olson's answer to Lasswell's question raises two further concerns: how is it that some groups become organized, given the free-rider problem, and what exactly is it about the political process that gives the advantage to those that are organized? With respect to the first question, Olson argued that small groups – or more precisely, groups where the benefits of collective action are concentrated among a small number of members – more easily overcome barriers to organization, as an individual member with claim to a large share of a collective benefit cares less if others are free riding on her efforts. Political action may also be taken by large groups, but Olson suggested that this would be more a "by-product" of the provision of selective incentives. Thus, those same students who are taught that the spoils of politics accrue to the organized also learn that a small number of Florida and Louisiana sugar companies benefit at the expense of numerous sugar consumers and that environmental organizations encourage participation by providing T-shirts to contributors.

There has been much debate on the question of how the collective-action problem is overcome and whether Olson's inferences about the role of group size were right.[1] This is not my focus. Rather, I am concerned with the second issue raised above: how it is that those who have overcome their collective-action problems seize the political initiative. I think at times we have been too quick to assume that groups, once organized, can credibly promise whatever politicians value in return for favorable policy treatment. As a consequence, we perhaps have been too ready to conclude that bias in the provision of collective goods arises primarily from the fact that some groups are organized, whereas others are not.

In this chapter I discuss the consequences of collective action when some aspects of agreements between politicians and organized interests are unenforceable, or in the language of the economic theory of contracts, "noncontractible." I focus on the inability of organized economic sectors to credibly promise that their members will pay more taxes in return for favorable policy treatment. Taxation by its nature invites free riding, as economic actors receive the collective goods paid for out of tax revenue whether or not they pay taxes themselves. In principle the logic of repeated interaction might prevent this, but the inability of firms to fully monitor each others' tax compliance makes this unlikely.[2] Politicians thus understand that some firms will by their nature be more tax compliant than others, so the anticipated tax compliance of economic sectors helps to determine policy choice (e.g., Levi, 1988; Bates, 1989; Haggard, 1990; Steinmo, 1993; Cheibub, 1998).

---

[1] On group size in particular, see, for example, Frohlich and Oppenheimer (1970); Chamberlin (1974); Hardin (1982); Sandler (1992); and Grier, Munger, and Roberts (1994). Works in this tradition typically stress the benefits of participation; Brady, Verba, and Schlozman (1995) focus instead on the costs (see also Verba, Schlozman, and Brady, 1995). For a review of the literature on collective action, see Tarrow (1998).

[2] The difficulty of designing mechanisms to prevent tax evasion among economic actors can be seen in the periodic discussions between Vladimir Putin's Kremlin and Russia's "oligarchs" (often represented formally by the Russian Union of Industrialists and Entrepreneurs) of a "social contract" by which the state would provide property-rights protection in return for tax compliance and other socially responsible behavior on the part of business. That such agreements needed to be repeatedly proposed illustrates their failure to stick. Part of the problem may have been that there was no good enforcement mechanism within the Union to enforce cooperation among its members (Tompson, 2005). On meetings between Putin and the oligarchs, see, for example, Rutland (2004) and Guriev and Rachinsky (2005) in reference to the first meeting on July 28, 2000; "Putin Asks Oligarchs for a Handout," *Moscow Times*, January 25, 2001; "Reshili ne mel'chit'," *Vedomosti*, July 22, 2003; "RSPP sozrel do sotsial'noi otvetstvennosti biznesa," *Vedomosti*, July 31, 2003; and "Putin urges Russian business to pay taxes, show patriotism," BBC Monitoring, November 16, 2004. In the first of these meetings Putin apparently also emphasized that the oligarchs should refrain from participation in politics.

I argue in particular that bargaining between politicians and organized sectors over the provision of collective goods is influenced by the recognition that firms will evade taxes to the extent that they can get away with it, so the anticipated tax compliance of firms in both organized and unorganized sectors determines the division of gains from any policy that a politician might adopt.[3] This is the logic of "representation through taxation." Formally, the model I present below is an adaptation of the well-known lobbying model of Grossman and Helpman (1994, 2001). The Grossman–Helpman model captures in a stylized, useful, and admittedly crass way the strategic calculations of those involved in lobbying by treating the politician as an auctioneer who literally sells policy to special interests. This model is itself a particular case of a more general class of "menu auction" models (Bernheim and Whinston, 1986), and as that name suggests, it is as if each lobby provides the politician with a menu, where next to every policy that could in principle be chosen is the price that the lobby promises to pay if that policy is implemented. In some settings this promise may be explicit, but in general it is best to think of these promises as implicit, where one way or another the lobbies merely make their preferences known. Having collected menus from every bidder, the seller then weighs the sum total of contributions promised from all bidders for any particular policy, factors in her own preferences over the policy outcome, and chooses the policy that provides her with the greatest overall benefit.

Grossman and Helpman show that if a reasonable assumption is made about the nature of the contributions promised by special interests, then equilibrium policy maximizes a weighted sum of the politician's policy preferences and those of organized special interests.[4] The particular innovation

---

[3] The idea that the division of gains ex post affects investment incentives ex ante when contracts are incomplete is central to the literature on the economic theory of the firm (Coase, 1937; Williamson, 1975, 1985; Klein, Crawford, and Alchian, 1978; Grossman and Hart, 1986; Hart and Moore, 1990). Shleifer and Vishny (1994) extend the theory of the firm to business–state relations, but they consider only bargaining between a politician and a single firm. Acemoglu (2005) develops a model in which the incentive of a revenue-maximizing ruler to invest in public goods depends on the state's fiscal capacity, but he does not extend the analysis to consider differences across sectors in the ability to tax.

[4] This is a special case of a more general result by Bernheim and Whinston (1986), who show that any equilibrium of a menu-auction game is jointly efficient when bidders' "contribution schedules" – the contributions promised for every possible policy that could be implemented – are "truthful," that is, when any differences in the bidder's promised contributions reflect differences in the payoff received from different policies. Grossman and Helpman, who refer to such contribution schedules as "compensating," assume – as do I – that for both politician and organized groups the marginal utility from an additional dollar of

of my model is that the policy preferences of both the politician and special interests are themselves derived from the anticipated tax compliance of the various sectors to which collective goods can be provided. The politician values tax revenue from both organized and disorganized sectors, so she is more inclined to provide collective goods to a sector when firms in a sector find it especially difficult to hide revenues from the state (i.e., when those firms are more "taxable"). At the same time, she is made through the promise of contributions to care about the welfare of organized groups, which for a given level of collective-goods provision is less when the firms in that sector are more easily taxed.

The political value of a sector thus depends on both its taxability and organization, as well as on the relative value the politician places on tax revenue and contributions from organized sectors. When tax revenue is a first-order political concern and economic sectors differ greatly in their anticipated tax compliance, as was the case in much of the postcommunist world during the 1990s, then unorganized sectors that are easy to tax may benefit from better collective-goods provision than organized sectors that are hard to tax. Alternatively, organized sectors may receive better policy treatment than unorganized sectors, but because of their taxability rather than their organization.

The model I present below is "reduced-form" in the sense that it assumes that politicians value tax revenue and whatever can be credibly promised by organized groups rather than deriving those assumptions from first principles. With respect to the analysis of postcommunist political economy, this comes at some loss, as it obscures important variation in postcommunist political systems. Nonetheless, it is general enough to incorporate fundamental differences in the relationship between the state and economic interests, and as I will show it does a very good job of explaining patterns of collective-goods provision – justice, police protection, and so on – across postcommunist space. At the same time, the argument extends beyond the political economy of postcommunism that is my empirical focus. In the developing world, as in many postcommunist countries, fiscal capacity is typically weak. Tax administrations consequently focus their energies on a few highly taxable sectors, letting others escape the revenue net. To the extent that this is the case, the model I propose may help to explain political-economic outcomes.

contributions paid or received is constant and independent of the policy chosen. This implies that the jointly efficient outcome takes the form that they describe.

Beyond the political economy of taxation, the theoretical framework I advance in this chapter can be used to analyze any situation where politicians have preferences over policy outcomes that cannot be achieved through direct negotiation with organized groups. The precise nature of bargaining and policy choice depends on the context, but the essential elements of the process are the same: organized groups promise what they can credibly deliver, and in choosing policy the politician takes into account not only those promises but also the uncoordinated actions of members of both organized and unorganized groups. When there are large differences in the anticipated behavior of groups with respect to what is noncontractible but politically important, viewing politics through the lens provided here may be more revealing than relying on a narrow Olsonian perspective.

The value of this theoretical framework may be especially large during periods of "extraordinary" politics, when politicians are concerned as much with how to induce a desired policy outcome as with the blandishments of organized groups. During such periods – possible, for example, during times of war or economic crisis – the uncoordinated actions of group members can have particular relevance, with politicians inclined to favor those who by their nature happen to contribute to the preferred policy outcome, regardless of whether they are organized. In contrast, during periods of "normal" politics the usual, Olsonian concerns should predominate.

3.1 Theoretical Framework

In this section I present in detail the logic of representation through taxation. I formalize this logic in the appendix to this chapter.

In my model there are three sets of actors: a politician who decides on the allocation of collective goods across economic sectors, some subset of which is organized; firms that populate those sectors; and lobbies that represent organized sectors. Collective goods are sector specific and serve to enhance the production of firms in that sector and no other; in Section 3.2, I relax this assumption to allow for the possibility that collective goods may benefit more than one sector. The politician has at her disposal a fixed budget from which to allocate funds to collective goods for different sectors. In deciding on this allocation she takes into consideration two factors: the tax revenue produced by that sector and the contributions promised by organized-sector lobbies. Organized-sector lobbies may credibly promise contributions in return for the provision of collective goods to their sectors, but they are unable to credibly promise that their members will fully report their revenues to tax authorities in exchange for collective goods. Rather, individual firms hide what they can get away with, even if that implies that the politician will allocate fewer collective goods to their sector.

In particular, I assume that the politician maximizes a weighted average of tax revenue and contributions. The distinction between the two is not that the politician favors one over the other – the relative weight given to each is one of the key parameters of the model, but I do not require that the weight take any particular value – but rather that organized groups can only credibly promise contributions in return for favorable policy treatment. Even in the special case of the model where contributions and tax revenue have exactly the same value to the politician, the provision of collective goods across sectors may be determined more by considerations of tax revenue if sectors differ greatly in their anticipated tax compliance.

A sector, in my telling, is a set of firms that share a common organization (or lack thereof) – they are represented by a common lobby, if organized – and a common technology. In particular, all firms in a sector are assumed to have the same taxability, meaning that they find it equally costly to hide revenues from tax authorities. The more taxable is a sector, the more costly it is for firms in that sector to hide revenues. Given that tax compliance is "noncontractible," firms hide what they can get away with regardless of what has been agreed to by the politician and organized-sector lobbies, with firms in sectors that are more taxable therefore hiding less.

As is evident from the analysis of the BEEPS data in the previous chapter, the taxability of a sector may be determined by many factors, some technological and others organizational. For example, small firms generally deal more in cash than do large firms and so may find it easier to hide transactions from tax authorities. The same is true of service and retail firms, a reality I have often encountered in Moscow stores where the credit-card machine was "broken" for months on end to encourage cash transactions that could be kept off the books. Conversely, natural-resource firms may find it relatively difficult to hide revenues from tax authorities, as their output is more likely to travel through government-controlled bottlenecks such as ports and pipelines. The government may also have an information advantage vis-à-vis certain firms (e.g., state-owned enterprises or monopolies) that makes it harder for those firms to hide revenues from the state. Finally, the loss of reputation from being caught hiding revenues may be especially costly for certain firms; conversations I have had with representatives of multinational firms in postcommunist countries suggest that this may apply in part to their companies.

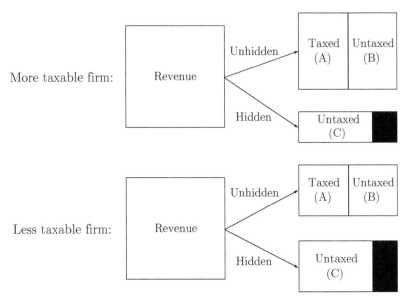

Figure 3.1 The allocation of revenue for a firm that is more and less taxable, respectively. The solid areas represent revenue that is destroyed in the process of hiding. Total untaxed revenue is greater for the less taxable firm. A politician cares about those regions labeled *A* for all sectors and also cares about those regions labeled *B* and *C* (in proportion to the degree that the politician values contributions versus tax revenue) for sectors that are organized.

Moreover, as the analysis in the previous chapter showed, these firm characteristics may interact in important ways with the tax systems of the countries in which firms are located. For example, the emphasis on communist-era revenue sources in the former Soviet Union meant that firms that were "naturally" more taxable – large, monopolistic enterprises in particular industries – were especially easy to tax relative to firms in sectors less prevalent under communism. In contrast, in Eastern Europe the difference between more and less taxable sectors was less stark, the result of decisions made in the early 1990s to build tax systems structured around new revenue sources.

Figure 3.1 shows how the taxability of a firm determines the allocation of revenue between the firm and the state. Hiding revenue is costly for any firm – foreign bank accounts and sham firms must be established and frequently rotated to avoid the detection of tax authorities,[5] extra accountants

---

[5] The Russian term for such firms – *odnodnevki* "one-day firms" – reflects their short lives. Yakovlev (2001) describes the use of such firms to evade taxes.

must be hired, and so on – but firms that are more taxable destroy more revenue in the process of hiding it than do those that are less taxable. Consequently, firms that are more taxable opt for a lower level of hiding, thus surrendering a greater proportion of their revenue to tax authorities and keeping a smaller proportion for themselves.[6]

Implicit in this discussion is the assumption that tax *rates* are the same for all sectors. As a first-order approximation this is certainly correct: for example, governments do not generally maintain separate profit taxes for individual sectors. Nonetheless, some exceptions are possible. In Section 3.2, I therefore explore the empirical implications of relaxing the assumption that the tax rate is fixed and constant across sectors. As I will show in Chapter 4, evidence from postcommunist states is inconsistent with this alternative conceptualization.

The logic of representation through taxation is that the taxability of a sector determines the division of gains from collective-goods provision and hence the incentive of politicians to provide collective goods to that sector. A politician always cares about tax revenue: those regions labeled *A* in Figure 3.1. It is not, however, the case that the politician always cares *exclusively* about tax revenue. Rather, when a sector is organized the politician is made to care about that portion of revenue that is retained by firms in a sector, that is, about those regions labeled *B* and *C*, because to not care means sacrificing the contributions that firms in the sector are willing to pay to increase the value of their share of production. The relative importance to the politician of tax revenue and contributions determines the weight she gives to revenue surrendered by all firms as taxes versus revenue retained by firms in organized sectors.

Thus, the *importance* of a sector to a politician is a function of three factors:

1. The taxability of the sector, which determines the allocation of revenue between the state (in Figure 3.1, region *A*) and firms in the sector (regions *B* and *C*).
2. Whether the sector is organized, which determines whether a politician cares about revenue retained by firms in the sector (regions *B* and *C*) as well as tax revenue (region *A*).

---

[6] In the figure, the more taxable firm retains 9/16 of total revenue, versus 5/8 > 9/16 for the less taxable firm. The formalization in the appendix to this chapter shows it is generally the case that firms that are less taxable retain a larger proportion of revenue from production.

3. The degree to which the politician values tax revenue relative to contributions, which determines the weight she gives to tax revenue (region A) and, if the sector is organized, to revenue retained by firms in the sector (regions B and C).

Given that the politician has a limited budget for collective goods at her disposal, she allocates more collective goods to sectors that are more important.

3.2 Empirical Predictions

In this section I describe the empirical predictions that follow from the logic of representation through taxation. As first discussed in the previous chapter, the BEEPS survey of firms I use to test these predictions includes a question on the degree to which firms hide revenues from tax authorities. I therefore present the empirical predictions in terms of the degree of revenue hiding by firms in a sector, though in the discussion I often refer to the taxability of the sector. So long as the tax rate is fixed and constant across sectors, these two concepts are analytically equivalent: firms that are more taxable hide less. This result, though theoretically trivial, is a first testable empirical prediction, one for which I found support in Chapter 2.

Prediction 1. When tax rates are constant across sectors, firms in sectors that are more taxable, that is, those whose firms find it more costly to hide revenues from the state, hide less of their revenue from tax authorities.

As the previous section describes, unorganized sectors are always more politically important, the more tax revenue the politician expects from them. We should therefore expect the provision of collective goods to be greater for unorganized sectors whose firms hide less than for those whose firms hide more. For example, a small-business sector that has failed to overcome its collective-action problems and therefore cannot promise contributions in return for collective goods can nonetheless expect support from the government to the extent that it provides politically valuable tax revenue. This does not mean, however, that small enterprises choose to hide less from the state for the sake of stronger property-rights protection or a better regulatory framework. Rather, every firm continues to hide what it can get away with, even if all such firms would be better off if they could somehow agree to be tax compliant.

That said, it is important to stress that a sector that receives more collective goods because it is highly taxable is not necessarily better off in absolute terms than a sector that is less taxable. The nature of representation through taxation is imperfect: it is entirely possible that the tax revenue surrendered is greater in value to firms than the collective goods received in return. Thus, just because we observe an "exchange" of tax revenue for collective goods, we should not immediately jump to the conclusion that this exchange is mutually beneficial.[7]

The impact of taxability on organized sectors is more subtle. Organized sectors that are less taxable – those whose firms hide more – are obviously less important to the politician for the tax revenue they provide. At the same time, such sectors are willing to provide larger contributions to the politician in return for collective goods, as they retain a greater share of the revenue that those goods generate. The first consideration dominates when the politician especially values tax revenue relative to contributions. Together with the result that the importance to the politician of unorganized sectors is always increasing in those sectors' taxability, this implies that when tax revenue is sufficiently politically important, the provision of collective goods to any sector – organized or unorganized – is greater when firms in that sector hide less from tax authorities. In contrast, when tax revenue is relatively less important, then the relationship between revenue hiding and collective-goods provision runs the opposite direction for unorganized and organized firms.

Prediction 2. Holding constant the taxability and organization of other sectors, the provision of collective goods

- to an unorganized sector is always decreasing in the proportion of revenues hidden by firms in that sector and
- to an organized sector is decreasing in the proportion of revenues hidden by firms in that sector so long as tax revenue is sufficiently important to the politician and is increasing otherwise.

Now consider a series of thought experiments. First, take two sectors that are equally taxable, one organized and the other not, and make it easier for each of them to hide revenues from the state. The politician thus

---

[7] Scholars of postcommunist political economy have been particularly interested in the degree to which business–state relations are characterized by "capture" or "exchange." See, for example, Hellman, Jones, and Kaufmann (2000); Frye (2002*a*); Jones Luong and Weinthal (2004); and Slinko, Yakovlev, and Zhuravskaya (2005).

values each sector less for the tax revenue it provides, but which of the two suffers the larger drop in collective-goods provision? The unorganized sector does. A decrease in expected tax revenue can only decrease the importance of an unorganized sector to the politician. But for the organized sector that decreased importance is at least partially offset by the greater willingness of firms in the sector to *pay* for collective-goods provision, as they surrender less of their revenue to the state. Thus, even though the politician expects to receive less of the production that results from collective-goods provision in the form of tax revenue, she anticipates being rewarded with a larger contribution in return for her largesse. In terms of Figure 3.1, an increase in the ability of firms to hide revenue from tax authorities decreases A but increases $B + C$. Because the politician values only A for unorganized sectors, but also $B + C$ for organized sectors, she is therefore more responsive to a decrease in taxability for unorganized sectors.

Prediction 3. For a given level of revenue hiding, an increase in the ability of firms in an unorganized sector to hide revenues results in a larger drop in collective-goods provision than an increase in the ability of firms in an organized sector to hide revenues.

Suppose next that there are two sectors, one organized and the other unorganized, but that the unorganized sector is relatively easy to tax. In other words, the unorganized sector is composed of firms like those in the top panel of Figure 3.1, whereas the organized sector is made up of firms like those in the bottom panel. Which of the two sectors receives a larger portion of the politician's budget for collective goods? The politician faces a trade-off. By providing collective goods to the unorganized sector, she receives more tax revenue but foregoes the contributions she would receive if she instead provided collective goods to the organized sector. For her to favor the unorganized sector she must place a sufficiently large value on tax revenue relative to contributions. The situation in Pskov oblast described in Chapter 1 is an example: the oblast government was desperate for tax revenue, and the unorganized vodka sector was easy to tax relative to organized interests in the region.

Prediction 4. Firms in a sector that is not organized may receive better provision of collective goods than firms in a sector that is organized when

- politicians especially care about tax revenue and

- the unorganized sector is more taxable than the organized sector, that is, when firms in the unorganized sector hide less of their revenues from tax authorities.

This prediction places sharp limits on the conventional understanding of the consequences of collective action. Organized groups may have an advantage in the competition for influence because of their ability to coordinate contributions of time and money by their members, but this advantage may be eroded if members of the group engage in politically damaging behavior in spheres of activity not governable by agreements with policy makers. When differences across groups with respect to these "noncontractible" provisions is large, then the anticipated behavior of unorganized groups may outweigh anything that organized groups can credibly promise.

What if we do observe an organized group that benefits disproportionately in the making of public policy? Should we immediately assume that this advantage arises from the group's lobbying power? As Daniel Carpenter notes (Carpenter, 2004), this is the conventional inference, especially in the study of regulatory policy, where the advantageous position enjoyed by large, established firms is assumed to follow from their "capture" of key agencies (Bernstein, 1955; Stigler, 1971; Peltzman, 1976). But the same characteristics that provide political access may also determine the behavior of organized interests with respect to actions that are politically important but outside the scope of what may be credibly promised to policy makers. Large firms and monopolies, for example, may suffer less from collective-action problems, but they may also find it harder to hide revenues from tax authorities. Thus, any particular advantage enjoyed by these firms in the provision of collective goods may arise as much or more from their (noncontractible) tax compliance as from their ability to lobby policy makers directly.

Consider, then, a final thought experiment. Suppose there are two sectors, one organized and the other not, and that the politician cares much more about tax revenue than about contributions. Which of the two sectors receives a larger share of the budget for collective-goods provision? The answer may well be the organized sector, but only if that sector is more taxable than the unorganized sector. "Capture," in this case, is implicit, unrelated to any particular access the organized sector has to the politician.

Prediction 5. When politicians especially care about tax revenue, then firms in an organized sector may benefit in the provision of collective goods at the expense of firms in an unorganized sector not because they are organized, but because they are more taxable, that is, because they hide less of their revenue from tax authorities.

I put Predictions 1–5 to the test in Chapter 4. In doing so, I also make use of two extensions to the model that I now describe. First, I constrain policy choice by limiting the ability of the politician to discriminate in the provision of collective goods across sectors. Second, I relax a constraint by allowing the politician to choose a separate tax rate for each sector rather than imposing an exogenous tax rate that applies to all sectors. Like the baseline model, each of these extensions should be viewed as a stylized representation of some political-economic environments but not others. As I will show in Chapter 4, the first extension helps to explain patterns of collective-goods provision in postcommunist states. The second extension finds less empirical support.

Until now I have assumed that the politician can perfectly discriminate across sectors in the provision of collective goods. Although strong, this assumption seems to be approximately correct for some goods in some political-economic environments, and we should not automatically assume that it does not hold in others even when we observe *outcomes* in which collective goods are provided equally across sectors. Work by Haber, Razo, and Maurer (2003) on economic policy during and after the Díaz dictatorship in Mexico shows that property-rights protection – often considered a pure public good – can in fact be selectively provided for a very long period of time. Similarly, public agencies that we typically think of as providing nonexcludable goods have frequently been employed to the advantage of one sector or another in postcommunist states. For example, in the early 1990s the Russian Central Bank provided sector- and firm-specific credits (Shleifer and Treisman, 2000), and the military and security services often became involved in business disputes (Latynina, 1999; Łoś and Zybertow-icz, 2000; Volkov, 2002).[8]

That said, it may be technically difficult to discriminate in the provision of certain goods. Goods provided on a territorial basis – postal and telephone service, electricity, and so on – fall particularly into this category. Although individual recipients might still be excluded, in practice the cost of exclusion is often prohibitive. Thus, any investment in the general

[8] A similar issue arises in the study of fiscal federalism, where the traditional assumption that national politicians are constrained to provide local public goods equally across jurisdictions has been challenged in recent years. See, for example, Seabright (1996), Persson and Tabellini (2000, ch. 9), Besley and Coate (2003), and Gehlbach (2007).

capacity to deliver such goods may benefit all who reside in a particular region, even though only a few of those residents may be politically important in the sense that I have defined the term. To the extent that such limits exist, politicians will be less responsive to increases in the political importance of any particular sector, as to respond means increasing collective-goods provision not only to that sector but also to others.

Prediction 6. The impact on collective-goods provision of an increase or decrease in the importance of a sector is greater for goods that are more excludable than for those that are less so.

Consider now the consequences for both revenue hiding and the provision of collective goods of assuming that the politician may choose a separate tax rate for each sector. In a strict sense this is nowhere true: corporate tax rates are typically constant across industries, and income and payroll taxes normally do not vary with an individual's place of employment. That said, there are at least three exceptions to this general rule. First, loopholes may be written into the tax code that have the practical effect of lowering the tax rate for certain sectors. Second, in many countries taxes are assessed differently on small enterprises, in part due to the particular difficulty of observing the activity of such firms. Finally, indirect taxes such as excises and customs duties fall more on some types of business activity than on others.

A politician who values a sector only for the tax revenue it provides chooses a tax rate for that sector that is revenue maximizing. In selecting this rate, the politician faces a trade-off: higher rates imply a larger share of a smaller pie. In terms of Figure 3.1, a higher rate translates into a larger proportion of unhidden revenue that is taxed ($A/(A+B)$), but a smaller proportion of unhidden revenue overall ($A+B$). The second effect is smaller for firms that find it more costly to hide revenues from tax authorities: such firms hide little in any event and so are less responsive to changes in tax rates. Thus, the revenue-maximizing rate is higher for more taxable sectors.

For sectors that are organized, this effect may be partially offset if the politician can be encouraged through the promise of contributions to value such sectors' untaxed production: tax *rates* may be contractible, even if tax compliance is not. Clearly, untaxed (and total) revenue is maximized when the tax rate is set at zero: firms keep the entirety of unhidden production and so have no incentive to hide revenue from the state as doing so is costly. In Figure 3.1, all revenue falls into region B when the tax rate is zero. In practice, of course, the desire for tax revenue typically encourages some taxation of even organized sectors. Where between zero and the revenue-maximizing level the tax rate falls depends on how much the politician values contributions versus tax revenue.

What are the implications for revenue hiding of assuming that the politician sets tax rates separately for each sector? In contrast to the baseline model, firms in sectors that are more taxable do not necessarily hide less of their revenue from tax authorities, as politicians are inclined to set higher tax rates for sectors that are more taxable, and firms respond to higher rates by hiding more. But revenue hiding is correlated with a sector's organization: sectors that are more organized are rewarded with lower tax rates, and so firms in organized sectors hide less.

Prediction 7. When the politician sets tax rates separately for each sector, revenue hiding is uncorrelated with a sector's taxability but is smaller for sectors that are organized than for those that are not.

As in the baseline model, highly taxable sectors are still important sources of tax revenue, as the politician is able to tax such sectors at higher rates. Nonetheless, any observed correlation between revenue hiding and the provision of collective goods would reflect not a tendency to favor sectors that are more taxable – again, revenue hiding is uncorrelated with taxability when the politician sets tax rates separately for each sector – but rather an inclination to support sectors that are organized (and so hide less) over those that are not.

3.3 Summary

Politicians care about policy for its own sake and because they are made to care by organized groups with a stake in the policy outcome. Yet there are limits to what organized groups can credibly promise in return for favorable policy treatment. Agreements with politicians that require the subsequent participation of individual group members may be unenforceable. In making policy choices, politicians therefore weigh credible promises made by organized groups against the anticipated behavior of members of both organized and unorganized groups with respect to "noncontractible" provisions.

The inability of organized groups to credibly promise that their members will be tax compliant in return for collective-goods provision has particular consequences for policy choice. Because tax compliance is noncontractible, bargaining between organized interests and politicians is influenced by the taxability of economic actors and thus the division of gains from collective-goods provision between those actors and the state. When differences in taxability across sectors are large and tax revenue is politically important, the allocation of collective goods may be determined as much by the anticipated tax compliance of sectors as by their organization.

This general proposition suggests a strategy for investigating the political-economic consequences of the variation in postcommunist tax systems documented in the previous chapter. As we saw there, "natural" differences in taxability – large enterprises are more taxable than small firms, monopolies more than firms in competitive industries – were exaggerated in the former Soviet Union, where tax systems were structured around revenue sources familiar from the communist era. Simply put, the difference between more and less taxable sectors was far greater in the eastern half of the postcommunist world. Moreover, the political importance of any differences in the tax compliance of firms may have been larger in the former Soviet Union, given the greater reliance on enterprise taxation. We might therefore expect politicians in post-Soviet states to have had particularly strong incentives to favor highly taxable sectors in the provision of collective goods.

In the next chapter I examine the extent to which patterns of collective-goods provision diverge in this way. I use the model presented here to guide this investigation by checking patterns observed in the data against a number of more specific predictions consistent with the logic of representation through taxation but not necessarily with any alternative theoretical framework. In doing so, I rely on a key advantage of exercises in deductive reasoning of the sort presented in this chapter: the derivation of heterogeneous causal effects, without which it would be more difficult to reject one theoretical framework in favor of another.

3.A Appendix: The Formal Logic of Representation through Taxation

In this section I present the formal model on which the discussion above is based. I begin by describing the model. I then solve for equilibrium behavior and derive certain comparative-static results. Finally, I extend the model to consider the impact of limits on the ability of the politician to discriminate in the provision of collective goods, as well as the consequences for revenue hiding and the provision of collective goods when the politician chooses tax rates separately for each sector.

3.A.1 Model

The actors in the model are firms that make up organized and unorganized sectors, organized-sector lobbies, and a politician. I consider each in turn.

Firms There is a set O of organized sectors and a set U of unorganized sectors, each made up of a finite number of firms. Index sectors by s and firms by i. Each firm i is endowed with k_i units of capital. To focus on the incentive effects of taxation, assume that all sectors are of an equal size normalized to one unit of capital, that is, assume $\sum_{i \in s} k_i = 1$ for all sectors s. I relax this assumption in Chapter 5 when considering the interaction of collective-goods provision and factor mobility.

Each firm allocates its capital to "hidden" and "unhidden" economic activity, choosing $H_i \in [0, 1]$, where H_i refers to the proportion of revenues hidden by firm i. Unhidden activity is taxed at an exogenous tax rate τ; hidden activity is not taxed. However, hiding revenues comes at a cost, assumed for simplicity to be equal to fraction $\alpha_s / 2 \, (H_i)^2$ of the firm's capital.[9] The parameter α_s captures the cost of hiding revenues for firms in sector s. I assume that $\alpha_s > \tau$ for all s, which assures an interior solution in which revenue hiding is sufficiently costly that firms choose to keep some portion of their activity unhidden. I refer to α_s as the taxability of sector s, as in equilibrium firms that find it more costly to hide revenues choose to hide less of their revenues from tax authorities.

Both hidden and unhidden activity benefit from the provision of sector-specific collective goods. Let g_s be the per-capita provision of collective goods to sector s (to be chosen by the politician), with $k_i g_s^\beta$ the resulting production of firm i in sector s, where β is a parameter of the model. Assume $\beta \in (0, 1)$, so there are decreasing returns to the provision of collective goods. Given the exogenous tax rate τ, the proportion of capital allocated to hidden economic activity H_i (chosen by the firm), and the provision of collective goods g_s (chosen by the politician), the after-tax production of firm i in sector s is

$$\left[(1 - \tau)(1 - H_i) + \left(H_i - \frac{\alpha_s}{2} (H_i)^2\right)\right] k_i g_s^\beta. \qquad (3.1)$$

---

[9] Any cost function $h(H, \alpha_s)$ satisfying $h_H, h_{HH}, h_{H\alpha_s} > 0$ (where subscripts denote derivatives) and standard boundary conditions produces the same qualitative results.

76

The first term in brackets represents the proportion of capital unhidden and remaining after taxation, whereas the second is the untaxed (because hidden) remainder, less the proportion of capital lost while hiding revenues.

Organized-Sector Lobbies Organized-sector lobbies attempt to influence the provision of collective goods to their sectors. They do so by promising a contribution $C_s \geq 0$ for every allocation of collective goods across sectors; I denote the vector of such allocations g_s by $\mathbf{g}$. Formally, each lobby s offers a contribution schedule $C_s (\mathbf{g})$, with $C_s (\mathbf{g}) \geq 0$ for all $\mathbf{g}$. Organized-sector lobbies maximize the joint welfare of their members:

$$\sum_{i \in s} \left[(1 - \tau)(1 - H_i) + \left(H_i - \frac{\alpha_s}{2} (H_i)^2 \right) \right] k_i g_s^\beta - C_s (\mathbf{g}) .$$

Politician The politician values both tax revenue and contributions from the organized-sector lobbies. She has at her disposal a fixed sum of money that she may allocate in any way to the provision of collective goods for the various organized and unorganized sectors.[10] I normalize this sum of money to be equal to 1, so that the set of allocations must satisfy $\sum_s g_s = 1$. Having received the contribution schedules C_s, the politician thus chooses a vector of collective-good allocations $\mathbf{g}$ to maximize

$$\sum_{s \in O} C_s (\mathbf{g}) + \gamma \sum_s T_s (g_s) ,$$

where $T_s (g_s)$ is the total tax revenue collected from sector s to be derived below. The parameter γ represents the degree to which the politician values tax revenue relative to contributions from the organized-sector lobbies. I assume only that $\gamma > 0$.

The sequence of play is as follows: (1) organized-sector lobbies simultaneously and noncooperatively submit contribution schedules and (2) the politician allocates funds to collective-goods provision and firms simultaneously and noncooperatively choose a level of revenue hiding. (The equilibrium outcome is the same regardless of whether the politician and firms move simultaneously or firms move after the politician.)

---

[10] At the expense of additional notation, analogous results can be obtained by assuming that the politician values both contributions and that portion of tax revenue not allocated to collective-goods production, where tax revenue is in turn augmented by the provision of collective goods.

3.A.2 Equilibrium

I solve for the subgame-perfect Nash equilibrium of this extensive game with perfect information, beginning with firms' allocation of capital between hidden and unhidden economic activity. Each firm i chooses H_i to maximize Expression (3.1). The solution to this problem is

$$H_i^* = \frac{\tau}{\alpha_s}. \tag{3.2}$$

A firm hides more, the larger is the exogenous tax rate, and the smaller is its cost of hiding revenues. Because all firms within a sector share the same cost α_s of hiding revenues, Expression (3.1) and Equation (3.2) together imply that the after-tax production of sector s is

$$\sum_{i \in s}\left[(1-\tau)(1-H_i^*) + \left(H_i^* - \frac{\alpha_s}{2}(H_i^*)^2\right)\right]k_i g_s^\beta = \left(1 - \tau + \frac{\tau^2}{2\alpha_s}\right)g_s^\beta.$$

(Recall that the total capital of all firms in any sector s is normalized to 1.) Holding g_s constant, after-tax production in any sector s is a decreasing function of the tax rate τ and of the taxability α_s of the sector. However, g_s is itself a function of τ and α_s, as the incentive for the politician to provide collective goods to a sector depends on the possibility of collecting tax revenue from that sector. In particular, note that we can derive $T_s(g_s)$, the total tax revenue collected from sector s, as

$$\sum_{i \in s}\left[\tau(1-H_i^*)\right]k_i g_s^\beta = \left(\tau - \frac{\tau^2}{\alpha_s}\right)g_s^\beta,$$

which is an increasing function of α_s.

Anticipating this behavior, the politician chooses the optimal allocation **g** of collective goods across sectors, taking into account the contribution schedules $C_s(\mathbf{g})$ offered by the organized-sector lobbies. Grossman and Helpman (1994, 2001) show that if attention is restricted to contribution schedules that are "truthful" – those for which differences in an organized sector's promised contributions reflect differences in the utility that would be received from different policies – then in equilibrium the politician maximizes a social welfare function that gives a weight of 1 to the policy payoff of organized groups and a weight of γ to the politician's other concerns (in Grossman and Helpman, social welfare; here, tax revenue):[11]

$$\sum_{s \in O} \left(1 - \tau + \frac{\tau^2}{2\alpha_s}\right) g_s^\beta + \gamma \sum_s \left(\tau - \frac{\tau^2}{\alpha_s}\right) g_s^\beta. \qquad (3.3)$$

Maximizing this expression subject to the constraint that $\sum_s g_s = 1$ gives the equilibrium provision of collective goods to each sector.

Proposition 1. If contribution schedules are "truthful," then the equilibrium provision of collective goods to any two sectors s and t satisfies

$$\frac{g_s}{g_t} = \left(\frac{\Pi_s}{\Pi_t}\right)^{\frac{1}{1-\beta}}, \qquad (3.4)$$

where for any sector s,

$$\Pi_s = \gamma \left(\tau - \frac{\tau^2}{\alpha_s}\right) \qquad (3.5)$$

if the sector is unorganized and

$$\Pi_s = \left(1 - \tau + \frac{\tau^2}{2\alpha_s}\right) + \gamma \left(\tau - \frac{\tau^2}{\alpha_s}\right) \qquad (3.6)$$

if the sector is organized.

Proof. Defining Π_s as in Equations (3.5) and (3.6), Expression (3.3) can be rewritten as $\sum_s \Pi_s g_s^\beta$. Maximizing this expression subject to the constraint that $\sum_s g_s = 1$ gives the following first-order condition for any s:

$$\beta \Pi_s g_s^{\beta-1} - \lambda = 0.$$

The Langrange multiplier on the constraint $\sum_s g_s = 1$ is denoted by λ. Rearranging terms for any two sectors s and t gives Equation (3.4). $\square$

Proposition 1 says that provision of collective goods to one sector is larger than that to another if the *joint* importance of the first sector's

---

[11] More generally, any truthful equilibrium of a menu-auction game is jointly efficient; see Bernheim and Whinston (1986). Note that joint efficiency is defined only with respect to what is contractible: in this model there are typically unrealized gains from trade due to the inability of organized-sector lobbies to commit that their members will pay taxes in full. Grossman and Helpman refer to truthful equilibria as "compensating" equilibria, which captures the idea that differences across policies in promised contributions compensate a lobby for any differences in its policy payoff.

production to the politician (because of tax revenue) and to the firms in that sector (but only if organized) is greater than that of the other sector. That importance is captured in Π_s, defined in Equations (3.5) and (3.6), which express the nature of influence in the model:

- When tax revenue is relatively unimportant to the politician (i.e., when γ is small), then the collective-action effect dominates: sectors tend to be favored when they are organized (because Π_s is typically larger for organized than for unorganized sectors).
- When tax revenue is relatively important to the politician (i.e., when γ is large), then the taxability effect dominates: sectors tend to be favored when they are easier to tax (because Π_s is relatively large only when α_s is large).

3.A.3 Comparative Statics

The difference between Equations (3.5) and (3.6) reflects the different incentives the politician has to support organized and unorganized sectors. Unorganized sectors are important to the politician only for the tax revenue they provide. In contrast, organized sectors are politically important both because of their tax potential and because they may compensate the politician for providing collective goods. Politicians are less inclined to provide collective goods to sectors that are hard to tax, as they receive little tax revenue from such sectors. However, sectors whose firms hide more from tax authorities are willing to *pay* more for collective goods, as they retain more of the resulting production. The first effect outweighs the second when tax revenue is relatively important. When it is not, the provision of collective goods to an organized sector is increasing, not decreasing, in the proportion of revenues hidden by firms in the sector. (Note that the arguments in this section take advantage of the assumption that the tax rate τ is exogenous and constant across firms, which implies that differences in revenue hiding across sectors are due entirely to differences in taxability α_s. I relax this assumption further below.)

Proposition 2. Holding constant the taxability and organization of other sectors, the provision of collective goods

- to an unorganized sector is always decreasing in the proportion of revenues hidden by firms in that sector and

- to an organized sector is decreasing in the proportion of revenues hidden by firms in that sector so long as tax revenue is sufficiently important to the politician and is increasing otherwise.

Proof. Proposition 1 states that the provision of collective goods to any sector s is increasing in Π_s, defined by Equations (3.5) and (3.6). Letting H_s^* be the level of revenue hiding by firms in sector s, Equation (3.5) can be rewritten as $\gamma\tau\,(1 - H_s^*)$, which is always decreasing in H_s^*. Similarly, Equation (3.6) can be rewritten as $(1 - \tau + \gamma\tau) + H_s^*\tau\,(1/2 - \gamma)$, which is decreasing in H_s^* for $\gamma > 1/2$ and increasing for $\gamma < 1/2$. □

Given that revenue hiding cuts both ways for organized sectors, one might expect the politician to punish unorganized sectors more for revenue hiding than they do organized sectors, as an unorganized sector is valuable only to the extent that it provides tax revenue. The following proposition shows this to be the case so long as the value of tax revenue to the politician is sufficiently small (so whether a sector is organized is relatively important) or there are sufficient diminishing returns to the provision of collective goods (so the politician is responsive to changes in the importance of any sector).

Proposition 3. For a given level of revenue hiding, for γ or β sufficiently small an increase in the ability of firms in an unorganized sector to hide revenues results in a larger drop in collective-goods provision than an increase in the ability of firms in an organized sector to hide revenues.

Proof. Using Proposition 1 and the constraint $\sum g_s = 1$, the value of collective-goods provision for any sector t can be derived as $g_t = [(\Pi_t)^{\frac{1}{1-\beta}}]/[\sum_s (\Pi_s)^{\frac{1}{1-\beta}}]$. Consider some unorganized sector u and organized sector o. Differentiating g_u with respect to H_u^* gives

$$\frac{\partial \Pi_u}{\partial H_u^*} \cdot \frac{(\Pi_u)^{\frac{\beta}{1-\beta}}\left[\sum_{s\neq u}(\Pi_s)^{\frac{1}{1-\beta}}\right]}{(1-\beta)\left[\sum_s(\Pi_s)^{\frac{1}{1-\beta}}\right]^2} = -\gamma\tau\frac{(\Pi_u)^{\frac{\beta}{1-\beta}}\left[\sum_{s\neq u}(\Pi_s)^{\frac{1}{1-\beta}}\right]}{(1-\beta)\left[\sum_s(\Pi_s)^{\frac{1}{1-\beta}}\right]^2}, \quad (3.7)$$

where, following the proof to Proposition 2, $\Pi_u = \gamma\tau\,(1 - H_u^*)$. Similarly, differentiating g_o with respect to H_o^* gives

$$\frac{\partial \Pi_o}{\partial H_o^*} \cdot \frac{(\Pi_o)^{\frac{\beta}{1-\beta}}\left[\sum_{s\neq o}(\Pi_s)^{\frac{1}{1-\beta}}\right]}{(1-\beta)\left[\sum_s(\Pi_s)^{\frac{1}{1-\beta}}\right]^2} = \tau\left(\frac{1}{2} - \gamma\right)\frac{(\Pi_o)^{\frac{\beta}{1-\beta}}\left[\sum_{s\neq o}(\Pi_s)^{\frac{1}{1-\beta}}\right]}{(1-\beta)\left[\sum_s(\Pi_s)^{\frac{1}{1-\beta}}\right]^2}, \quad (3.8)$$

where $\Pi_o = (1 - \tau + \gamma\tau) + H_o^*\tau\left(\frac{1}{2} - \gamma\right)$. Clearly, Expression (3.7) is less than Expression (3.8) when $\gamma \leq 1/2$. With respect to diminishing returns, note that as β approaches zero, Expression (3.7) approaches $-\gamma\tau[\sum_{s\neq u}(\Pi_s)]/[\sum_s \Pi_s]^2$, whereas Expression (3.8) approaches $\tau(1/2 - \gamma)[\sum_{s\neq o}(\Pi_s)]/[\sum_s \Pi_s]^2$; in that case, Expression (3.7) is less than Expression (3.8), as $\sum_{s\neq o} \Pi_s < \sum_{s\neq u} \Pi_s$ (because $\Pi_u < \Pi_o$ when $H_u^* = H_o^*$, which is the premise of the proposition). $\qquad\square$

Together, Propositions 1, 2, and 3 suggest that the predictions and inferences we make about the consequences of collective action may be very different when tax revenue is politically important and differences in taxability across sectors are large. The following two propositions show explicitly how our conventional understanding of politics should change under these conditions.

Proposition 4. Firms in a sector that is not organized may receive better provision of collective goods than firms in a sector that is organized when

- politicians especially care about tax revenue and
- the unorganized sector is more taxable than the organized sector, that is, when firms in the unorganized sector hide less of their revenues from tax authorities.

Proof. Consider an unorganized sector u and an organized sector o. Equation (3.4) says that $g_u > g_o$ if and only if

$$\gamma\left(\tau - \frac{\tau^2}{\alpha_u}\right) > \left(1 - \tau + \frac{\tau^2}{2\alpha_o}\right) + \gamma\left(\tau - \frac{\tau^2}{\alpha_o}\right).$$

Rewriting this as

$$\gamma\left(\alpha_u - \alpha_o\right) > \frac{\alpha_u\alpha_o}{\tau^2}\left(1 - \tau + \frac{\tau^2}{2\alpha_o}\right),$$

we see that the unorganized sector is favored when $\gamma\left(\alpha_u - \alpha_o\right)$ is positive and large. With respect to revenue hiding, recall that for any firm i in any sector s, H_i^* is a decreasing function of α_s. $\qquad\square$

Proposition 5. When politicians especially care about tax revenue, then firms in an organized sector benefit in the provision of collective goods at the expense of firms in an unorganized sector if and only if the organized sector is more taxable, that is, if and only if firms in the organized sector hide less of their revenue from tax authorities.

Proof. Consider an unorganized sector u and an organized sector o, and let γ approach infinity. Then by Proposition 1, the ratio of collective-goods provision g_o/g_u is

$$\lim_{\gamma \to \infty} \left(\frac{\Pi_o}{\Pi_u} \right)^{\frac{1}{1-\beta}} = \left(\frac{1 - \frac{\tau}{\alpha_o}}{1 - \frac{\tau}{\alpha_u}} \right)^{\frac{1}{1-\beta}},$$

which is greater than 1 if and only if $\alpha_o > \alpha_u$, that is, if and only if firms in sector o hide less than do those in sector u. □

3.A.4 Extensions

Limits on the Ability to Discriminate Technological and other constraints may reduce the ability of politicians to discriminate in the provision of collective goods at the sectoral level. We may consider the impact of limits in the ability to discriminate in the provision of collective goods by partitioning the set of sectors into "territories," where the politician can provide only territory-specific collective goods. Formally, partition the set of sectors such that there are θ sectors in each territory, and assume that the number of sectors is divisible by θ. Label territories $r = a, b, \ldots$, and refer to the set of all territories as R. Then the politician chooses a vector $\mathbf{g} = (g_a, g_b, \ldots)$ to maximize $\sum_{r \in R} \sum_{s \in r} \Pi_s g_r^\beta$, subject to the constraint $\sum_{r \in R} \theta g_r = 1$. (With respect to the θ term in the constraint, recall from the basic model that g_s refers to per-capita provision of collective goods to sector s and that the size of each sector is normalized to 1.)

The first-order condition for the Lagrangian of this problem for any territory r is

$$\beta \sum_{s \in r} \Pi_s g_r^{\beta-1} - \theta \lambda = 0,$$

where λ is the Langrange multiplier on the constraint. Then the provision of collective goods g_a to any territory a is

$$g_a = \frac{\left(\sum_{s \in a} \Pi_s \right)^{\frac{1}{1-\beta}}}{\theta \sum_{r \in R} \left(\sum_{s \in r} \Pi_s \right)^{\frac{1}{1-\beta}}}.$$

The following proposition follows from this expression.

Proposition 6. For β sufficiently small, the impact of an increase or decrease in Π_s (a change in organization, or a change in taxability) is less as the partition becomes coarser, that is, as sectors are partitioned into fewer territories.

Proof. Consider the impact of a marginal change in Π_s on g_a, where sector s is in territory a (for a change in organization the effect would be discrete, but the logic is analogous):

$$\frac{\partial g_a}{\partial \Pi_s} = \frac{\left(\sum_{s \in a} \Pi_s\right)^{\frac{\beta}{1-\beta}} \left[\sum_{r \neq a} \left(\sum_{s \in r} \Pi_s\right)^{\frac{1}{1-\beta}}\right]}{\theta (1 - \beta) \left[\sum_{r \in R} \left(\sum_{s \in r} \Pi_s\right)^{\frac{1}{1-\beta}}\right]^2}.$$

Clearly this expression is decreasing in θ, the number of sectors in any territory. However, in addition we must consider the impact of a coarsening on the definition of territories, which is also a part of this expression. As with Proposition 3, let β approach zero, which captures the idea that diminishing returns to the provision of collective goods are sufficiently great that the politician is responsive to changes in the importance of any territory:

$$\lim_{\beta \to 0} \frac{\partial g_a}{\partial \Pi_s} = \frac{\sum_{s \notin a} \Pi_s}{\theta \left(\sum_s \Pi_s\right)^2}.$$

Examining this expression, we see that as the size of a territory increases, the number of sectors not in that territory decreases, such that the numerator of the right-hand-side term decreases. □

Endogenous Tax Rates The analysis so far has assumed that the tax rate τ is fixed and constant across sectors. To consider the outcome when the tax rate as well as the provision of collective goods is endogenous and organized-sector lobbies promise contributions for every vector of such policies, assume that the politician maximizes Expression (3.3) with respect to both $\mathbf{g}$ and a vector of sector-specific tax rates $\tau = (\tau_1, \ldots \tau_s, \ldots)$. (In this alternative formulation the natural timing assumption is for firms to choose a level of revenue hiding after policy has been chosen.) Then in equilibrium $\tau_s^* = \alpha_s (\gamma - 1)/(2\gamma - 1)$ if the sector is organized and $\tau_s^* = \alpha_s /2$ if it is not. (If we want to avoid the possibility of "negative taxes," we may assume that $\gamma \geq 1$.) Given that $H_i^* = \tau_s^* /\alpha_s$, the following proposition immediately follows.

Proposition 7. When the politician sets tax rates separately for each sector, the level of revenue hiding is $H_i^* = (\gamma - 1)/(2\gamma - 1)$ for all firms in organized sectors and is $H_i^* = 1/2$ for all firms in unorganized sectors.

Thus, the level of revenue hiding is uncorrelated with a sector's taxability but is smaller for sectors that are organized than for those that are not.

Proof. Omitted. □

Two conclusions follow. First, revenue hiding is correlated only with the organization of a sector, not with its taxability. (This argument holds when the cost of revenue hiding takes the more general form $\frac{\alpha_s}{x} (H_i)^x$, with $\alpha_s, x > 1$; see Gehlbach, 2003.) Second, because the level of revenue hiding in this extension depends only on whether a firm belongs to an organized sector, any observed correlation between revenue hiding and the provision of collective goods is attributable not to taxability but to organization.

4

Patterns of Collective-Goods Provision

In Chapter 2, I showed how two very different tax systems took shape in the postcommunist world during the 1990s. In the former Soviet Union, various structural characteristics – highly concentrated industrial structures, distance from the West and the pull of the European Union, and relatively low levels of economic development – encouraged states to rely on corporate taxes and taxes on goods and services, both key Soviet-era revenue sources. In Eastern Europe, in contrast, there was greater emphasis on taxation of individuals, a revenue source not central under communism.[1] Such differences were reflected in patterns of tax compliance, as tax authorities concentrated to a greater or lesser degree on collecting taxes from revenue sources with which they were familiar. In the former Soviet Union, the heavy emphasis on taxation of large, often monopolistic, enterprises of the sort that populated the Soviet economic landscape left other firms comparatively free to hide revenues from tax authorities. Meanwhile, in Eastern Europe, the revenue net was cast more widely, resulting in smaller systematic differences in tax compliance across economic sectors.

The model in Chapter 3 helps us to predict the consequences of these patterns of revenue collection and tax compliance for provision of sector-specific collective goods. Generally speaking, we should expect politicians in the former Soviet Union to have been more inclined than their counterparts in Eastern Europe to promote sectors that were relatively easy to

---

[1] Here, as elsewhere in the book, I follow convention by often referring to the countries of the Commonwealth of Independent States – the CIS, which excludes the Baltic states of Estonia, Latvia, and Lithuania – as the "former Soviet Union" and by using the term "Eastern Europe" to mean countries in both Eastern Europe and the Baltics.

tax. Not only were differences in tax compliance across economic sectors larger in the eastern half of the postcommunist world, but such differences carried greater political weight due to the heavier reliance on enterprise taxation.

In this chapter I test this prediction and others generated by the model in the previous chapter, using data from the survey of enterprises in twenty-five postcommunist countries – the Business Environment and Enterprise Performance Survey (BEEPS) – first discussed in Chapter 2. I begin by introducing the variables to be used in the subsequent analysis. I then take a first look at patterns of collective-goods provision in the postcommunist world. Roughly speaking, the provision of collective goods to respondent firms is determined by three variables: the degree to which firms hide revenues from the state (firms that hide more revenues receive fewer collective goods), size (the larger the firm, the better the provision of collective goods), and monopoly status (monopolies receive more collective goods than nonmonopolies). The logic of representation through taxation thus passes a first-blush examination: of these three characteristics, the logic of collective action predicts only that size and monopoly status should matter, whereas the model presented in Chapter 3 suggests anticipated tax compliance should also be important.

Following this general examination, I take up the question of whether the sharp differences in tax systems documented in Chapter 2 translate into distinct patterns of collective-goods provision. I begin by looking separately at firms in the former Soviet Union and in Eastern Europe. As expected, revenue hiding is a stronger predictor of collective-goods provision in the eastern half of the postcommunist world: firms in the former Soviet Union that are less tax compliant suffer from substantially worse collective-goods provision, whereas those in Eastern Europe do not. At the same time, there is some evidence that politicians in Eastern Europe punish unorganized sectors that hide revenues even as they reward organized sectors that do so, an empirical finding consistent with the model in Chapter 3. Patterns of collective-goods provision thus suggest that the anticipated tax compliance of sectors influences bargaining between economic actors and the state throughout the postcommunist world but that politicians penalize sectors that hide revenues to a much greater degree in the former Soviet Union than in Eastern Europe.

Finally, moving beyond the crude division of the postcommunist world into eastern and western halves, I find that revenue hiding matters most for collective-goods provision in countries whose tax structures are oriented heavily around corporate taxation, with little difference between countries reliant on individual taxation and those focused more on indirect taxation. Thus, anticipated tax compliance is the strongest predictor of collective-goods provision precisely where the discussion in previous chapters suggests it should be: in those countries, largely in the former Soviet Union, whose tax systems are structured around taxation of enterprises.

The empirical work I present is thus broadly consistent with the theoretical predictions of the model in the previous chapter. Further below I discuss various robustness checks and alternative explanations, but one important caveat merits mention here. The data I use in this chapter are cross-sectional in nature, drawn from a survey conducted a decade into the transition. Ideally, one would track patterns of tax compliance and collective-goods provision for the same firms over time, both because changing patterns can illuminate the evolving nature of business–state relations and because panel data can help to resolve identification issues. Unfortunately, the 1999 BEEPS was the first survey of firms carried out with a common survey instrument in nearly every postcommunist country. It is, moreover, the only survey conducted in a large number of transition countries with both the tax-compliance and collective-goods questions that are central to my analysis. Later rounds of the BEEPS retain the revenue-hiding question first introduced in Chapter 2 but omit the battery of questions that I use to measure provision of collective goods and do not generally follow the same firms from round to round. I am therefore forced to draw inferences about patterns of collective-goods provision in the postcommunist world from a snapshot at a particular point in time.

This is an unfortunate constraint but one that the theoretical exploration in Chapter 3 helps to relax. The argument that I developed there does not take the simple form "A causes B." Rather, the model of representation through taxation predicts that the relationship between taxability and collective-goods provision should vary across countries, sectors, and collective goods. This causal heterogeneity provides empirical leverage. As I show below, various alternative theories are consistent with some of my empirical results but inconsistent with others. In contrast, the logic of representation through taxation provides a plausible explanatory framework for all of the relationships documented here. It is an illustration of what I believe distinguishes social science from more purely experimental traditions: the use of theory to identify causal relationships.

4.1 *Data*

To explore patterns of collective-goods provision in postcommunist countries, I return to the Business Environment and Enterprise Performance Survey (BEEPS) that I introduced in Chapter 2. Participants in the BEEPS were asked to "rate the overall quality and efficiency of services delivered" by fourteen "*public* agencies or services" (emphasis in original) on a six-point scale ranging from "very bad" to "very good." The variables and their frequency distributions are given in Table 4.1. As can be seen, the distribution for most variables is roughly bell shaped.

I use these evaluations as proxies for the actual quality and efficiency of services delivered to the respondent firm, that is, as proxies for the level of collective-goods provision available to the firm. Obviously, this is appropriate only if firms that rate more highly the quality and efficiency of a public agency or service actually do receive better collective-goods provision. One possible objection to this assumption is that firms in some sectors may rate certain public agencies or services positively or negatively merely because they consider the goods provided unimportant. The particular battery of questions in the BEEPS minimizes this risk, as the public agencies or services listed are in general valuable to all firms, not merely those in certain sectors. The one obvious exception is customs, which is of direct use only for importing and exporting firms.[2]

The theoretical framework presented in Chapter 3 suggests that any variation in the provision of collective goods due to capacity for collective action or anticipated tax compliance will be greater when the politician is better able to discriminate in the provision of these goods. To make it easier to evaluate whether this is in fact the case, throughout this chapter I order public services or agencies according to their excludability, that is, the degree to which goods may be provided to some firms but not to

---

[2] An alternative approach would be to treat protection from rent-seeking bureaucrats as a collective good, as bureaucratic corruption is generally recognized as a key obstacle to doing business in postcommunist countries. In fact, the BEEPS includes a measure of bribe ("unofficial") payments to public officials that can be used for this purpose. All of the key results reported in this chapter go through if I treat the proportion of revenues *not* paid as bribes as the dependent variable rather than the measures of collective-goods provision discussed here. I choose not to emphasize this result because it is unclear which public officials are in receipt of such bribes, and I do not want to confuse the provision of collective goods with contributions provided to politicians in return for such goods.

Table 4.1. *Quality and efficiency of public agencies and services*

	Courts	Police	Military	Government	Parliament	Central Bank	Health	Education	Roads	Post	Telephone	Electricity	Water	Customs
Very bad	9.29	9.99	7.55	15.28	17.83	7.70	10.05	5.40	12.95	1.86	3.12	4.10	4.55	5.96
Bad	20.72	17.79	12.91	16.77	22.05	11.98	23.74	13.99	23.88	6.57	8.98	8.56	10.84	13.45
Slightly bad	25.96	23.26	15.43	22.37	25.09	15.15	24.31	20.21	22.78	10.06	12.51	10.31	13.62	19.45
Slightly good	25.24	23.70	24.17	21.90	18.62	24.90	21.50	30.06	22.56	31.13	27.52	26.36	25.96	28.35
Good	17.17	22.23	34.55	19.53	14.29	34.08	18.34	27.72	16.43	46.04	42.28	45.18	40.95	28.83
Very good	1.61	3.03	5.40	4.16	2.13	6.19	2.05	2.62	1.40	4.34	5.60	5.49	4.08	3.97
N	3,035	3,603	2,611	3,416	3,388	3,181	3,702	3,553	3,560	3,758	3,910	3,900	3,802	2,921

Note. Percentage of respondents rating public agency or service at given level of quality and efficiency. Full names of variables: judiciary/courts, police, armed forces/military, central government leadership (president/PM/cabinet), parliament, central bank, public health care service/hospitals, education services/schools, roads department/public works, postal service/agency, telephone service/agency, electric power company/agency, water/sewerage service/agency, and customs service/agency.

others. The ordering is inevitably a bit crude, based on my own prior beliefs about which goods are more and which less excludable. My interpretation of certain results will be valid to the extent that these beliefs are correct.

In particular, both in Table 4.1 and the figures to follow, I have grouped thirteen of the fourteen public services and agencies into distinct groups, in descending order of excludability. Beyond this rough classification, I have no particular expectation about the relative excludability of different collective goods, and so within groups I maintain the ordering in the BEEPS questionnaire.[3]

1. Courts, police, military: Justice and police protection can clearly be provided on a discriminatory basis, often at the level of the individual firm. Moreover, in postcommunist countries, interior-ministry troops can and do sometimes become involved in business disputes, a fact of commercial life that enlivens both popular (e.g., Latynina, 1999) and scholarly (e.g., Łoś and Zybertowicz, 2000; Volkov, 2002) accounts of postcommunist entrepreneurship.
2. Government, parliament, central bank: As branches of government that provide collective goods, the government and parliament are able to discriminate to the extent that they have control over any goods that are excludable. Central banks provide the public good of macroeconomic stability, of course, but in postcommunist countries they often also channel credits to specific sectors (Shleifer and Treisman, 2000).
3. Health and education: The general provision of health and education obviously involves a significant degree of nonexcludability. That said, health care was frequently provided at the sectoral or firm level under communism through designated clinics, and many day-care centers (an integral part of the Soviet educational system) were attached to particular enterprises. In the postcommunist era, the status of these social assets was often fiercely contested (e.g., Juurikkala and Lazareva, 2006).
4. Roads, post, telephone, electricity, and water: These goods are typically provided on a territorial basis, limiting their excludability.

[3] The original ordering in the BEEPS questionnaire is as follows: customs, courts, roads, post, telephone, electricity, water, health, education, police, military, government, parliament, central bank.

Moreover, the design of Soviet-era infrastructure is such that turning off electricity or water to individual consumers is often technologically difficult (Way and Collier, 2004).

Customs, the one remaining public service or agency, is conceptually distinct from the other thirteen. Customs law and regulation may, of course, be highly discriminatory, and one might expect sectors with greater capacity for collective action to receive more favorable treatment. At the same time, the customs service functions more as tax collector than as provider of productivity-enhancing collective goods, so that the effect of anticipated tax compliance on customs practice is unclear.

What firm characteristics should we expect to be correlated with these proxies for collective-goods provision? The traditional theory of collective action suggests that the quality and efficiency of services delivered to an economic sector is related to the ability and incentive of members of that sector to overcome their collective-action problems. I examine several measures in particular:

- Membership in a "trade association or lobby group," as collective action is less expensive when the cost of organization has already been sunk. I use a dummy variable equal to one if the firm is a member.
- The employment of the firm, as large firms may have greater bargaining power with state officials. (In essence, one may think of a firm as a set of economic actors who have overcome their collective-action problems.) I use the log of employment, as there may be decreasing marginal returns to scale in the political arena. Qualitatively similar results obtain if employment without the log transformation is used instead.
- The degree of competition, as collective action may be more likely if benefits are concentrated among a small number of firms. The BEEPS questionnaire asks firms whether they have no competitors in their major product line in the domestic market, one to three competitors, or more than three competitors. I use dummy variables for the first two categories.
- Past and present ownership, as both current and former state-owned firms may have access to government officials that enterprises that emerged during the postcommunist transition ("de novo" firms) do

not. I include dummy variables for both majority state ownership and de novo status.

These variables and others used as covariates were introduced in Chapter 2; summary statistics are provided in Table 2.A.5 in the appendix to that chapter.

The taxability model presented in the previous chapter stresses instead the importance of revenue hiding in determining the provision of collective goods. As discussed in Chapter 2, firms surveyed in the BEEPS were asked, "What percentage of the sales of a typical firm in your area of activity would you estimate is reported to the tax authorities, bearing in mind difficulties with complying with taxes and other regulations?" For the empirical work below I recode this variable as the *proportion* of sales *hidden* from tax authorities. The indirect wording of this question – firms are queried not about their own behavior but about that of a "typical firm" in their "area of activity" – fortuitously suggests a sectoral characteristic, as the taxability model suggests should be important for politicians discriminating in the provision of sector-specific collective goods.

All of the empirical models that I estimate control for firm characteristics that may be correlated with either the collective-action or revenue-hiding variables, on the one hand, and the measures of collective-goods provision, on the other, independently of their effect on the collective-action and revenue-hiding variables: foreign ownership, whether the firm exports any goods directly, and industry (with nine dummy variables corresponding to the ten industries reported in Table 2.A.5).[4] Throughout I control for institutional variation at the country level by including country dummies.[5] In addition, in all empirical models I include town-size dummies as a rough control for any institutional variation within countries, as the BEEPS does not code the exact physical location of firms within a country; I obtain very similar results when these dummies are excluded.

---

[4] For discussion of industry characteristics that may be associated with capacity for collective action, see, for example, Frieden (1992) and Alt and Gilligan (1994).

[5] In principle, this can be problematic for the empirical strategy I describe below, as in contrast to fixed-effects linear models, one cannot consistently estimate fixed-effects probit models by simply including group-level dummies. In practice, however, unreasonable estimates appear to be a problem only when the number of observations per group is small, as is not the case with the BEEPS data. See http://www.stata.com/statalist/archive/2003-09/msg00103.html for discussion.

4.2 Representation through Collective Action versus Representation through Taxation

To what extent is postcommunist politics governed by the Olsonian considerations of interest-group representation versus the revenue concerns that the theory of representation through taxation suggests should be important in much of the postcommunist world? In this section I approach this question by examining the provision of collective goods to firms in the full BEEPS sample, assuming for the moment that the incentives of politicians are constant across postcommunist space. In the following section I explore the extent to which these incentives diverged across countries in Eastern Europe and the former Soviet Union.

I begin by estimating a "pure" collective-action model on the full sample of firms, where the key determinants of collective-goods provision are (a) whether the firm belongs to a trade association or lobby group, (b) (the log of) firm employment, (c) the absence of competition in the firm's major product line in the domestic market (dummy variables reflecting whether the firm is a monopoly or has one to three competitors), and (d) access to government officials arising from current or former state ownership (dummy variables for majority state ownership and de novo status). Formally, my empirical model is

$$y_i^* = z_i\eta + x_i\beta + \epsilon_i, \tag{4.1}$$

where y_i^* is the quality or efficiency of some public agency or service, as experienced by firm i; z_i is the vector of collective-action variables for firm i; x_i is a vector of other firm characteristics included as control variables, including industry, country, and town-size dummy variables; ϵ_i is the unobserved residual; and η and β are vectors of parameters to be estimated.

As discussed above, we do not observe y_i^* directly but only a categorical rating y_i ("very good," "good," etc.) of the quality and efficiency of the public agency or service. However, one may assume that there exist common thresholds (cutpoints) that determine when a firm that experiences y_i^* switches from one categorical rating y_i to another. If one further assumes that ϵ_i is distributed as a standard normal, then this is the ordered-probit model, which may be estimated by maximum likelihood. In this model, the cutpoints are parameters to be estimated.

How well does the theory of collective action fare in explaining variation in collective-goods provision in postcommunist countries? Table 4.A.1 in the appendix to this chapter presents estimation results for each of the fourteen public agencies and services whose quality and efficiency firms were asked to rate.[6] Most striking in the results is the absolutely negligible effect of membership in a trade association or lobby group, a finding consistent with other studies of postcommunist lobbying, as I discuss below. Figure 4.1 illustrates the impact of association membership graphically, showing the estimated difference between members and nonmembers in the probability that the respondent is generally satisfied with the quality or efficiency of a public agency or service, that is, that the respondent rates the quality or efficiency as "very good," "good," or "slightly good." (I use the same scale for this and subsequent figures to allow easy comparison across firm characteristics and models.) Only for roads is the estimated effect of membership in a business association significantly different from zero (though the point estimate for military is approximately the same), and for this variable the effect of association membership has opposite the expected sign.

In contrast, the estimated impact of firm size is always positive, with the estimated coefficient on log employment statistically significant at conventional levels for eight of the fourteen public services or agencies. Further, for those collective goods the estimated effect of employment is substantively large. As illustrated in Figure 4.2, the estimated change in satisfaction with a public agency or service as employment increases from 1 to 100 ranges from 5.5 percent for water to nearly 14 percent for the police. Size, not formal membership in a business association, seems to guarantee better treatment by government officials. Moreover, as expected, the estimated impact of firm size is largest for those collective goods that are

---

[6] For all empirical models in this chapter, I report heteroskedasticity-robust standard errors, with associated significance levels and confidence intervals. Arguably, one should instead report standard errors robust to correlation among observations within countries, the primary sampling unit, i.e., one should "cluster by country." Unfortunately, the CLARIFY package that I use to produce the data for estimated effects often breaks down when the cluster option is invoked, though (nonclustered) robust standard errors are supported. For purposes of consistency with estimated effects I therefore report robust standard errors in all tables of estimation results. However, I reran all models – including those discussed in the text but not presented graphically – clustering by country and checked significance levels against those with robust standard errors. Although a few estimated coefficients are significant at the 10-percent level when clustering by country while significant at the 5-percent level with robust standard errors, and a very small number of estimated coefficients lose significance entirely, all key qualitative results are unaffected.

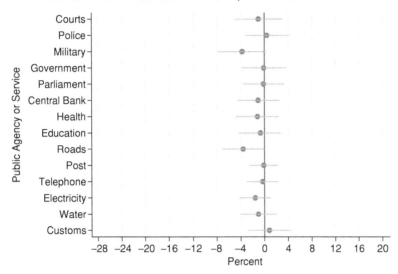

Figure 4.1 Collective-action model: business-association membership and collective-goods provision. Difference between members and nonmembers of business associations in probability satisfied with public agency or service. All other variables held at mean values. Dots represent point estimates, and lines represent 95-percent confidence intervals.

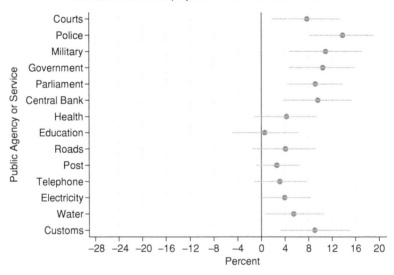

Figure 4.2 Collective-action model: size and collective-goods provision. Change in probability satisfied with public agency or service as employment increases from one to one hundred. All other variables held at mean values. Dots represent point estimates, and lines represent 95-percent confidence intervals.

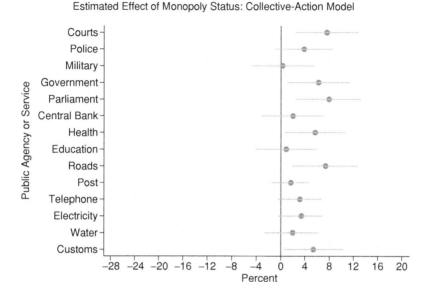

Figure 4.3 Collective-action model: competition and collective-goods provision. Difference between monopolies and firms with more than three competitors in probability satisfied with public agency or service. All other variables held at mean values. Dots represent point estimates, and lines represent 95-percent confidence intervals.

presumably more excludable. Size matters for satisfaction with the police and government, not the post office or telephone company.

Of the remaining collective-action variables, for only two are the estimated effects even occasionally significant: monopoly status and de novo status. As expected, monopolies generally report greater satisfaction with collective-goods provision than do firms in more competitive industries, though as shown in Figure 4.3 the estimated difference between monopolies and firms with more than three competitors is significantly different from zero for only six of the fourteen public agencies or services. New firms also report occasionally less satisfaction with collective-goods provision, though as shown below this effect largely disappears after controlling for revenue hiding.

These results are generally consistent with other analyses of collective action in postcommunist countries, though there are a few differences. Closest to the model here is Timothy Frye's work on business lobbying in Russia (Frye, 2002a), which uses different data but includes a nearly identical set of collective-action variables. As with my results, Frye finds that size is positively correlated with success in lobbying and that de novo status is occasionally negatively correlated; in contrast to my results, he also generally finds a positive effect of membership in a business organization but no effect of monopoly status.[7] Other studies using different specifications have consistently found that small firms in postcommunist countries suffer from poor collective-goods provision (e.g., Hellman, Jones, and Kaufmann, 2000; Frye, 2004), even while noting substantial differences in this effect across countries (e.g., Frye and Shleifer, 1997; Johnson, McMillan, and Woodruff, 2000). The insignificant effect of business-association membership that I find is consistent with evidence that the primary function of postcommunist business associations is to provide trade information and other services to their members, rather than to act as intermediaries between firms and the state (Johnson, McMillan, and Woodruff, 2002; Pyle, 2006a; see, however, Hendley, Murrell, and Ryterman, 2000).

Thus, of the various collective-action variables, firm size has the largest and most consistently significant effect on collective-goods provision. But what accounts for the size effect? The model of representation through taxation presented in the previous chapter suggests that large firms may benefit from better provision of collective goods if they are more taxable and not just because they are less subject to collective-action problems. In Chapter 2, I showed that large firms surveyed in the BEEPS report greater tax compliance than do small firms, a result consistent with the intuition that large enterprises find it more costly to hide revenues from tax authorities. More generally, I found support for the argument, formalized as Prediction 1 in the taxability model, that firms in sectors that are more taxable hide less of their revenue from tax authorities. (Here, as in the previous chapter, I use the term "sector" to denote any group of firms that share a common organization and a common technology. This definition implies groupings finer grained than the industries – personal service, manufacturing, and so on – for which I include dummy variables in the empirical analysis. In the case discussed in Chapter 1, for example, private vodka retailers and the state-owned distribution company Pskovalko would constitute two separate sectors.) To the extent that such tax compliance is anticipated by politicians, we might expect to see the provision of collective goods negatively correlated with revenue hiding.

---

[7] Firms in Frye's study were asked whether they could influence legislation or normative acts, whereas my dependent variables measure satisfaction with the level of collective-goods provision. Frye also distinguishes among lobbying at various levels of government.

I test the predictions of the taxability model by adding the proportion of revenues hidden H_i to the basic collective-action model already estimated [Equation (4.1)]:

$$y_i^* = H_i \delta + \mathbf{z}_i \eta + \mathbf{x}_i \beta + \epsilon_i. \qquad (4.2)$$

As before, $\mathbf{z}_i$ is the vector of collective-action variables for firm i, and $\mathbf{x}_i$ is the vector of other firm characteristics included as control variables, including industry, town-size, and country dummy variables. Because the determinants of revenue hiding examined in Chapter 2 are included in $\mathbf{z}_i$ and $\mathbf{x}_i$, I thus implicitly assume that there are other characteristics of the sector – broadly defined – to which the firm belongs that are observable to political actors and convey information about the level of revenue hiding in that sector but that are unobservable in the data (and uncorrelated with ϵ_i). My experience in the postcommunist world suggests that this assumption is plausible. Politicians in these countries seem to know with a great deal of precision which types of firms pay their taxes and which do not, even if in the short run they can do little about it. The vodka case in Chapter 1 provides an example: the BEEPS data indicate whether a firm engages in wholesale trade, retail trade, manufacturing, and so on, but vodka trade differs in its taxability from other firms in wholesale and retail trade, as does vodka production from other types of manufacturing.

Table 4.A.2 in the appendix to this chapter presents the estimation results. The estimated coefficient on revenue hiding is always negative and is significantly different from zero at conventional levels for all public agencies or services but the central bank, post, and customs. As Figure 4.4 shows, the estimated effect of revenue hiding on collective-goods provision is large, comparable in magnitude to that of employment in the basic collective-action model. (Revenue hiding of zero and 50 percent represent values approximately one standard deviation either side of the mean.)

Thus, as Prediction 2 of the theoretical model presented in the previous chapter hypothesizes, firms in sectors that hide less of their revenues from tax authorities generally benefit from better collective-goods provision. Moreover, as with the impact of employment in the collective-action model, the effect of revenue hiding is generally greatest for those collective goods presumed to be most excludable (Prediction 6 of the taxability model), though there are a few exceptions. At the same time, both Predictions 2 and 3 suggest that such effects may be different for firms in organized rather than unorganized sectors. I address this possibility in the following

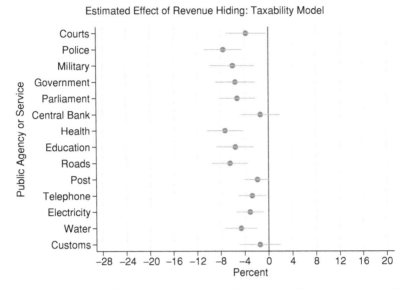

Figure 4.4 Taxability model: revenue hiding and collective-goods provision. Change in probability satisfied with public agency or service as revenue hiding increases from zero to 50 percent. All other variables held at mean values. Dots represent point estimates, and lines represent 95-percent confidence intervals.

section in the context of regional differences in patterns of collective-goods provision.

Predictions 4 and 5 of the model of representation through taxation deal directly with the difference between the basic collective-action model and the taxability model. Prediction 4 says that when tax revenue is especially important to politicians, then a sector that is unorganized but easy to tax may benefit from greater collective-goods provision than one that is organized but hard to tax. The empirical results reported above and in Table 4.A.2 suggest that this is indeed possible, as membership in a trade association or lobby group is estimated to have no effect, whereas the estimated impact of revenue hiding is generally quite large. Prediction 5 says that firms that are organized may benefit from better collective-goods provision not just because they are organized but because they are more taxable. In terms of the empirical model, we should thus expect the estimated coefficient on size and monopoly status to trend toward zero with the inclusion of revenue hiding. Comparison of Tables 4.A.1 and 4.A.2 in the appendix to this chapter shows this to generally be the case. I consider this prediction in more detail further below when examining the impact of employment on collective-goods provision in the two halves of the postcommunist world.

The logic of representation through taxation thus fares well in explaining general patterns of collective-goods provision across the postcommunist world. Capacity for collective action matters in determining who gets what in politics – size and monopoly status are particularly important – but a pure collective-action model both overstates the impact of this capacity and misses the effect of anticipated tax compliance on the provision of collective goods. But does the logic of representation through taxation have the same effect in all postcommunist countries, as the cursory examination in this section implicitly assumes? The empirical and theoretical analysis of the previous two chapters suggests that it should not. In the following section I relax the assumption of causal homogeneity and explore the relationship between taxability and the provision of collective goods across different institutional environments.

4.3 Divergent Patterns of Collective-Goods Provision

In Chapter 2, I demonstrated the existence of a sharp divide in the nature of tax systems that emerged following the collapse of communism in the Soviet Union and Eastern Europe. Roughly speaking, countries in the former Soviet Union continued to rely on "old" revenue sources, building tax systems around corporate taxes and taxes on goods and services. In contrast, the postcommunist states of Eastern Europe moved to a greater reliance on taxation of individuals through income, social security, and payroll taxes. This difference had important implications for tax compliance, as tax authorities in the former Soviet Union concentrated especially on encouraging tax payments by large, monopolistic firms in particular sectors, much as they had done in the communist era, whereas those in Eastern Europe focused more on learning how to coax revenues out of new sources. The result was that "natural" differences in taxability across sectors – for example, large enterprises are more taxable than are small ones and monopolies are more taxable than are firms in more competitive industries – were exaggerated in the former Soviet Union. To put a fine point on it, post-Soviet states knew only how to tax that which is relatively easy to tax everywhere, whereas states in Eastern Europe were better at raising revenues from a variety of sources.

The consequence of this divergence in tax systems should have been less incentive in Eastern Europe than in the former Soviet Union to

Table 4.2. *Causal heterogeneity in taxability model: summary of predictions*

Comparisons across regions: CIS (CIS) vs. EE/Baltics (EEB)	
Excludable goods	$\Delta_{CIS} < \Delta_{EEB}$
Nonexcludable goods	$\Delta_{CIS} = \Delta_{EEB} = 0$
Comparisons within regions: unorganized (U) vs. organized (O)	
Excludable goods	
CIS	$\Delta_U < \Delta_O \; (\Delta_O < 0?)$
Eastern Europe and Baltics	$\Delta_U < \Delta_O \; (\Delta_O > 0?)$
Nonexcludable goods	
CIS	$\Delta_U = \Delta_O = 0$
Eastern Europe and Baltics	$\Delta_U = \Delta_O = 0$
Comparisons across tax systems: corporate (ENT) vs. indirect (GS) vs. individual (LAB)	
Excludable goods	$\Delta_{ENT} < \Delta_{GS}, \Delta_{ENT} < \Delta_{LAB}$
Nonexcludable goods	$\Delta_{ENT} = \Delta_{GS} = \Delta_{LAB} = 0$

Note: The variable Δ denotes predicted change (negative values indicate decreases and positive values increases) in probability satisfied with public agency or service as revenue hiding increases.

disproportionately provide collective goods to sectors that are relatively easy to tax. Having lived a few years in East Central Europe, I find it hard to imagine a Czech or Hungarian government structuring its political economy around a highly taxable industry like vodka, such as we saw in the Russian region of Pskov in Chapter 1. With few *systematic* differences in revenue hiding across firms, and with enterprise taxation less important as a general source of revenue, there would not have been the perverse incentive to provide collective goods to especially taxable sectors.

To test this hypothesis, and more generally to explore variation in the impact of anticipated tax compliance on the provision of collective goods, I conduct comparisons across regions, within regions, and across tax systems. Table 4.2 summarizes the heterogenous causal relationships between revenue hiding and collective-goods provision predicted by the model of the previous chapter. First, I simply divide the sample into two – firms in the CIS and those in Eastern Europe and the Baltics – and reestimate the empirical taxability model (Equation (4.2)) for each subsample. To the extent that politicians in the former Soviet Union do have a disproportionate incentive to discriminate in favor of sectors relatively easy to tax, revenue hiding should be more negatively associated with collective-goods provision for firms in the eastern half of the postcommunist world. At the same time, any discrimination in the provision of collective goods should stronger for goods that are more excludable.

Second, for firms in each of these two regions I compare the effect of revenue hiding for organized and unorganized firms by interacting revenue hiding with the log of employment, the collective-action variable with the strongest impact on collective-goods provision. Prediction 3 of the taxability model in the previous chapter suggests that any discrimination against less taxable economic activity should be greater for small (presumably unorganized) than for large (presumably organized) firms, as unorganized sectors are politically important only to the extent that they produce tax revenue. In addition, however, Prediction 2 says that the impact of revenue hiding on the provision of collective goods to organized sectors may be *positive* when tax revenue is less important, as greater ability to hide revenues increases the incentive of organized sectors to lobby for collective goods. Given the lesser reliance on enterprise taxation in the western half of the postcommunist world, we might expect this outcome to be more likely for the subsample of firms in Eastern Europe and the Baltics.

Finally, I model the effect of revenue hiding on collective-goods provision as a function of the tax structure of the country in which a firm is located. If the hypothesis is correct that politicians have a greater incentive to favor sectors that are relatively taxable where tax systems are structured around enterprise taxation, then revenue hiding and collective-goods provision should be more negatively associated in countries where corporate taxes make up a larger share of total tax revenue. As with the previous exercises, I expect this pattern to hold more for collective goods that are relatively excludable.

For these comparisons to be informative, there must be variation across countries either in the value that politicians attach to tax revenue from firms or in the degree to which revenue hiding is systematically related to sectoral characteristics observable by politicians but not included in Equation (4.2). To the extent that this is not the case, any cross-country differences in the propensity of politicians to discriminate in favor of taxable sectors will be unidentified. As I show, this assumption appears to be valid: the strength of the relationship between revenue hiding and collective-goods provision varies across postcommunist countries in systematic and expected fashion.

Figure 4.5 illustrates results from the first of these comparisons, showing the estimated relationship between revenue hiding and collective-goods provision for firms in the CIS, on the one hand, and in Eastern Europe and the Baltics, on the other. (Estimated coefficients and standard errors are presented in Tables 4.A.3 and 4.A.4 in the appendix to this chapter.) The

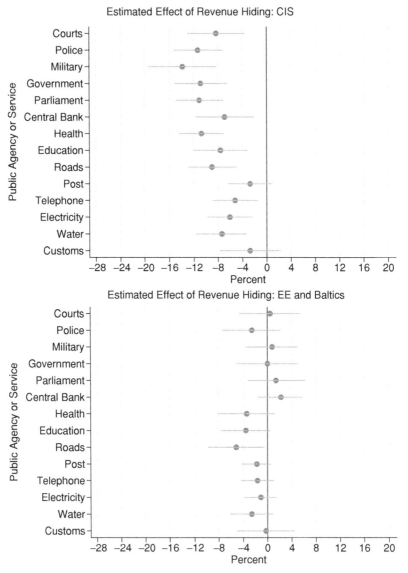

Figure 4.5 Taxability model: revenue hiding and collective-goods provision, CIS (top) versus Eastern Europe and Baltics (bottom). Change in probability satisfied with public agency or service as revenue hiding increases from zero to 50 percent. All other variables held at mean values. Dots represent point estimates, and lines represent 95-percent confidence intervals.

difference is stark. Revenue hiding is significantly and negatively associated with collective-goods provision for twelve of fourteen public agencies and services for the subsample of firms in the CIS. In contrast, there is essentially no systematic relationship between revenue hiding and collective-goods provision among firms in Eastern Europe and the Baltics: only the estimated effect on roads is significantly different from zero, and the point estimate is small. Consistent with prior expectations, politicians in the former Soviet Union appear to be quite inclined to discriminate in favor of sectors that are relatively easy to tax, whereas those in Eastern Europe seem not at all motivated to do so.

Moreover, the estimated revenue-hiding effect is generally largest in the former Soviet Union for those public agencies and services where it may be easiest to discriminate in the provision of collective goods. The estimated change in probability satisfied with a public service or agency as revenue hiding increases from zero to 50 percent is greater than eight percent for courts, police, military, government, parliament, health, and roads. With the exception of roads, these all lie in the set of collective goods identified above as presumably most excludable. In contrast, there is no systematic relationship between ability to discriminate and the estimated size of the revenue-hiding effect in Eastern Europe. Thus, rather than being uniformly greater in the former Soviet Union, the revenue-hiding effect is larger precisely for those public agencies and services where we would expect it to be.

The strong relationship between revenue hiding and collective-goods provision in the former Soviet Union suggests caution in drawing inferences from a pure collective-action model. Generally speaking, large firms in the former Soviet Union benefit from better collective-goods provision than do small firms. But approximately one-quarter of the effect of employment estimated in a pure collective-action model for the subsample of firms in the CIS disappears after controlling for revenue hiding. (For reasons of space I omit the relevant table and figures.) Large firms in the former Soviet Union benefit in the making of public policy not only because they are better able to overcome their collective-action problems but also because they are more important revenue sources. In contrast, the estimated size effect for firms in Eastern Europe is for most public agencies and services nearly identical in the collective-action and taxability models.

Figures 4.6 and 4.7 depict results from the second comparison, where for each regional subsample of firms I extend the empirical taxability model (Equation (4.2)) by including the interaction of the proportion of revenues

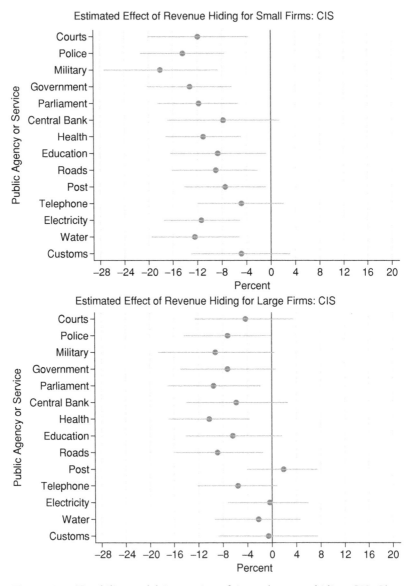

Figure 4.6 Taxability model: interaction of size and revenue hiding, CIS. Change in probability satisfied with public agency or service as revenue hiding increases from zero to 50 percent. Firms with 5 employees (top) versus firms with 500 employees (bottom). All other variables held at mean values. Dots represent point estimates, and lines represent 95-percent confidence intervals.

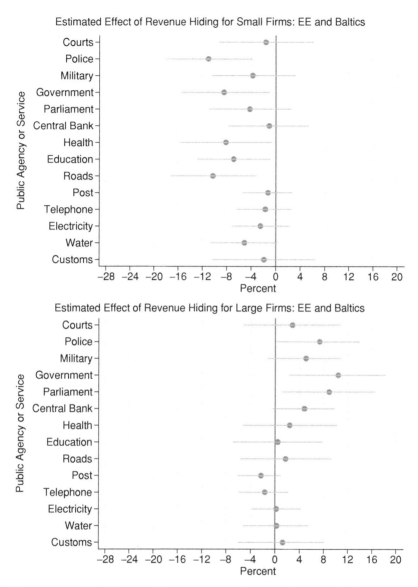

Figure 4.7 Taxability model: interaction of size and revenue hiding, Eastern Europe and Baltics. Change in probability satisfied with public agency or service as revenue hiding increases from zero to 50 percent. Firms with 5 employees (top) versus firms with 500 employees (bottom). All other variables held at mean values. Dots represent point estimates, and lines represent 95-percent confidence intervals.

hidden from tax authorities with the log of employment. (Estimation results are presented in Tables 4.A.5 and 4.A.6 in the appendix to this chapter.) As expected, in both regions there is a stronger negative association between revenue hiding and collective-goods provision for small (presumably unorganized) firms, with the effect especially pronounced for collective goods that are more excludable. What is most striking, however, is the *positive* relationship between revenue hiding and provision of the most excludable collective goods for large (presumably organized) firms in Eastern Europe. Although the estimated effect is statistically significant only for police, government, and parliament, the overall pattern is consistent with that predicted by the model in the previous chapter when tax revenue is relatively unimportant: organized sectors receive more collective goods when they are *less* taxable, as they retain more of the value those goods generate and so have a greater incentive to lobby for their provision. In contrast, even large (and presumably organized) firms in the former Soviet Union are punished for hiding revenues from tax authorities. The logic of representation through taxation thus produces sharply different outcomes in Eastern Europe, where governments were not generally reliant on enterprise taxes as a source of revenue, and the former Soviet Union, where corporate taxes were much more important.

The division of firms into regional subsamples illustrates the very different relationship between anticipated tax compliance and collective-goods provision in the two halves of the postcommunist world. As I have shown, this difference corresponds to the two ideal types of tax systems that emerged in the former Soviet Union and Eastern Europe following the collapse of communism. However, as with any ideal type, the characterization of a tax system as "post-Soviet" or "East European" is an oversimplification, obscuring important variation in tax structure within both regions. To the extent that tax systems determine the incentives of politicians to promote one type of economic activity over another, we might therefore expect to see variation in the relationship between revenue hiding and collective-goods provision across countries that mirrors variation in tax structure.

Thus, for the final comparison I model the impact of revenue hiding on collective-goods provision as a function of the tax structure in the country in which a firm is located. To do so, I estimate a model for the full sample in which I include not only the proportion of revenues hidden from tax authorities but also the interaction of this variable with the compositional variables for average tax structure discussed in Chapter 2 and presented in

Table 2.A.1 in the appendix to that chapter. (I drop firms in Bosnia and the Serb Republic in Bosnia from the analysis, as tax-structure data are unavailable for those governments.) As the compositional variables sum to 1, one of the four interaction terms must be omitted from the model; which of the four is omitted is immaterial to the results. I thus interact the proportion of revenues hidden with the average proportion of tax revenue collected by the country in which the firm is located during the period 1994–2000 from (a) corporate taxes; (b) taxes on goods and services; and (c) income, social security, and payroll taxes, respectively.[8]

Estimation results for this model are presented in Table 4.A.7 in the appendix to this chapter. However, the results here are difficult to interpret from estimated coefficients and standard errors alone for reasons that go beyond the usual issues with ordered-probit models. Because revenue hiding is interacted with compositional variables (variables that sum to 1 and are bounded between zero and 1), any counterfactual must take into account that an increase in one of the compositional variables necessarily entails a decrease in the others. For example, an increase in the proportion of revenues collected from corporate taxes from 0.10 to 0.20 must be accompanied by a decrease in the proportion of all other taxes collected of 0.10. However, with more than two compositional variables, there is no unique way to allocate the decrease among the remaining variables: all of the reduction could come from taxes on goods and services, some from taxes on goods and services and some from other taxes, and so on.[9]

I deal with this issue by formulating counterfactuals in an especially simple way: I construct ideal types of tax structures, where three of the four tax categories are fixed at a baseline level, and the fourth category is disproportionately high. In particular, I choose the following baseline division of taxes:

- corporate taxes: 0.05
- taxes on goods and services: 0.30
- income, social security, and payroll taxes: 0.40
- other taxes: 0.10

I then allocate the remaining 0.15 in turn to each of the first three taxes to represent "corporate," "indirect," and "individual" tax structures. As

---

[8] I obtain qualitatively similar results from a random-coefficient model (treating the dependent variable as continuous rather than discrete), where I model the effect of revenue hiding as a function of tax structure and an unobserved country effect (Western, 1998; Beck, 2001).

[9] For discussion of these points, see Adolph (2004, 2005).

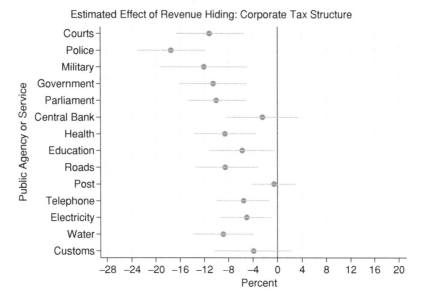

Figure 4.8 Taxability model with tax-structure interactions: revenue hiding and collective-goods provision, "corporate" tax structure. Change in probability satisfied with public agency or service as revenue hiding increases from zero to 50 percent. Assumed tax structure: corporate taxes, 0.20; taxes on goods and services, 0.30; income, social security, and payroll taxes, 0.40; other taxes, 0.10. All other variables held at mean values. Dots represent point estimates, and lines represent 95-percent confidence intervals.

constructed, each of these ideal types corresponds roughly to the maximum observed proportion of revenues collected from that tax.

Figures 4.8–4.10 illustrate the estimated impact of revenue hiding on collective-goods provision for these three ideal types. As shown in Figure 4.8, a "corporate" tax structure is strongly associated with discrimination in the provision of collective goods based on the taxability of economic activity, with estimated effects similar to those depicted in Figure 4.5 for the subsample of firms in the CIS. In contrast, neither a tax structure oriented around taxation of goods and services, nor one focused on taxation of individuals, seems to encourage discrimination based on anticipated tax compliance.

Thus, of the two "old" taxes predominant in the former Soviet Union, the emphasis on corporate taxes best explains the divergent patterns of collective-goods provision in the two halves of the postcommunist world. Having built tax systems especially focused on the taxation of certain key

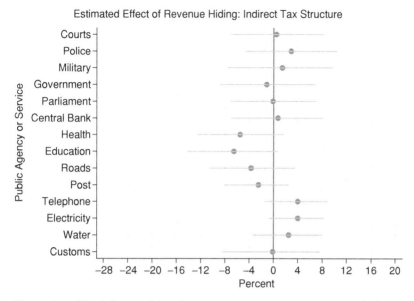

Figure 4.9 Taxability model with tax-structure interactions: revenue hiding and collective-goods provision, "indirect" tax structure. Change in probability satisfied with public agency or service as revenue hiding increases from zero to 50 percent. Assumed tax structure: corporate taxes, 0.05; taxes on goods and services, 0.45; income, social security, and payroll taxes, 0.40; other taxes, 0.10. All other variables held at mean values. Dots represent point estimates, and lines represent 95-percent confidence intervals.

enterprises, politicians in post-Soviet states seem inclined to allocate goods and services in such a way as to ensure that those enterprises remain an important part of the tax base.

In summary, the results of this section are broadly consistent with the logic of representation through taxation. The incentives of postcommunist politicians to provide collective goods appear to be structured by the tax systems put in place early in the 1990s. Where those tax systems emphasized "old" over "new" revenue sources – and especially, as was generally the case in the former Soviet Union, where they were built around the collection of corporate taxes – politicians rewarded sectors that were relatively more tax compliant, while neglecting those that were less so. As expected, this effect was especially pronounced for public services and agencies where discrimination in the provision of collective goods may be easier. It was also larger for small, and presumably disorganized, firms: with little other reason

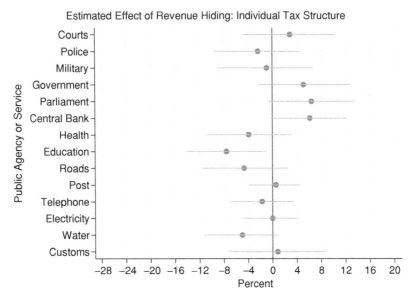

Estimated Effect of Revenue Hiding: Individual Tax Structure

Figure 4.10 Taxability model with tax-structure interactions: revenue hiding and collective-goods provision, "individual" tax structure. Change in probability satisfied with public agency or service as revenue hiding increases from zero to 50 percent. Assumed tax structure: corporate taxes, 0.05; taxes on goods and services, 0.30; income, social security, and payroll taxes, 0.55; other taxes, 0.10. All other variables held at mean values. Dots represent point estimates, and lines represent 95-percent confidence intervals.

to support such firms, politicians were especially sensitive to differences in their presumed tax compliance.

In contrast, where tax systems emphasized "new" over "old" revenue sources, as was generally the case in Eastern Europe, politicians were on average less responsive to differences in the taxability of sectors. Even so, there is important variation in treatment of firms within these countries, with large, presumably organized firms in some cases receiving more collective goods when they hid more revenues from the state. This counterintuitive finding is consistent with the model presented in the previous chapter, which predicts that when tax revenue is less important politically, tax evasion may actually increase the political importance of organized sectors, as those sectors retain more of the gain from collective goods and so lobby harder for their provision.

Thus, the logic of representation through taxation not only helps to explain general patterns of collective-goods provision across postcommunist countries but also provides a framework for understanding more subtle variation in business–state relations. In the following section I examine various alternative explanations for these empirical relationships and check the robustness of the results to changes in specification and sample.

4.4 Robustness Checks and Alternative Explanations

The central empirical finding of this chapter is that revenue hiding is negatively associated with the quality and efficiency of public agencies and services experienced by firms in postcommunist countries, more so for firms in the former Soviet Union than in Eastern Europe, and more so in countries with "corporate" tax structures than elsewhere. My interpretation of this result is that politicians in (parts of) the postcommunist world favored sectors that were important sources of tax revenue. An alternative reading of the data is that firms that were satisfied with collective-goods provision hid less of their revenue from tax authorities. Such behavior would be consistent with Levi's (1988) concept of "quasi-voluntary compliance," where rulers – not free to extract revenues "as they please" – are compelled to provide collective goods and prevent free riding by other taxpayers to encourage compliance.[10] To the extent that this is the case, the negative relationship between revenue hiding and collective-goods provision would reflect at least in part the greater willingness of firms that benefit from good collective-goods provision to pay taxes.

There are two reasons to doubt this alternative explanation for the patterns of collective-goods provision documented here. First, my focus is on the behavior of firms, not individual taxpayers. Although individuals may engage in self-sacrificing behavior when they feel they have been treated unfairly (e.g., Rabin, 1993), competitive pressure should reduce such behavior among enterprises. In particular, firms that hide less than they can get away with due to satisfaction with the provision of collective goods will find themselves at a disadvantage vis-à-vis their competitors and over time will form a progressively smaller portion of the market, either because they are run out of business or because they have fewer funds available for expansion. Second, the dramatically different relationship between revenue hiding and provision of collective goods in various parts of the postcommunist world is

---

[10] A related argument is that "tax morale" is improved when taxpayers feel they have been treated fairly by tax authorities; see, for example, Feld and Frey (2002, 2007). Berenson (2006*a,b*) provides evidence for such behavior from a survey of individual taxpayers in Russia, Poland, and Ukraine.

hard to reconcile with notions of reciprocity. If collective-goods provision is driving tax compliance among firms, rather than the reverse, then it is doing so only in the former Soviet Union. It seems implausible that norms of tax compliance based on reciprocity could have evolved so dramatically during the first decade of transition in the former Soviet Union but not at all in Eastern Europe. The more likely explanation is that poorly developed norms of tax compliance interacted in the former Soviet Union with the decision to construct tax systems around familiar revenue sources, producing a period of "extraordinary" politics in which politicians favored sectors that were relatively easy to tax, even at the expense of those that were better organized.

Another interpretation of the relationship between taxation and collective-goods provision is that firms have a choice between operating in a "formal" sector, where taxes are paid and the state provides access to collective goods, and an "informal" sector, where taxes are unpaid and access to collective goods is forfeited (de Soto, 1990; Johnson, Kaufmann, and Shleifer, 1997; Frye and Zhuravskaya, 2000; Frye, 2002b; Roland and Verdier, 2003; Bueno de Mesquita and Hafer, 2008). In this understanding, firms respond to poor collective-goods provision by exiting to the "informal" sector, so that underprovision of collective-goods drives tax evasion rather than the reverse. Here, too, there are two reasons to doubt this alternative explanation for the negative correlation between revenue hiding and collective-goods provision. First, all firms in the BEEPS sample are in fact officially registered enterprises operating in the "formal" sector, regardless of the degree to which they hide revenues from tax authorities. The only exit that has taken place is from the firm's tax obligations, which for the reasons discussed above should not be driven by collective-goods provision. Second, even if one allows the possibility that the revenue-hiding measure could represent exit to an "informal" sector, it makes little sense that firms in one half of the postcommunist world should base their exit decision on the quality of collective goods available in the "formal" sector, whereas those in the other half should not. As with the question of reciprocity, the dissimilarity between the former Soviet Union and Eastern Europe in patterns of collective-goods provision is better explained by the difference in tax systems in those two regions.

Another possible explanation relates to firms' tax-avoidance strategies. One can think of firms as having two options: they may hide revenues from tax authorities, or they may report their revenues but then refuse to meet their tax obligations (Ponomareva and Zhuravskaya, 2004;

Radaev, 2002). The latter strategy is likely to be employed by politically powerful firms, which may not only find it simpler to run up tax arrears than to hide revenues from tax authorities but which also may be better able to lobby for collective goods. Thus, if the variable "political power" is not completely captured by observable characteristics, the negative correlation between revenue hiding and collective-goods provision could be spurious.

As discussed in Chapter 2, the BEEPS includes a question that may be used to evaluate this possibility. Respondents were asked whether the firm received "subsidies (including tolerance of tax arrears) from local or national government." (In all, 11 percent of firms answered that they did.) In fact, responses to this question are uncorrelated with the proportion of revenues hidden from tax authorities after controlling for other firm characteristics, counter to what one would expect if revenue hiding and nonpayment of taxes on reported revenues were substitutes. Thus, there is little reason to think that the negative correlation between revenue hiding and collective-goods provision merely reflects choice of one tax-avoidance strategy over another based on a firm's political power. (We may, of course, add the subsidy variable to the empirical taxability model in Equation (4.2) to control for any otherwise unobserved characteristics correlated with both forgiveness of tax arrears and provision of collective goods. As expected given the lack of correlation between revenue hiding and the subsidy variable, this leaves the estimated impact of revenue hiding virtually unchanged.)

Firms may also differ in profitability, with more profitable firms choosing to hide more of their revenues from the state (Morozov, 1996; Hanousek and Palda, 2003). Unfortunately, the BEEPS questionnaire contains no measure of profitability, which may not be completely captured by observable characteristics. Nonetheless, it is implausible that more profitable sectors – those whose firms may hide more – would receive *fewer* collective goods. Rather, profitability should be associated with greater provision of collective goods, either because more profitable firms can pay for better provision or because they are more profitable precisely because they have been better provided for.

Similarly, sectors may differ in size, with politicians inclined to provide more collective goods to sectors that are relatively large. (The BEEPS contains no variables by which the size of a sector, as defined here, may be measured.) Because factors of production in turn migrate to sectors to which collective goods have been provided, this implies a potential simultaneity bias in the results reported here. This logic suggests an alternative, complementary explanation for the observed correlations between revenue hiding and collective-goods provision. As I discuss in Chapter 5, both factor allocation and collective-goods provision "tipped" during the 1990s toward old, relatively more taxable activity in the former Soviet Union and toward new, relatively less taxable activity in Eastern Europe. This is, of course, consistent with the sharp divide in patterns of collective-goods provision between the two halves of the postcommunist world that I document in this chapter. However, it suggests that such patterns might be due not only to revenue concerns when the BEEPS was conducted in 1999 but also to such considerations earlier in the decade.

The model presented in the previous chapter assumes that tax revenue is equally valuable to the politician, regardless of the sector from which it is collected. Although that seems reasonable in a unitary state, it is possible that in a federal system revenue-sharing agreements between different levels of government would render this assumption invalid. For example, in the case study in Chapter 1, provisions in Russian tax law that allocated excise revenue to the federal and regional governments changed from year to year, thus likely affecting the incentive of regional officials to promote the local vodka sector. Similarly, as discussed in Chapter 2, regional officials in federal systems might collude with tax inspectors and local firms to hide tax revenue from central tax administrations. Such collusion may be easier to organize for some types of enterprises than for others. If the degree to which tax revenue from different sectors is valued is systematically correlated with the taxability of those sectors, then the negative correlation between revenue hiding and collective-goods provision might reflect the tendency of politicians to allocate more collective goods to sectors that are important sources of tax revenue but not only or primarily for the reasons stressed here.

This theoretical possibility is further suggested by the large number of firms in the sample located in Russia, the most truly federal system in the former Soviet Union and thus the most likely to suffer from fiscal pathologies of this sort. To check that such considerations are not driving the results, I reestimated the empirical taxability model (Equation (4.2)) for firms in the CIS, dropping all Russian firms from the sample. The key qualitative results are virtually unchanged from those for the full sample of firms in the CIS. In particular, revenue hiding is negatively associated with collective-goods provision, with effects that are statistically significant at conventional levels, for firms in the subsample for all public agencies and services but customs.

116

Similarly, the empirical predictions tested in this chapter are based on the version of the taxability model presented in Chapter 3 that assumes that the tax rate is fixed and constant across sectors. But what if the politician sets a tax rate separately for each sector, as when the politician writes tax breaks for individual sectors into the tax code? As shown in Section 3.2, this possibility is easily incorporated into the theoretical model. The empirical prediction that emerges from this analysis – Prediction 7 in the previous chapter – is that when tax rates are endogenous, revenue hiding will be correlated only with the organization of a sector, not with its taxability. But as we have seen, this appears not to be the case: revenue hiding is systematically correlated with firm characteristics other than the collective-action variables (which may themselves be correlated with revenue hiding for reasons other than the ability of firms to lobby state officials).

Further, because the level of revenue hiding in the version of the theoretical model with endogenous tax rates depends only on whether a firm belongs to an organized sector, any observed correlation between revenue hiding and the provision of collective goods should be due only to the revenue hiding variable's picking up unmeasured capacity for collective action. But then the divergence in patterns of collective-goods provision between the former Soviet Union and Eastern Europe makes little sense. As shown above, collective action does seem to matter for public policy in Eastern Europe, as in the former Soviet Union. However, that implies that revenue hiding – in this alternative story, correlated with unmeasured capacity for collective action – should be associated with collective-goods provision in both halves of the postcommunist world, which is not true.

As a final note, it is worth stressing again that the data not only exhibit a strong correlation between revenue hiding and collective-goods provision in those parts of the postcommunist world where we most expect it, but also generally support the more subtle predictions of the theoretical model presented in Chapter 3: the interaction between collective action and anticipated tax compliance (Prediction 3), including the surprising result that poor tax compliance can sometimes increase the political value of organized sectors, and the different impact of revenue hiding for collective goods that are more and less excludable (Prediction 6). As stressed above, the derivation of heterogeneous causal effects is one of the key advantages of deductive reasoning. That there is support for all of the predictions of the model increases the confidence with which we can reject alternative theories of collective-goods provision in favor of the logic of representation through taxation.

4.5 Summary

The logic of representation through taxation suggests that the anticipated tax compliance of sectors interacts with the organization of interests to determine collective-goods provision. The survey data examined here provide broad support for a number of specific predictions that follow from this general proposition. Firms that are more taxable, as evidenced by higher reported tax compliance, receive better collective-goods provision from a variety of public agencies. Among traditional collective-action variables, only enterprise size has a similarly consistent effect. Moreover, the importance of taxability as a determinant of favorable policy treatment is largest for those public services and agencies where discrimination in the provision of collective goods is easiest.

At the same time, there is substantial variation across postcommunist states in the strength of these relationships. In the former Soviet Union, where tax systems were structured around familiar revenue sources, taxability is a powerful determinant of "who gets what" out of government, with collective goods disproportionately provided to sectors that are relatively easy to tax. In contrast, politicians in Eastern Europe seem little inclined to punish sectors that are poor providers of tax revenue, and they may even reward organized sectors to the extent that their members hide revenue from tax authorities and so have a greater incentive to lobby for collective goods. Roughly speaking, post-Soviet politicians fit the image of the revenue-maximizing politician who cares little about sectors that are difficult to tax, whereas their East European counterparts are more akin to the Olsonian policy maker subject to influence by organized but not unorganized groups. Beyond this general regional distinction, variation across postcommunist countries follows the contours of tax policy noted in Chapter 2. Countries with revenue systems oriented around enterprise taxation have political economies disproportionately supportive of important revenue sources; others do not.

As a consequence, certain types of enterprises – small firms in competitive industries, which is to say most new firms – had two strikes against them in post-Soviet states. Not only did they suffer the disadvantage of unorganized interests everywhere, but they had the additional shortcoming that the tax systems created in the 1990s were focused elsewhere, leaving them free to hide much of their revenue from the state. In principle, of course, this could have spurred growth of these enterprises, as the greater retention of revenues encouraged investment and compensated for the general weakness of financial markets in postcommunist states. In practice, however, this advantage seems to have been outweighed by postcommunist politicians' lack of interest in providing the collective goods necessary for small enterprise to flourish, as other revenue sources were far more important.

The outcome, which I describe in the next chapter, is that the small-business sector in the former Soviet Union lagged far behind its counterpart in Eastern Europe. Counter to the expectations of the architects of post-communist privatization, the large transfer of assets to private hands was insufficient to spur politicians in post-Soviet countries to provide collective goods to truly new private enterprise. This disappointing outcome, I argue, can be traced to the failure of "normal" politics to emerge soon enough. Desperate for revenue, and confronted with the reality that post-communist tax systems had been built around familiar revenue sources, post-Soviet politicians largely ignored any political weight acquired by the new private sector and focused instead on its meager contribution to the public purse. The poor provision of collective goods to the new private sector, in turn, discouraged the migration to it of labor and capital, thus further undermining the incentive of politicians to provide support. Post-Soviet political economies were caught in a "revenue trap."

4.A Appendix: Supplementary Tables

Table 4.A.1. *Collective-action model*

	Courts	Police	Military	Government	Parliament	Central Bank	Health	Education	Roads	Post	Telephone	Electricity	Water	Customs
Association member	-0.025	0.011	-0.100	-0.004	-0.005	-0.029	-0.031	-0.017	-0.096*	-0.003	-0.009	-0.054	-0.032	0.021
	(0.052)	(0.047)	(0.057)	(0.049)	(0.049)	(0.050)	(0.047)	(0.047)	(0.048)	(0.048)	(0.045)	(0.046)	(0.047)	(0.050)
Log employment	0.044*	0.076**	0.063**	0.059**	0.058**	0.055**	0.024	0.003	0.024	0.022	0.022	0.028	0.034*	0.051**
	(0.017)	(0.015)	(0.018)	(0.016)	(0.016)	(0.017)	(0.016)	(0.016)	(0.016)	(0.016)	(0.015)	(0.015)	(0.016)	(0.017)
Monopoly	0.190**	0.097	0.010	0.156*	0.209**	0.057	0.144*	0.024	0.189**	0.072	0.111	0.126	0.060	0.146*
	(0.067)	(0.062)	(0.074)	(0.067)	(0.071)	(0.075)	(0.065)	(0.069)	(0.069)	(0.067)	(0.064)	(0.071)	(0.070)	(0.070)
1–3 competitors	0.047	-0.012	-0.047	-0.020	-0.024	0.005	-0.025	-0.046	-0.025	-0.129*	-0.054	-0.030	-0.001	0.103
	(0.059)	(0.057)	(0.068)	(0.054)	(0.056)	(0.057)	(0.055)	(0.054)	(0.055)	(0.057)	(0.054)	(0.057)	(0.055)	(0.060)
State owned	-0.046	0.063	0.078	0.118	0.077	0.070	-0.032	0.029	0.100	0.085	0.088	0.089	0.057	0.021
	(0.064)	(0.060)	(0.072)	(0.063)	(0.064)	(0.066)	(0.059)	(0.062)	(0.063)	(0.062)	(0.060)	(0.062)	(0.061)	(0.066)
De novo	-0.101	-0.057	-0.132*	-0.093	-0.081	0.006	-0.110*	-0.094*	-0.144**	-0.105*	0.004	-0.031	-0.107*	-0.089
	(0.051)	(0.046)	(0.056)	(0.048)	(0.047)	(0.049)	(0.045)	(0.046)	(0.047)	(0.047)	(0.046)	(0.045)	(0.047)	(0.052)
Foreign ownership	0.020	-0.070	-0.098	-0.011	0.031	0.020	0.007	-0.101	-0.069	-0.087	0.015	0.048	-0.036	-0.012
	(0.062)	(0.056)	(0.067)	(0.054)	(0.056)	(0.059)	(0.056)	(0.058)	(0.059)	(0.057)	(0.057)	(0.056)	(0.054)	(0.056)
Exporter	-0.040	-0.036	-0.141*	0.023	-0.022	0.072	-0.032	-0.027	-0.003	-0.002	0.037	-0.027	0.047	0.001
	(0.052)	(0.050)	(0.061)	(0.051)	(0.051)	(0.054)	(0.049)	(0.050)	(0.051)	(0.050)	(0.049)	(0.051)	(0.050)	(0.052)
Cutpoint 1	-1.072	-0.701	-0.887	-0.136	-0.272	-0.537	-1.005	-1.396	-1.289	-2.015	-1.701	-1.805	-1.765	-1.361
	(0.121)	(0.110)	(0.124)	(0.112)	(0.110)	(0.115)	(0.104)	(0.109)	(0.110)	(0.120)	(0.114)	(0.109)	(0.113)	(0.122)
Cutpoint 2	-0.262	0.044	-0.206	0.504	0.447	0.099	-0.101	-0.602	-0.428	-1.245	-0.938	-1.123	-1.021	-0.626
	(0.118)	(0.109)	(0.121)	(0.112)	(0.110)	(0.115)	(0.102)	(0.107)	(0.108)	(0.111)	(0.107)	(0.105)	(0.107)	(0.119)
Cutpoint 3	0.440	0.731	0.341	1.193	1.164	0.643	0.563	0.039	0.205	-0.722	-0.412	-0.659	-0.495	0.007
	(0.118)	(0.109)	(0.121)	(0.113)	(0.111)	(0.115)	(0.103)	(0.107)	(0.108)	(0.110)	(0.107)	(0.104)	(0.106)	(0.118)
Cutpoint 4	1.204	1.462	1.070	1.929	1.844	1.390	1.233	0.880	0.934	0.251	0.396	0.148	0.248	0.814
	(0.119)	(0.111)	(0.123)	(0.115)	(0.113)	(0.117)	(0.104)	(0.108)	(0.108)	(0.109)	(0.106)	(0.103)	(0.106)	(0.119)
Cutpoint 5	2.527	2.823	2.629	3.145	3.052	2.856	2.544	2.424	2.308	2.137	2.093	1.920	2.001	2.251
	(0.134)	(0.120)	(0.133)	(0.125)	(0.127)	(0.124)	(0.116)	(0.121)	(0.123)	(0.115)	(0.111)	(0.109)	(0.114)	(0.126)
N	2,943	3,492	2,529	3,314	3,284	3,083	3,591	3,444	3,454	3,641	3,791	3,779	3,686	2,833
Log pseudolikelihood	-4661.29	-5447.97	-3765.66	-5143.75	-5136.36	-4630.58	-5675.46	-5174.94	-5392.86	-4612.29	-5247.03	-5116.70	-5225.31	-4308.12

Note. Ordered-probit model. Dependent variable is quality and efficiency of public agency or service. Industry, town-size, and country dummies included. Heteroskedasticity-robust standard errors in parentheses. Significance levels: ** = 0.01, * = 0.05.

Table 4.A.2. *Taxability model*

	Courts	Police	Military	Government	Parliament	Central Bank	Health	Education	Roads	Post	Telephone	Electricity	Water	Customs
Revenue hiding	−0.192*	−0.379**	−0.320*	−0.283**	−0.293**	−0.073	−0.375**	−0.287**	−0.339**	−0.146	−0.181*	−0.215**	−0.276**	−0.075
	(0.088)	(0.084)	(0.103)	(0.086)	(0.086)	(0.089)	(0.081)	(0.083)	(0.082)	(0.085)	(0.079)	(0.080)	(0.081)	(0.093)
Association member	0.006	0.020	−0.098	0.000	−0.009	−0.031	−0.023	−0.026	−0.089	−0.006	0.009	−0.039	−0.015	0.027
	(0.054)	(0.050)	(0.059)	(0.051)	(0.051)	(0.052)	(0.048)	(0.049)	(0.051)	(0.051)	(0.047)	(0.048)	(0.050)	(0.052)
Log employment	0.047**	0.070**	0.059**	0.055**	0.054**	0.063**	0.026	0.001	0.017	0.028	0.024	0.025	0.025	0.047**
	(0.018)	(0.016)	(0.019)	(0.017)	(0.017)	(0.018)	(0.016)	(0.017)	(0.017)	(0.016)	(0.016)	(0.016)	(0.016)	(0.017)
Monopoly	0.190**	0.077	−0.015	0.116	0.185*	0.025	0.136*	0.034	0.148*	0.058	0.082	0.092	0.059	0.153*
	(0.071)	(0.066)	(0.078)	(0.070)	(0.073)	(0.078)	(0.067)	(0.071)	(0.073)	(0.070)	(0.068)	(0.075)	(0.074)	(0.073)
1–3 competitors	0.034	0.011	−0.045	0.002	−0.013	0.012	−0.014	−0.024	−0.026	−0.095	−0.046	−0.010	0.018	0.113
	(0.061)	(0.059)	(0.069)	(0.057)	(0.058)	(0.058)	(0.057)	(0.056)	(0.057)	(0.059)	(0.056)	(0.059)	(0.057)	(0.062)
State owned	−0.049	0.058	0.055	0.105	0.069	0.058	−0.018	0.030	0.096	0.067	0.072	0.080	0.044	0.038
	(0.067)	(0.063)	(0.074)	(0.065)	(0.066)	(0.068)	(0.061)	(0.064)	(0.063)	(0.064)	(0.061)	(0.064)	(0.063)	(0.068)
De novo	−0.060	−0.047	−0.120*	−0.068	−0.057	0.029	−0.075	−0.076	−0.108*	−0.080	0.015	−0.009	−0.087	−0.083
	(0.053)	(0.048)	(0.059)	(0.050)	(0.049)	(0.051)	(0.046)	(0.048)	(0.049)	(0.049)	(0.048)	(0.047)	(0.049)	(0.054)
Foreign ownership	0.007	−0.107	−0.120	−0.046	0.005	−0.020	−0.036	−0.125*	−0.108	−0.142*	−0.036	0.037	−0.074	−0.013
	(0.064)	(0.059)	(0.070)	(0.056)	(0.058)	(0.061)	(0.058)	(0.060)	(0.062)	(0.059)	(0.060)	(0.058)	(0.057)	(0.058)
Exporter	−0.046	−0.062	−0.176**	0.017	−0.026	0.072	−0.044	−0.045	−0.022	−0.027	0.025	−0.041	0.056	0.000
	(0.055)	(0.053)	(0.063)	(0.053)	(0.053)	(0.056)	(0.051)	(0.051)	(0.052)	(0.053)	(0.051)	(0.052)	(0.052)	(0.054)
Cutpoint 1	−1.101	−0.819	−0.955	−0.221	−0.355	−0.550	−1.084	−1.462	−1.415	−2.041	−1.759	−1.903	−1.899	−1.364
	(0.127)	(0.117)	(0.132)	(0.120)	(0.118)	(0.123)	(0.110)	(0.116)	(0.117)	(0.126)	(0.121)	(0.117)	(0.120)	(0.129)
Cutpoint 2	−0.284	−0.060	−0.278	0.425	0.368	0.087	−0.163	−0.665	−0.542	−1.275	−0.998	−1.205	−1.141	−0.636
	(0.124)	(0.115)	(0.129)	(0.120)	(0.118)	(0.123)	(0.108)	(0.112)	(0.115)	(0.117)	(0.114)	(0.112)	(0.115)	(0.125)
Cutpoint 3	0.431	0.622	0.267	1.126	1.092	0.644	0.505	−0.029	0.099	−0.748	−0.479	−0.736	−0.613	0.003
	(0.124)	(0.115)	(0.129)	(0.121)	(0.119)	(0.124)	(0.108)	(0.112)	(0.114)	(0.115)	(0.113)	(0.111)	(0.113)	(0.125)
Cutpoint 4	1.198	1.365	0.995	1.857	1.766	1.395	1.189	0.816	0.838	0.228	0.331	0.081	0.139	0.814
	(0.126)	(0.117)	(0.131)	(0.123)	(0.121)	(0.125)	(0.109)	(0.114)	(0.115)	(0.115)	(0.112)	(0.110)	(0.113)	(0.126)
Cutpoint 5	2.534	2.708	2.550	3.068	2.979	2.840	2.481	2.350	2.267	2.105	2.036	1.855	1.889	2.252
	(0.142)	(0.126)	(0.140)	(0.134)	(0.135)	(0.133)	(0.121)	(0.127)	(0.132)	(0.121)	(0.118)	(0.116)	(0.120)	(0.134)
N	2,760	3,250	2,387	3,094	3,069	2,877	3,358	3,226	3,223	3,386	3,528	3,518	3,434	2,649
Log pseudolikelihood	−4355.59	−5062.65	−3561.19	−4793.86	−4789.05	−4336.59	−5285.75	−4849.95	−4989.52	−4300.30	−4874.39	−4751.03	−4861.39	−4029.82

Note. Ordered-probit model. Dependent variable is quality and efficiency of public agency or service. Revenue hiding is proportion of revenues hidden. Industry, town-size, and country dummies included. Heteroskedasticity-robust standard errors in parentheses. Significance levels: ** $= 0.01$, * $= 0.05$.

Table 4.A.3. *Taxability model: subsample of firms in CIS*

	Courts	Police	Military	Government	Parliament	Central Bank	Health	Education	Roads	Post	Telephone	Electricity	Water	Customs
Revenue hiding	−0.428**	−0.621**	−0.700**	−0.594**	−0.676**	−0.346**	−0.633**	−0.379**	−0.486**	−0.173	−0.287**	−0.347**	−0.395**	−0.139
	(0.123)	(0.115)	(0.143)	(0.119)	(0.122)	(0.123)	(0.114)	(0.114)	(0.112)	(0.118)	(0.107)	(0.111)	(0.110)	(0.126)
Association member	0.047	−0.066	−0.254**	−0.159*	−0.150	−0.103	−0.047	0.042	−0.134	−0.045	0.045	−0.064	−0.002	−0.032
	(0.086)	(0.080)	(0.094)	(0.079)	(0.082)	(0.080)	(0.077)	(0.081)	(0.079)	(0.075)	(0.072)	(0.075)	(0.077)	(0.084)
Log employment	0.067*	0.063*	0.046	0.073**	0.065*	0.038	0.026	0.020	0.009	0.009	0.006	0.002	0.058*	0.046
	(0.029)	(0.025)	(0.030)	(0.028)	(0.027)	(0.028)	(0.024)	(0.025)	(0.026)	(0.025)	(0.024)	(0.025)	(0.025)	(0.025)
Monopoly	0.110	0.118	0.052	0.046	0.123	0.022	0.160	−0.003	0.119	0.030	−0.063	0.060	0.015	0.120
	(0.103)	(0.094)	(0.114)	(0.094)	(0.100)	(0.109)	(0.100)	(0.105)	(0.106)	(0.099)	(0.097)	(0.099)	(0.106)	(0.105)
1–3 competitors	0.025	0.056	−0.029	−0.083	−0.095	0.083	−0.004	0.045	−0.069	0.055	−0.048	0.071	−0.001	0.116
	(0.099)	(0.087)	(0.104)	(0.089)	(0.094)	(0.087)	(0.087)	(0.085)	(0.091)	(0.093)	(0.085)	(0.088)	(0.087)	(0.097)
State owned	−0.023	−0.002	−0.050	0.076	0.036	0.051	−0.038	0.025	0.041	−0.020	0.090	0.035	−0.048	−0.040
	(0.101)	(0.089)	(0.106)	(0.092)	(0.095)	(0.095)	(0.089)	(0.090)	(0.088)	(0.089)	(0.085)	(0.090)	(0.090)	(0.101)
De novo	−0.048	−0.035	−0.177*	−0.043	−0.046	−0.018	−0.016	−0.079	−0.205**	−0.072	0.036	−0.040	−0.060	−0.083
	(0.076)	(0.067)	(0.082)	(0.073)	(0.072)	(0.072)	(0.064)	(0.065)	(0.066)	(0.069)	(0.065)	(0.066)	(0.067)	(0.076)
Foreign ownership	−0.023	−0.247**	−0.352**	−0.071	0.032	−0.063	−0.112	−0.161	−0.181	−0.205*	−0.147	0.034	−0.098	0.080
	(0.120)	(0.096)	(0.108)	(0.088)	(0.097)	(0.098)	(0.093)	(0.097)	(0.098)	(0.094)	(0.095)	(0.091)	(0.088)	(0.095)
Exporter	0.057	−0.070	−0.067	−0.017	−0.035	0.095	−0.074	−0.020	−0.191*	−0.025	0.055	−0.025	0.176*	−0.044
	(0.092)	(0.089)	(0.101)	(0.085)	(0.087)	(0.090)	(0.084)	(0.080)	(0.083)	(0.087)	(0.083)	(0.088)	(0.087)	(0.086)
Cutpoint 1	−1.273	−1.037	−1.401	−0.434	−0.509	−0.897	−1.497	−1.386	−1.943	−2.313	−2.043	−2.390	−2.009	−1.545
	(0.198)	(0.168)	(0.199)	(0.183)	(0.178)	(0.183)	(0.155)	(0.163)	(0.168)	(0.176)	(0.167)	(0.166)	(0.173)	(0.173)
Cutpoint 2	−0.484	−0.276	−0.582	0.286	0.232	−0.180	−0.492	−0.534	−1.015	−1.486	−1.243	−1.625	−1.244	−0.787
	(0.194)	(0.165)	(0.194)	(0.182)	(0.178)	(0.182)	(0.152)	(0.160)	(0.165)	(0.167)	(0.157)	(0.159)	(0.166)	(0.172)
Cutpoint 3	0.346	0.473	−0.014	1.086	1.011	0.450	0.291	0.122	−0.293	−0.980	−0.713	−1.090	−0.659	−0.095
	(0.193)	(0.165)	(0.193)	(0.183)	(0.180)	(0.182)	(0.152)	(0.160)	(0.163)	(0.164)	(0.155)	(0.157)	(0.163)	(0.172)
Cutpoint 4	1.173	1.201	0.718	1.768	1.653	1.205	0.976	1.010	0.469	0.022	0.110	−0.222	0.115	0.779
	(0.196)	(0.167)	(0.194)	(0.186)	(0.182)	(0.184)	(0.153)	(0.162)	(0.162)	(0.163)	(0.154)	(0.156)	(0.163)	(0.175)
Cutpoint 5	2.756	2.514	2.154	3.093	2.899	2.506	2.273	2.523	1.865	2.000	1.934	1.655	1.986	2.183
	(0.251)	(0.187)	(0.214)	(0.204)	(0.207)	(0.197)	(0.183)	(0.191)	(0.187)	(0.183)	(0.171)	(0.173)	(0.184)	(0.197)
N	1,284	1,592	1,145	1,522	1,491	1,383	1,666	1,617	1,625	1,622	1,740	1,748	1,700	1,233
Log pseudolikelihood	−1955.48	−2481.12	−1786.93	−2236.87	−2254.92	−2180.36	−2531.68	−2481.15	−2490.05	−2175.07	−2514.06	−2448.42	−2479.08	−1903.39

Note. Ordered-probit model. Dependent variable is quality and efficiency of public agency or service. Revenue hiding is proportion of revenues hidden. Industry, town-size, and country dummies included. Heteroskedasticity-robust standard errors in parentheses. Significance levels: ** $= 0.01$, * $= 0.05$.

Table 4.A.4. *Taxability model: subsample of firms in Eastern Europe and Baltics*

	Courts	Police	Military	Government	Parliament	Central Bank	Health	Education	Roads	Post	Telephone	Electricity	Water	Customs
Revenue hiding	0.022	-0.133	0.052	-0.000	0.073	0.160	-0.175	-0.213	-0.269*	-0.183	-0.145	-0.100	-0.186	-0.016
	(0.129)	(0.127)	(0.157)	(0.128)	(0.127)	(0.134)	(0.121)	(0.125)	(0.124)	(0.125)	(0.121)	(0.121)	(0.125)	(0.142)
Association member	-0.012	0.079	0.007	0.102	0.092	0.031	-0.016	-0.056	-0.059	0.017	-0.020	-0.018	-0.021	0.067
	(0.068)	(0.063)	(0.076)	(0.067)	(0.066)	(0.070)	(0.062)	(0.062)	(0.066)	(0.067)	(0.060)	(0.061)	(0.064)	(0.066)
Log employment	0.034	0.066**	0.063*	0.041	0.044*	0.083**	0.024	-0.016	0.036	0.047*	0.040	0.045*	0.004	0.050*
	(0.024)	(0.022)	(0.025)	(0.022)	(0.022)	(0.023)	(0.021)	(0.022)	(0.023)	(0.022)	(0.023)	(0.022)	(0.022)	(0.025)
Monopoly	0.262**	0.063	-0.081	0.212*	0.276*	-0.000	0.115	0.071	0.207*	0.091	0.232*	0.128	0.110	0.164
	(0.101)	(0.093)	(0.109)	(0.107)	(0.109)	(0.112)	(0.094)	(0.098)	(0.103)	(0.099)	(0.095)	(0.116)	(0.106)	(0.106)
1–3 competitors	0.065	-0.010	-0.072	0.065	0.051	-0.084	-0.014	-0.096	0.022	-0.221**	-0.047	-0.074	0.035	0.097
	(0.078)	(0.081)	(0.094)	(0.075)	(0.074)	(0.079)	(0.078)	(0.074)	(0.073)	(0.076)	(0.075)	(0.079)	(0.075)	(0.081)
State owned	-0.083	0.129	0.176	0.100	0.070	0.055	-0.053	0.033	0.105	0.115	-0.008	0.108	0.105	0.077
	(0.092)	(0.091)	(0.108)	(0.096)	(0.095)	(0.101)	(0.089)	(0.094)	(0.094)	(0.095)	(0.091)	(0.094)	(0.093)	(0.095)
De novo	-0.095	-0.042	-0.039	-0.093	-0.060	0.077	-0.161*	-0.059	-0.010	-0.098	-0.042	0.011	-0.135	-0.089
	(0.076)	(0.073)	(0.088)	(0.072)	(0.069)	(0.074)	(0.069)	(0.073)	(0.076)	(0.073)	(0.073)	(0.070)	(0.072)	(0.079)
Foreign ownership	0.004	-0.033	0.030	-0.056	-0.036	-0.011	-0.020	-0.088	-0.142	-0.129	-0.005	0.014	-0.069	-0.054
	(0.077)	(0.076)	(0.093)	(0.075)	(0.075)	(0.081)	(0.075)	(0.078)	(0.081)	(0.077)	(0.079)	(0.077)	(0.076)	(0.076)
Exporter	-0.098	-0.049	-0.241**	0.045	-0.013	0.084	-0.032	-0.067	0.071	-0.029	0.030	-0.027	-0.004	0.021
	(0.068)	(0.066)	(0.081)	(0.068)	(0.068)	(0.072)	(0.065)	(0.067)	(0.067)	(0.066)	(0.065)	(0.065)	(0.065)	(0.071)
Cutpoint 1	-1.131	-1.166	-1.385	-1.258	-1.109	-1.719	-0.882	-1.815	-0.649	-2.320	-2.113	-1.856	-2.407	-1.635
	(0.167)	(0.159)	(0.187)	(0.158)	(0.154)	(0.174)	(0.157)	(0.167)	(0.166)	(0.178)	(0.173)	(0.174)	(0.166)	(0.184)
Cutpoint 2	-0.279	-0.405	-0.937	-0.685	-0.391	-1.219	-0.053	-1.115	0.191	-1.668	-1.412	-1.252	-1.645	-0.942
	(0.164)	(0.156)	(0.182)	(0.157)	(0.153)	(0.174)	(0.155)	(0.160)	(0.166)	(0.166)	(0.163)	(0.164)	(0.157)	(0.179)
Cutpoint 3	0.347	0.211	-0.402	-0.059	0.301	-0.756	0.512	-0.499	0.764	-1.091	-0.892	-0.871	-1.184	-0.355
	(0.164)	(0.156)	(0.180)	(0.156)	(0.153)	(0.174)	(0.155)	(0.159)	(0.168)	(0.162)	(0.163)	(0.163)	(0.155)	(0.179)
Cutpoint 4	1.079	0.976	0.342	0.718	1.011	0.011	1.212	0.316	1.499	-0.130	-0.080	-0.106	-0.447	0.414
	(0.165)	(0.157)	(0.179)	(0.157)	(0.153)	(0.173)	(0.157)	(0.160)	(0.170)	(0.160)	(0.161)	(0.161)	(0.153)	(0.179)
Cutpoint 5	2.320	2.342	1.970	1.880	2.219	1.540	2.522	1.879	2.976	1.722	1.588	1.641	1.264	1.884
	(0.177)	(0.167)	(0.184)	(0.169)	(0.169)	(0.178)	(0.168)	(0.169)	(0.191)	(0.162)	(0.163)	(0.163)	(0.154)	(0.183)
N	1,476	1,658	1,242	1,572	1,578	1,494	1,692	1,609	1,598	1,764	1,788	1,770	1,734	1,416
Log pseudolikelihood	-2364.41	-2560.87	-1732.08	-2520.65	-2504.90	-2122.52	-2709.86	-2350.55	-2456.41	-2100.69	-2329.07	-2274.39	-2356.83	-2108.19

Note. Ordered-probit model. Dependent variable is quality and efficiency of public agency or service. Revenue hiding is proportion of revenues hidden. Industry, town-size, and country dummies included. Heteroskedasticity-robust standard errors in parentheses. Significance levels: ** $= 0.01$, * $= 0.05$.

Table 4.A.5. *Taxability model with employment interaction: subsample of firms in CIS*

	Courts	Police	Military	Government	Parliament	Central Bank	Health	Education	Roads	Post	Telephone	Electricity	Water	Customs
Revenue hiding	−0.792*	−1.027**	−1.103**	−0.947**	−0.900**	−0.428	−0.708*	−0.476	−0.494	−0.683*	−0.250	−0.879**	−0.827**	−0.317
	(0.337)	(0.307)	(0.371)	(0.319)	(0.337)	(0.366)	(0.291)	(0.308)	(0.297)	(0.311)	(0.295)	(0.277)	(0.294)	(0.317)
Revenue hiding × log employment	0.092	0.104	0.103	0.092	0.058	0.021	0.020	0.025	0.002	0.130	−0.010	0.138*	0.113	0.046
	(0.078)	(0.070)	(0.088)	(0.075)	(0.081)	(0.084)	(0.070)	(0.073)	(0.072)	(0.072)	(0.068)	(0.066)	(0.071)	(0.075)
Association member	0.045	−0.069	−0.254**	−0.159*	−0.150	−0.103	−0.048	0.042	−0.134	−0.047	0.045	−0.068	−0.005	−0.033
	(0.086)	(0.080)	(0.094)	(0.079)	(0.082)	(0.080)	(0.077)	(0.081)	(0.079)	(0.075)	(0.072)	(0.075)	(0.078)	(0.083)
Log employment	0.045	0.039	0.022	0.051	0.052	0.033	0.021	0.014	0.009	−0.022	0.009	−0.030	0.032	0.035
	(0.034)	(0.029)	(0.035)	(0.032)	(0.032)	(0.032)	(0.029)	(0.030)	(0.030)	(0.030)	(0.030)	(0.029)	(0.029)	(0.032)
Monopoly	0.112	0.119	0.054	0.046	0.123	0.022	0.160	−0.003	0.119	0.032	−0.063	0.061	0.018	0.121
	(0.103)	(0.093)	(0.114)	(0.094)	(0.100)	(0.109)	(0.100)	(0.105)	(0.106)	(0.099)	(0.097)	(0.099)	(0.105)	(0.106)
1–3 competitors	0.023	0.051	−0.031	−0.087	−0.098	0.082	−0.005	0.044	−0.069	0.050	−0.048	0.065	−0.005	0.114
	(0.099)	(0.087)	(0.104)	(0.089)	(0.094)	(0.087)	(0.087)	(0.085)	(0.091)	(0.093)	(0.085)	(0.087)	(0.087)	(0.097)
State owned	−0.022	−0.002	−0.049	0.077	0.037	0.052	−0.038	0.025	0.041	−0.021	0.090	0.035	−0.049	−0.040
	(0.101)	(0.089)	(0.106)	(0.092)	(0.095)	(0.095)	(0.089)	(0.090)	(0.088)	(0.088)	(0.085)	(0.089)	(0.090)	(0.101)
De novo	−0.050	−0.037	−0.181*	−0.046	−0.048	−0.019	−0.017	−0.080	−0.205**	−0.075	0.036	−0.043	−0.063	−0.085
	(0.077)	(0.067)	(0.082)	(0.073)	(0.072)	(0.072)	(0.064)	(0.065)	(0.066)	(0.069)	(0.065)	(0.066)	(0.067)	(0.076)
Foreign ownership	−0.031	−0.257**	−0.362**	−0.080	0.026	−0.065	−0.113	−0.164	−0.181	−0.218*	−0.146	0.022	−0.108	0.075
	(0.120)	(0.097)	(0.109)	(0.088)	(0.098)	(0.098)	(0.093)	(0.097)	(0.099)	(0.095)	(0.095)	(0.092)	(0.089)	(0.096)
Exporter	0.060	−0.064	−0.065	−0.013	−0.034	0.096	−0.073	−0.018	−0.191*	−0.020	0.055	−0.019	0.181*	−0.042
	(0.092)	(0.089)	(0.101)	(0.085)	(0.087)	(0.090)	(0.083)	(0.080)	(0.083)	(0.087)	(0.083)	(0.088)	(0.087)	(0.086)
Cutpoint 1	−1.371	−1.146	−1.512	−0.531	−0.568	−0.918	−1.517	−1.412	−1.945	−2.454	−2.033	−2.536	−2.127	−1.595
	(0.219)	(0.184)	(0.219)	(0.198)	(0.198)	(0.197)	(0.170)	(0.179)	(0.181)	(0.190)	(0.185)	(0.181)	(0.189)	(0.195)
Cutpoint 2	−0.581	−0.385	−0.694	0.188	0.173	−0.202	−0.512	−0.560	−1.017	−1.626	−1.233	−1.771	−1.362	−0.837
	(0.214)	(0.181)	(0.214)	(0.197)	(0.198)	(0.197)	(0.167)	(0.176)	(0.177)	(0.181)	(0.177)	(0.174)	(0.181)	(0.194)
Cutpoint 3	0.250	0.365	−0.125	0.989	0.953	0.428	0.271	0.096	−0.295	−1.120	−0.703	−1.235	−0.776	−0.145
	(0.213)	(0.180)	(0.213)	(0.199)	(0.199)	(0.198)	(0.167)	(0.176)	(0.176)	(0.179)	(0.175)	(0.172)	(0.179)	(0.193)
Cutpoint 4	1.077	1.094	0.608	1.671	1.596	1.184	0.957	0.984	0.467	−0.117	0.121	−0.366	−0.001	0.729
	(0.216)	(0.182)	(0.213)	(0.201)	(0.201)	(0.199)	(0.168)	(0.178)	(0.175)	(0.178)	(0.175)	(0.170)	(0.178)	(0.196)
Cutpoint 5	2.661	2.406	2.045	2.999	2.841	2.485	2.253	2.497	1.863	1.864	1.944	1.514	1.872	2.134
	(0.269)	(0.199)	(0.234)	(0.218)	(0.222)	(0.209)	(0.192)	(0.203)	(0.197)	(0.196)	(0.190)	(0.185)	(0.197)	(0.217)
N	1,284	1,592	1,145	1,522	1,491	1,383	1,666	1,617	1,625	1,622	1,740	1,748	1,700	1,233
Log pseudolikelihood	−1954.76	−2479.92	−1786.11	−2236.02	−2254.60	−2180.32	−2531.64	−2481.09	−2490.05	−2173.31	−2514.05	−2446.23	−2477.67	−1903.20

Note. Ordered-probit model. Dependent variable is quality and efficiency of public agency or service. Revenue hiding is proportion of revenues hidden. Industry, town-size, and country dummies included. Heteroskedasticity-robust standard errors in parentheses. Significance levels: ** = 0.01, * = 0.05.

Table 4.A.6. *Taxability model with employment interaction: subsample of firms in Eastern Europe and Baltics*

	Courts	Police	Military	Government	Parliament	Central Bank	Health	Education	Roads	Post	Telephone	Electricity	Water	Customs
Revenue hiding	-0.159	-0.898**	-0.474	-0.767**	-0.471	-0.240	-0.597*	-0.557*	-0.768**	-0.063	-0.125	-0.275	-0.477	-0.173
	(0.300)	(0.282)	(0.332)	(0.276)	(0.278)	(0.306)	(0.283)	(0.272)	(0.280)	(0.281)	(0.273)	(0.281)	(0.280)	(0.344)
Revenue hiding × log employment	0.048	0.212**	0.146	0.209**	0.148*	0.108	0.116	0.094	0.137*	-0.033	-0.005	0.049	0.080	0.041
	(0.069)	(0.067)	(0.083)	(0.066)	(0.066)	(0.074)	(0.067)	(0.066)	(0.065)	(0.067)	(0.065)	(0.069)	(0.065)	(0.079)
Association member	-0.013	0.077	0.005	0.099	0.091	0.031	-0.017	-0.057	-0.060	0.017	-0.020	-0.019	-0.021	0.067
	(0.068)	(0.063)	(0.076)	(0.067)	(0.066)	(0.070)	(0.062)	(0.062)	(0.066)	(0.067)	(0.060)	(0.061)	(0.064)	(0.066)
Log employment	0.024	0.026	0.036	0.000	0.015	0.062*	0.002	-0.035	0.010	0.053*	0.041	0.035	-0.012	0.043
	(0.027)	(0.025)	(0.029)	(0.025)	(0.025)	(0.026)	(0.024)	(0.026)	(0.026)	(0.025)	(0.025)	(0.025)	(0.024)	(0.028)
Monopoly	0.268**	0.095	-0.060	0.240*	0.296**	0.015	0.130	0.084	0.226*	0.086	0.231*	0.135	0.121	0.169
	(0.101)	(0.093)	(0.110)	(0.107)	(0.110)	(0.113)	(0.093)	(0.099)	(0.103)	(0.100)	(0.095)	(0.115)	(0.107)	(0.106)
1–3 competitors	0.067	0.003	-0.066	0.081	0.061	-0.078	-0.009	-0.090	0.030	-0.222**	-0.047	-0.071	0.040	0.099
	(0.078)	(0.081)	(0.095)	(0.075)	(0.074)	(0.078)	(0.078)	(0.074)	(0.073)	(0.077)	(0.076)	(0.080)	(0.075)	(0.081)
State owned	-0.087	0.117	0.168	0.087	0.061	0.050	-0.061	0.025	0.094	0.118	-0.008	0.104	0.099	0.074
	(0.092)	(0.091)	(0.108)	(0.096)	(0.095)	(0.101)	(0.089)	(0.094)	(0.095)	(0.095)	(0.091)	(0.094)	(0.093)	(0.096)
De novo	-0.096	-0.036	-0.036	-0.091	-0.058	0.079	-0.159*	-0.057	-0.011	-0.098	-0.042	0.011	-0.133	-0.088
	(0.076)	(0.073)	(0.088)	(0.072)	(0.069)	(0.074)	(0.069)	(0.073)	(0.076)	(0.073)	(0.073)	(0.070)	(0.072)	(0.079)
Foreign ownership	0.006	-0.031	0.034	-0.053	-0.034	-0.008	-0.018	-0.088	-0.140	-0.130	-0.005	0.015	-0.068	-0.053
	(0.077)	(0.077)	(0.093)	(0.075)	(0.075)	(0.081)	(0.075)	(0.078)	(0.082)	(0.077)	(0.079)	(0.077)	(0.076)	(0.076)
Exporter	-0.099	-0.054	-0.239**	0.041	-0.015	0.083	-0.036	-0.069	0.068	-0.028	0.031	-0.028	-0.006	0.020
	(0.068)	(0.066)	(0.081)	(0.068)	(0.068)	(0.072)	(0.065)	(0.067)	(0.067)	(0.065)	(0.065)	(0.064)	(0.066)	(0.071)
Cutpoint 1	-1.170	-1.326	-1.486	-1.422	-1.222	-1.807	-0.970	-1.889	-0.755	-2.294	-2.109	-1.893	-2.471	-1.665
	(0.175)	(0.168)	(0.191)	(0.164)	(0.161)	(0.179)	(0.162)	(0.174)	(0.173)	(0.185)	(0.180)	(0.181)	(0.172)	(0.190)
Cutpoint 2	-0.318	-0.561	-1.038	-0.846	-0.502	-1.305	-0.139	-1.189	0.087	-1.643	-1.408	-1.289	-1.707	-0.972
	(0.173)	(0.165)	(0.187)	(0.164)	(0.161)	(0.179)	(0.160)	(0.167)	(0.173)	(0.185)	(0.171)	(0.172)	(0.163)	(0.185)
Cutpoint 3	0.309	0.058	-0.504	-0.219	0.191	-0.841	0.426	-0.573	0.661	-1.066	-0.888	-0.908	-1.245	-0.385
	(0.172)	(0.165)	(0.184)	(0.163)	(0.160)	(0.179)	(0.160)	(0.166)	(0.175)	(0.167)	(0.170)	(0.171)	(0.160)	(0.184)
Cutpoint 4	1.041	0.826	0.242	0.560	0.902	-0.074	1.127	0.243	1.397	-0.106	-0.076	-0.142	-0.508	0.384
	(0.173)	(0.165)	(0.183)	(0.164)	(0.161)	(0.178)	(0.162)	(0.166)	(0.177)	(0.165)	(0.168)	(0.168)	(0.159)	(0.184)
Cutpoint 5	2.282	2.194	1.873	1.728	2.114	1.456	2.438	1.807	2.873	1.747	1.592	1.604	1.203	1.855
	(0.185)	(0.174)	(0.188)	(0.176)	(0.177)	(0.183)	(0.172)	(0.175)	(0.198)	(0.167)	(0.171)	(0.171)	(0.160)	(0.187)
N	1,476	1,658	1,242	1,572	1,578	1,494	1,692	1,609	1,598	1,764	1,788	1,770	1,734	1,416
Log pseudolikelihood	-2364.15	-2555.52	-1730.28	-2515.59	-2502.35	-2121.32	-2708.16	-2349.51	-2454.19	-2100.55	-2329.07	-2274.09	-2356.03	-2108.03

Note. Ordered-probit model. Dependent variable is quality and efficiency of public agency or service. Revenue hiding is proportion of revenues hidden. Industry, town-size, and country dummies included. Heteroskedasticity-robust standard errors in parentheses. Significance levels: ** = 0.01, * = 0.05.

Table 4.A.7. *Taxability model with tax-structure interactions*

	Courts	Police	Military	Government	Parliament	Central Bank	Health	Education	Roads	Post	Telephone	Electricity	Water	Customs
Revenue hiding	2.148	0.771	-2.461	1.270	0.719	-1.953	-3.249	-4.062*	-2.284	-0.234	-4.505*	-5.852**	-2.287	0.772
	(2.348)	(2.315)	(2.877)	(2.156)	(2.283)	(2.285)	(2.012)	(2.049)	(2.154)	(2.047)	(2.012)	(2.043)	(2.149)	(2.262)
Revenue hiding × corporate	-6.595*	-6.540*	-1.334	-5.508	-5.475	0.178	1.993	4.533	0.875	0.224	2.427	3.617	-0.195	-2.242
	(3.296)	(3.232)	(4.010)	(3.043)	(3.176)	(3.225)	(2.854)	(2.891)	(3.049)	(2.900)	(2.843)	(2.892)	(3.022)	(3.138)
Revenue hiding × indirect	-2.457	0.503	3.525	-2.218	-1.602	1.337	3.108	4.275	2.568	-0.705	6.800*	8.031**	4.354	-0.946
	(3.027)	(2.989)	(3.708)	(2.834)	(2.995)	(3.000)	(2.616)	(2.637)	(2.818)	(2.729)	(2.685)	(2.618)	(2.748)	(3.064)
Revenue hiding × individual	-1.707	-1.304	2.589	-0.128	0.663	3.466	3.666	3.926	2.217	0.893	4.063*	5.946**	1.264	-0.596
	(2.368)	(2.335)	(2.923)	(2.158)	(2.280)	(2.307)	(2.016)	(2.087)	(2.157)	(2.036)	(2.001)	(2.097)	(2.184)	(2.251)
Association member	0.046	0.034	-0.076	0.017	-0.003	-0.032	-0.015	-0.017	-0.083	0.003	0.008	-0.049	-0.005	0.042
	(0.056)	(0.052)	(0.062)	(0.053)	(0.053)	(0.054)	(0.050)	(0.051)	(0.053)	(0.053)	(0.049)	(0.051)	(0.051)	(0.055)
Log employment	0.032	0.071**	0.057**	0.037*	0.045*	0.062**	0.005	0.005	0.014	0.024	0.019	0.025	0.030	0.037*
	(0.019)	(0.017)	(0.020)	(0.018)	(0.018)	(0.018)	(0.017)	(0.017)	(0.017)	(0.017)	(0.017)	(0.017)	(0.017)	(0.018)
Monopoly	0.135	0.063	-0.050	0.088	0.173*	0.030	0.091	-0.025	0.107	0.069	0.110	0.094	0.041	0.130
	(0.075)	(0.070)	(0.083)	(0.074)	(0.078)	(0.082)	(0.070)	(0.074)	(0.077)	(0.074)	(0.070)	(0.077)	(0.078)	(0.078)
1–3 competitors	0.000	-0.018	-0.053	0.003	-0.006	0.004	-0.002	-0.054	-0.030	-0.053	-0.005	0.002	0.012	0.104
	(0.065)	(0.062)	(0.072)	(0.060)	(0.061)	(0.061)	(0.061)	(0.059)	(0.061)	(0.063)	(0.060)	(0.062)	(0.060)	(0.066)
State owned	-0.030	0.067	0.086	0.150**	0.083	0.037	-0.029	0.033	0.084	0.049	0.058	0.079	0.042	0.035
	(0.071)	(0.066)	(0.077)	(0.069)	(0.070)	(0.071)	(0.064)	(0.068)	(0.067)	(0.068)	(0.064)	(0.067)	(0.067)	(0.072)
De novo	-0.073	-0.038	-0.145*	-0.115*	-0.091	0.018	-0.096*	-0.077	-0.126*	-0.099	0.015	-0.023	-0.095	-0.089
	(0.055)	(0.050)	(0.061)	(0.052)	(0.051)	(0.053)	(0.048)	(0.050)	(0.051)	(0.051)	(0.050)	(0.049)	(0.050)	(0.056)
Foreign ownership	0.028	-0.124*	-0.115	-0.069	-0.027	-0.033	-0.049	-0.141*	-0.094	-0.138*	-0.011	0.026	-0.105	-0.012
	(0.065)	(0.061)	(0.073)	(0.059)	(0.062)	(0.064)	(0.062)	(0.062)	(0.064)	(0.060)	(0.062)	(0.061)	(0.060)	(0.061)
Exporter	-0.048	-0.059	-0.180**	0.046	0.002	0.067	-0.027	-0.051	0.013	-0.017	0.025	-0.030	0.065	0.033
	(0.058)	(0.056)	(0.066)	(0.056)	(0.056)	(0.058)	(0.054)	(0.054)	(0.056)	(0.055)	(0.054)	(0.055)	(0.055)	(0.057)
Cutpoint 1	-1.262	-0.872	-1.093	-0.362	-0.475	-0.607	-1.150	-1.523	-1.470	-2.114	-1.833	-2.044	-1.981	-1.409
	(0.134)	(0.125)	(0.142)	(0.128)	(0.125)	(0.130)	(0.116)	(0.124)	(0.123)	(0.136)	(0.129)	(0.127)	(0.129)	(0.136)
Cutpoint 2	-0.450	-0.109	-0.397	0.292	0.258	0.033	-0.231	-0.714	-0.590	-1.319	-1.078	-1.317	-1.226	-0.686
	(0.131)	(0.122)	(0.139)	(0.128)	(0.125)	(0.129)	(0.113)	(0.120)	(0.121)	(0.126)	(0.121)	(0.121)	(0.124)	(0.133)
Cutpoint 3	0.292	0.580	0.168	1.010	0.999	0.598	0.447	-0.074	0.071	-0.769	-0.556	-0.832	-0.676	-0.052
	(0.131)	(0.122)	(0.139)	(0.128)	(0.126)	(0.130)	(0.113)	(0.120)	(0.121)	(0.124)	(0.120)	(0.119)	(0.122)	(0.133)
Cutpoint 4	1.079	1.338	0.912	1.765	1.709	1.381	1.140	0.784	0.824	0.232	0.260	0.004	0.085	0.770
	(0.132)	(0.124)	(0.140)	(0.130)	(0.128)	(0.132)	(0.115)	(0.121)	(0.122)	(0.124)	(0.120)	(0.119)	(0.122)	(0.134)
Cutpoint 5	2.443	2.664	2.468	3.015	2.910	2.845	2.461	2.326	2.273	2.149	1.984	1.823	1.840	2.239
	(0.153)	(0.134)	(0.150)	(0.143)	(0.144)	(0.141)	(0.129)	(0.135)	(0.141)	(0.131)	(0.125)	(0.124)	(0.128)	(0.143)
N	2,535	2,999	2,208	2,835	2,814	2,656	3,079	2,965	2,951	3,121	3,242	3,230	3,153	2,412
Log pseudolikelihood	-3971.71	-4671.76	-3285.78	-4343.91	-4367.20	-3968.00	-4818.87	-4426.25	-4542.90	-3906.01	-4458.43	-4286.01	-4438.29	-3666.83

Note. Ordered-probit model. Dependent variable is quality and efficiency of public agency or service. Revenue hiding is proportion of revenues hidden. Tax-structure variables expressed as proportions. Industry, town-size, and country dummies included. Heteroskedasticity-robust standard errors in parentheses. Significance levels: ** = 0.01,* = 0.05.

5

Revenue Traps

The previous chapters present a story about the importance of initial conditions in determining political-economic outcomes in Eastern Europe and the former Soviet Union.[1] Facing diverse constraints in the early 1990s, postcommunist governments went about the task of creating tax systems in different ways. In the eastern half of the postcommunist world, a decision to focus on corporate taxation meant not only that tax revenue from enterprises would be politically important in general, but also that collections from firms that were familiar revenue sources – large enterprises, monopolies, and so on – would be especially critical to cash-starved governments. As I have shown, one apparent consequence of this decision is that post-Soviet governments disproportionately provided collective goods to sectors that were relatively easy to tax; in practice this amounted to a particular bias against new private enterprise. In contrast, the focus in Eastern Europe and the Baltics on new revenue sources created fewer incentives to discriminate in the provision of sector-specific collective goods based on the taxability of economic activity.

This is, so far, a story about the sensitivity of *outcomes* to initial conditions and the decisions made in the early years following the collapse of communism. Students of the region have presented a number of such explanations in recent years, linking economic and political performance in the postcommunist world to initial electoral outcomes and constitutional choice (Fish, 1998, 2005), proximity to the West (Kopstein and Reilly, 2000; Hanson, 2001; Janos, 2002; Pevehouse, 2005), initial macroeconomic

---

[1] As I have done throughout the book, I follow convention by often including the Baltic states of Estonia, Latvia, and Lithuania in "Eastern Europe" and by using the term "former Soviet Union" to refer to all post-Soviet states but those in the Baltics.

distortions (de Melo et al., 2001), the cultural legacy of communism (Jowitt, 1992; Ledeneva, 1998), the character of late-communist institutions (Bunce, 1999; Roeder, 2001), the nature of church institutions under communism (Wittenberg, 2006), and precommunist education (Darden and Grzymala-Busse, 2006), among other factors.[2] In short, history matters.

However, saying that history matters is not the same thing as saying that history matters in the long run. As Scott Page argues (Page, 2006), many processes exhibit "outcome dependence" but not "equilibrium dependence." Outcome dependence is merely the condition that the outcome at any point in time depends on what has happened in the past. This is, seemingly, a very weak condition (which is not to say that identifying the particular dependence is easy). Arguably more important is whether the long-run distribution of outcomes depends on these initial conditions and early decisions (what typically seems to be meant by the phrase "path dependence"), that is, whether the process of change exhibits equilibrium dependence. This requires not only that history matter but also that it matter in a way that creates positive and (especially) negative externalities, reinforcing earlier outcomes (Page, 2006, pp. 101–102, 109).[3] In principle, it is possible that despite initial differences all postcommunist countries will ultimately converge to the same outcome. If so, then the factors identified here and elsewhere as important to the postcommunist transition may have little long-run impact. To argue otherwise requires that we specify the feedback mechanisms that render early outcomes determinative.

In this chapter I identify one such feedback mechanism: factor mobility. (Obviously, I do not claim this mechanism to be unique.) When labor and capital are mobile across sectors, relatively small initial differences in the provision of collective goods across sectors can result in very large long-run differences in the distribution of economic activity across those sectors. With factors of production mobile, labor and capital are more likely to locate in sectors benefiting from good collective-goods provision. But to the extent that labor and capital do locate in such sectors, the incentive

---

[2] Kopstein (2003) and Pop-Eleches (2007) present fuller reviews. For discussion, see Kitschelt (2003).

[3] Although the existing literature on path dependence has largely concentrated on increasing returns, that is, on positive externalities (e.g., David, 1985; Arthur, 1994; Pierson, 2004), Page suggests that increasing returns are neither necessary nor sufficient for equilibrium dependence.

for politicians to favor those sectors and disfavor others in the provision of collective goods only increases. The upshot of this mutually reinforcing process is that factors of production and collective-goods provision tend to pool together in certain sectors rather than be distributed smoothly across sectors.

Under typical circumstances, these factor/collective-good configurations are stable: neither politicians nor factor owners have an incentive to abandon a sector, given the presence of the other. But circumstances in Eastern Europe and the former Soviet Union were far from typical during the 1990s. Taking advantage of what was seen as a period of "extraordinary" politics, policy makers had massively and intentionally reallocated labor and capital through a process of mass privatization, with the goal of effecting a shift to something resembling a Western capitalist economy: labor and capital largely employed in private enterprise and governments supportive of private economic activity. Political economies, in other words, were pushed into disequilibrium, with the hope that when the dust settled both politicians and factor owners would find that they had no choice but to allocate resources to the new, private economy.

In such an environment, any political bias in favor of either the old or new economy resonates strongly. As documented in the previous chapter, politics did not immediately revert to "normal" conditions, where the organization of interests is the primary determinant of policy choice. Rather, in much of the former Soviet Union politicians systematically favored economic sectors that provided critically important tax revenue, to the detriment of an emerging entrepreneurial sector. This decision to underprovide collective goods to the new, private economy meant that labor and capital were less likely to migrate there; that, in turn, only further discouraged politicians from providing those collective goods. As a consequence, the political economies in this part of the postcommunist world have not tipped in the way that the architects of privatization anticipated. Rather, they appear to be caught in a "revenue trap," with politicians dependent on existing sources of revenue in the old (state-owned or formerly state-owned) economy, even while the providers of that revenue rely on continued government support. In contrast, in much of Eastern Europe things have turned out as planned, with an increasing proportion of economic activity located in the new, private economy and politicians generally supportive of such activity.

A revenue trap is a coordination failure: both political and economic agents would be better off if political support and factors of production were allocated differently, but the mutual dependence of these agents on the status quo makes such a transition unlikely. Moreover, it is an especially pernicious coordination failure, one where the government is part of the problem rather than the solution. Unable to escape their own reliance on existing sources of revenue, politicians are in no position to provide the "big push" necessary for private economic agents to coordinate around productive economic activity (Rosenstein-Rodan, 1943; Murphy, Shleifer, and Vishny, 1989).

The vision of a government doggedly pursuing inefficient policies is central to the literature on economic development, exemplified (as I note in the introductory chapter) by Robert Bates's *Markets and States in Tropical Africa* (Bates, 1981). Yet the source of stubbornness that I emphasize is different from the organization of interests emphasized by Bates (see also Olson, 1982; Hellman, 1998).[4] The initial distribution of outcomes may "lock in" as politicians become dependent on the status quo, not (just) because the beneficiaries of existing policies lobby for their continuation but because of the revenue that recipients of government support provide regardless of their organization. Collective action can strengthen this dependence, but it is unnecessary for the basic mechanism to operate. What is necessary is simply that tax revenue be valued by politicians and that sector-specific collective goods be important to economic actors. These conditions seem to have been met in the postcommunist region.

It is too soon to say for sure that the distribution of outcomes I document is in fact the long-term configuration of political economies in Eastern Europe and the former Soviet Union.[5] The evidence I present here is preliminary and, relative to that in previous chapters, circumstantial. Yet the general direction of change seems consistent with the theoretical argument. In the following section I present this argument more fully.

---

[4] Some studies of comparative economic development stress instead the role of organized groups in promoting policy change and growth; see, for example, Putnam (1993), Martin and Swank (2004), and Sinha (2005). Evidence from cross-country empirical studies is ambiguous: Knack and Keefer (1995, 1997) find no effect of associational activity on growth, whereas Coates and Heckelman (2003) find positive effects on investment (and therefore presumably on growth) in some institutional environments but negative effects in others.

[5] As I discuss in the previous chapter, one missing piece of evidence is the nature of collective-goods provision across postcommunist countries in more recent years. Ideally, one would investigate whether the patterns of collective-goods provision identified there continued to hold into the second decade of transition. Unfortunately, two additional rounds of the BEEPS conducted by the World Bank in 2002 and 2005 omitted the evaluations of public agencies and services used in that analysis.

5.1 Revenue Dependence and Factor Mobility

The theoretical approach in Chapter 3 was to take the allocation of labor and capital as given and ask how politicians allocate collective goods across sectors based on the taxability and organization of those sectors. Although a useful starting point, this perspective ignores the tendency of labor and capital to migrate to sectors that benefit from better collective-goods provision. As we saw in Chapter 1, the vodka industry in Pskov oblast emerged from nothingness precisely because of the privileges bestowed on it by the administration of Pskov governor Evgeny Mikhailov. Absent that favorable treatment, labor and capital would likely have remained employed in other sectors.

Nonetheless, even though labor and capital are responsive to differences across sectors in relative collective-goods provision, politicians do not normally have a free hand in shaping factor allocation through the provision of collective goods. Mikhailov, for example, was eventually replaced by a local businessman ideologically opposed to favorable treatment of the vodka sector. Given that opposition, one might have expected regional policy to change course. As discussed in Chapter 1, this was not the case. After an initial flirtation with a different policy regime, the new administration reverted to the status quo ante, restoring the essential elements of the previous administration's approach. Vodka had simply become too important a revenue source to tamper with. Pskov authorities were caught in a revenue trap, with politicians reliant on the vodka sector for tax revenue, even as the vodka sector was dependent on Pskov authorities for political support.

In the language of game theory, collective-goods provision and factor allocation are strategic complements. Factor owners have limited supplies of labor and capital at their disposal and so allocate those factors to the economic activity that provides the greatest return. All other things being equal, that return is greatest in sectors to which the most productivity-enhancing collective goods have been provided. In particular, so long as no other sector is so inherently attractive to factor owners that they prefer it even in the absence of state support, factors of production will flow into a sector to the extent that collective goods have been provided to it.

Similarly, politicians have limited budgets of money, time, and political capital, and they allocate those resources where they receive the largest return. As discussed in Chapter 3, that return may be determined in part by the taxability of economic activity, as well as by the organization of sectors. In addition, however, if collective goods are not rival – if the use of a collective good by one enterprise does not preclude its use by another – then the return may be determined in part by the size of the sector: *ceteris paribus*, the larger the sector, the larger the return, as a fixed investment in collective goods can be spread over more economic activity.

As is typical in such strategic environments, multiple equilibria are possible. Factors of production and collective goods pool together in one sector or another, the allocation of one reinforcing the provision of the other. This is a logic well known to students of resource-rich countries, where political support, capital, and to some extent labor are often concentrated in the resource-extraction sector. Governments become reliant on revenues from this sector, developing "specialized agencies to monitor, regulate, and promote the activities of these few critical firms" (Shafer, 1994, p. 13), even while failing to "establish institutions to tax, monitor, regulate, or promote other sectors" (p. 14). "State frameworks for decision making [are] quickly molded to facilitate the perpetuation of oil-led [or other resource] development" (Karl, 1997, p. 197). Concurrently, given the lack of attention bestowed on other sectors, including an unwillingness to shield those sectors from the macroeconomic effects of resource booms, factors of production concentrate in the resource-extraction sector, reinforcing government incentives to support it. The argument, however, is more general than this example suggests. In principle many sectors could benefit from strategic complementarities of this sort, with politicians and factor owners trapped for better or worse in a mutually dependent relationship.

Although insightful, the perspective of multiple equilibria does nothing to explain how one sector might displace another, a criticism sometimes leveled more generally at work that emphasizes historical continuity. As Kathleen Thelen notes, many explanations that "emphasiz[e] the mechanisms through which previous patterns are reproduced . . . downplay the factors that might tell us how they can be changed" (Thelen, 1999, p. 396). But if we understand something about the incentives of various actors, then we may be able to identify moments of disequilibrium – "critical junctures," in the language of historical institutionalism (Lipset and Rokkan, 1967; Collier and Collier, 1991) – where a few key actions may tip the political economy toward one equilibrium or another. As I discuss in the following section, the years immediately after privatization were such a moment for the postcommunist states of Eastern Europe and the former Soviet Union.

5.2 The Political Economy of Privatization in Postsocialist States

In the early 1990s in postcommunist Europe, the key question for many policy makers, advisors, and scholars was how to effect a shift from a political economy in which the state was heavily involved in the economy and most individuals and capital were employed in state-owned enterprises, to one with state support for an economy in which private enterprise would be predominant. Privatization was seen as the central element of a strategy to make this happen. What was necessary was to create a "private property regime" – a "social and economic order defining a new set of expectations that individuals may have with respect to their ability to dispose of the assets recognized as 'theirs' by the legal system" (Frydman and Rapaczynski, 1994, p. 169) – and more generally to provide the necessary conditions for private property to be profitably employed. But, paradoxically, such an environment could not be created in the absence of private property, as the state would have no interest in providing the necessary institutions. Mass privatization would create the constituency necessary for these institutions to develop, providing political pressure on the state long after the privatizers had disappeared from the political scene (Klaus, 1994; Boycko, Shleifer, and Vishny, 1995; Frye, 1997; Gaidar, 1999; Åslund, 2002).

A particular model of the political process motivates this view of the political economy of privatization. First, whether because of pressure at the ballot box or from organized groups, politicians under normal circumstances respond to groups that are *numerous*. The key to mass privatization, then, is to transfer a sufficient proportion of assets into private hands, so that there is political pressure on politicians to supply the institutions that underpin a market economy. Those institutions having been provided, private enterprise will flourish, reinforcing the incentive of politicians to support it.

Second, a distinction is made between periods of "normal" and "extraordinary" politics (Balcerowicz, 1994; see also Lipton and Sachs, 1990, Sachs, 1994, Åslund, 1995), similar to that which I have used throughout this book. In the former, politicians respond to the usual pressures from voters and interest groups. In the latter, politics is driven more by the policy preferences of those in power. The first years after the collapse of communism were seen as a period of extraordinary politics. The old political constraints had been swept away, new ones had yet to emerge, and leaders were assumed to be more inclined than usual to make decisions for the greater good (Balcerowicz, 1994, p. 85). Consequently, the possibility

existed that a few decisions made at a key moment could result in a fundamental realignment of political and economic incentives.

This is a model of multiple equilibria with sensitivity to initial outcomes, similar in many respects to that which I outlined in the previous
section. In both cases, it is important to stress that a change in the behavior
of politicians is only a necessary condition for an equilibrium shift, not a
sufficient one. In particular, as discussed above, the strategic complemen-
tarity that encourages labor and capital to locate in the private economy
if politicians provide the necessary institutions must be sufficiently great
to overcome any inherent advantages of locating in whatever remains of
the communist-era economy. Moreover, any change in institutions must
be sufficiently rapid to offset the tendency of labor and capital to migrate
back to whatever sectors retain the support of unenlightened politicians,
thus undermining the impact of privatization on politicians' incentives.[6]

The key difference between this model and that which I sketched above
lies in the incentives assumed of postcommunist politicians. I believe that
for many politicians in the region the desire to raise revenue has been
a first-order concern, trumping the "normal" political considerations. In
other words, a period of "extraordinary" politics extended beyond the initial
breakthrough period, such that well into the first decade of transition, political decisions were driven not only or primarily by the usual calculations.
Rather than being motivated by far-sighted goals, however, politicians were
trapped by the immediate need to generate revenue to satisfy various constraints. My reading of the voluminous literature bequeathed to historians
by participants in the privatization debates of the early 1990s suggests that
this concern was not anticipated. On the contrary, the political impact of
privatization was seen to operate primarily through its direct effect on factor owners (e.g., Roland and Verdier, 1994; Schmidt, 2000). Recipients
of privatized assets would support free-market politicians; employees of
private firms would eventually do the same as the efficiency benefits of privatization took root (Przeworski, 1991). The more that owners and workers
benefited from privatization and other reforms, the more likely they would
be to support politicians who advocated free-market principles.

---

[6] It is interesting to note that a large change in institutions during the early years of transition –
if possible – could also have effected an equilibrium shift so long as resources then pooled
into the private economy more quickly than politicians and bureaucrats reverted to business
as usual. As a general rule, this strategy was not attempted (e.g., Clement and Murrell,
2001).

There is, in fact, evidence that individuals who benefited from privatization were more inclined to support market institutions. Survey evidence from the Czech Republic, which under Vaclav Klaus underwent mass privatization in the early 1990s, suggests that individuals who received and retained property through privatization were more likely to support "complete freedom" for private enterprise, less likely to believe that the state should increase price controls, and more likely to prefer a free-market system (Earle and Gehlbach, 2003). Further, economically liberal parties in East Central Europe (the Czech Republic, Slovakia, Hungary, and Poland) have often performed better in regions where new private enterprises have taken root, perhaps because of the comparatively high wages such enterprises pay (Fidrmuc, 2000*a,b*; Jackson, Klich, and Poznańska, 2005). More generally, regions of these four countries and of Russia with large numbers of winners from economic reform have consistently rewarded "new regime" parties, that is, those parties considered responsible for instituting reforms, even when postreform economic growth took place under the tutelage of "old regime" parties (Tucker, 2006).

That said, most countries in the region implemented some program of mass privatization, yet the political commitment to private enterprise – especially new firms – has been sharply uneven. At the same time, the new private sector (as distinct from the privatized formerly state-owned sector) that seems to have contributed to support for liberal economic policies in East Central Europe has manifestly failed to develop at the same pace in many other countries in the region, despite the general transfer of assets to private owners. As suggested above, these facts should be seen as interrelated: politicians have little incentive to support a new private sector where none exists, while entrepreneurs find it difficult to set up shop without a supportive business environment (see also Jackson, 2003; Malesky, 2006).

Figure 5.1 illustrates the scale of privatization in nine countries in Eastern Europe, the Baltics, and the CIS for the critical first decade after the collapse of communism. (I depict trends in these countries to allow comparison with Figure 5.3 below. In the appendix to this chapter, I provide statistics for all postcommunist countries; as can be seen, the experience of these nine countries with privatization is broadly representative of trends in the region.) With the exception of Belarus, privatization rapidly transferred the bulk of assets in all nine countries into private hands. Viewed from the perspective of the early 1990s, this was an enormous political accomplishment, one by no means preordained. And although one might

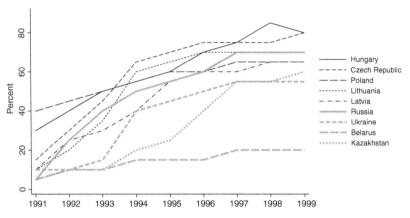

Figure 5.1   Private sector share in GDP, 1991–1999. Data source: EBRD (2000).

not have expected privatization to everywhere accomplish its primary goal – the realignment of incentives, with both politicians and factor owners committed to private enterprise – there is little reason to expect systematic differences across postcommunist space based on this picture alone.

Figure 5.2 makes much the same point, showing subjective indexes of progress with small-scale (retail establishments) and large-scale (industrial enterprises) privatization in the same nine countries. These indexes, issued annually by the European Bank for Reconstruction and Development, provide a score from 1 to 4+ for each country in the postcommunist world; Figure 5.2 shows the index for 1999.[7] (I give scores for all postcommunist countries in the appendix to this chapter.) Every country represented in the figure but Belarus receives a score of at least 3 for small-scale privatization, and every country but Ukraine and Belarus receives a score of at least 3 for large-scale privatization. Again, a similar message would be conveyed if other countries in the region were depicted: by the late 1990s, small privatization had been accomplished nearly everywhere, and large privatization had been carried out to a very high degree of completion in most countries.

---

[7] For small-scale privatization, a score of 1 signifies "little progress," whereas a score of 4+ indicates "standards and performance typical of advanced industrial economies; no state ownership of small enterprises; effective tradability of land." For large-scale privatization, a score of 1 corresponds to "little private ownership," whereas a score of 4+ reflects "standards and performance typical of advanced industrial economies; more than 75 per cent of enterprise assets in private ownership with effective corporate governance." See EBRD (2000, p. 15).

Small–Scale Privatization

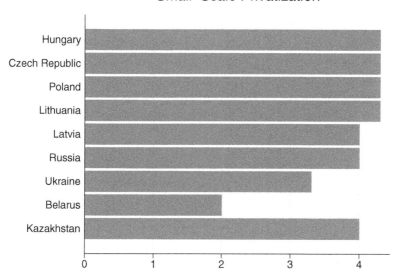

Large–Scale Privatization

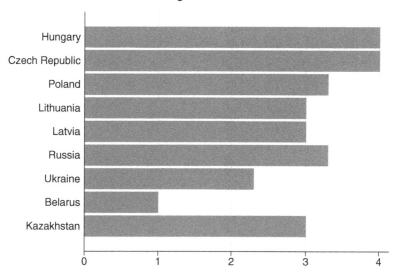

Figure 5.2 1999 EBRD index of small-scale and large-scale privatization. Data source: EBRD (2000).

Looking merely at the scale of privatization in postcommunist countries, we should thus expect little systematic variation in the degree to which privatization was successful in bringing about the shift in expectations and behavior hoped for by its designers. Yet such differences exist. One way of seeing this is to look at the economic impact of privatization on the firms that were privatized. Estimating these effects is difficult, in significant part because privatization agencies often selected enterprises for privatization whose productivity they judged to be higher or growing more quickly. However, most studies – including those that control one way or another for these selection effects – find that privatization had an economically large and statistically significant effect on firm performance in Eastern Europe and the Baltics but a small and often insignificant effect in the former Soviet Union less the Baltics (Megginson and Netter, 2001; Djankov and Murrell, 2002). In one of the best recent studies, David Brown, John Earle, and Almos Telegdy analyze panel data on the population of firms in four postcommunist countries, finding a 15 percent average increase in (multifactor) productivity for privatized firms in Romania, 8 percent in Hungary, 2 percent in Ukraine, and −3 (!) percent in Russia (Brown, Earle, and Telegdy, 2006).

The causes of these differences in privatization effects are not well understood, but a leading hypothesis is that variation across countries in the quality of government inputs plays a role (e.g., Djankov and Murrell, 2002). (Other possibilities include the method of privatization itself, e.g., whether firms were privatized to insiders or outsiders.) The economic logic is straightforward: if a firm's production function is augmented by sector-specific collective goods such as property-rights protection and a supportive legal system, then differences across countries in the relative provision of those goods to privatized and nonprivatized firms will result in different estimated effects of privatization. As we saw in Chapter 4, after controlling for other firm characteristics, there is little evidence of a systematic bias against private firms per se in the provision of collective goods in the former Soviet Union. But the possibility remains that the biases that are evident have disproportionately benefited sectors that are state owned. The history of vodka politics in Pskov oblast related in Chapter 1 provides an example: the profitability of the largely state-owned vodka sector was inflated through the intervention of regional authorities, but the cause of this intervention was due as much to the technological ease of taxing vodka as to state ownership of the sector.

Here, too, the recent work of Brown, Earle, and Telegdy offers insights. Although estimated privatization effects in Ukraine and Russia are negligible on average, there is considerable variation across sectors. In particular, in Russia the estimated effect of privatization is positive and statistically significant for three of ten sectors: textiles, other nonmetallic mineral products, and basic and fabricated metals. In Ukraine positive and statistically significant effects are found for the fuels, chemicals, rubber, and plastics sector and for other nonmetallic mineral products. With the exception of textiles, these sectors are in resource-intensive industries that as a general rule are highly taxable. In contrast, in Hungary and Romania the estimated effect of privatization is positive and significant in nearly every sector. The only exceptions (identical for the two countries) are textiles and fuels, chemicals, rubber, and plastics (Brown, Earle, and Telegdy, 2004). These differences are consistent with the evidence presented in the previous chapter that the political economies of the former Soviet Union, but not those of Eastern Europe, were oriented around support for highly taxable industries.[8]

Nonetheless, despite the large differences in privatization effects, there is little systematic evidence to date that labor and capital are flowing into privatized enterprises to a greater degree in Eastern Europe than in the former Soviet Union: the share of GDP in the private sector has stayed relatively constant since the end of privatization in most postcommunist countries. But if we look at one slice of the private sector – the small-business sector, roughly synonymous with *new* private enterprise in the postcommunist world because there were few small enterprises under communism[9] – then clear evidence of factor mobility is visible. Figure 5.3, which is taken from World Bank (2002), shows the development of the small-business sector (defined in the figure as firms with fewer than fifty employees) in the same nine countries as in the previous two figures. By the late 1990s, employment in small enterprises in Eastern Europe and the Baltics was approaching levels typically observed in Organisation for Economic Co-operation and

[8] Lane (2001) provides some supporting evidence, citing the many specialized departments in Russian ministries responsible for the highly taxable fuel and power sector.

[9] In the BEEPS data set used in previous chapters, 86 percent of new firms have fewer than 100 employees, versus 35 percent of old firms. Moreover, these relationships are quite similar in the two halves of the postcommunist world: 84 percent of new firms have fewer than 100 employees in the CIS, whereas 87 percent do in Eastern Europe and the Baltics. Although these cannot be taken as population estimates because the BEEPS is not a random sample, the general correlation is clear.

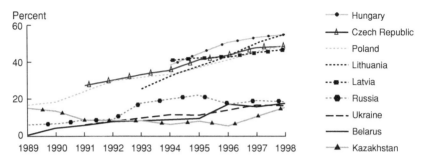

Figure 5.3 Share of employment in small enterprises, 1989–1998. Adapted from World Bank (2002).

Development (OECD) countries. In contrast, in the former Soviet Union less the Baltics, small-enterprise employment lagged far behind.[10]

Strikingly, the distribution of small-enterprise employment across countries in the region is "lumpy," exactly as a model with multiple equilibria would predict. Small-business employment is either high (Eastern Europe) or low (former Soviet Union). Further, if we extend our gaze beyond 1998, this pattern seems stable, with perhaps one exception. Table 5.1 presents data from an unpublished EBRD database on small and medium-sized enterprises (SMEs) in postcommunist countries.[11] As with the data reported in Figure 5.3, the numbers in this table should be taken as impressionistic, not precise estimates of the size of the small-business sector. Definitions of small and medium-sized enterprises vary from country to country and even across industries within countries depending on what is measured (employment or turnover).[12] Nonetheless, the general pattern in 2001 is the same as that reported in Figure 5.3 and hence largely unchanged despite the general economic rebound in the CIS following the 1998 Russian financial crisis: small enterprises constitute a much smaller share of employment and turnover in the former Soviet Union than in Eastern Europe. After an initial sorting into two groups,

---

[10] There is evidence of substantial reallocation of labor across enterprises in Russia and Ukraine (Brown and Earle, 2003, 2006). However, the data on small-business employment suggest limited reallocation out of Soviet-era enterprises into the new private sector.

[11] I report data from 2001, the last year for which a broad cross section is available.

[12] To maximize comparability, I calculate the share of small, not small and medium-sized, enterprises in total employment and turnover, as in many CIS countries medium-sized and large enterprises are collapsed into a single category. In practice, this means that "small" is defined, with some exceptions, to be firms with fewer than fifty employees.

Table 5.1. *Small-enterprise share of employment and turnover, 2001*

	Small-Enterprise Share of Total Employment, 2001	Small-Enterprise Share of Total Turnover, 2001
Eastern Europe and Baltics		
Albania	0.47	0.61
Bulgaria	0.67	
Croatia	0.32	0.40
Estonia	0.49	0.54
Hungary	0.36	0.21
Latvia	0.43	0.48
Macedonia	0.30	0.48
Poland	0.44	0.43
Romania	0.63	0.36
Slovakia	0.41	
Slovenia	0.29	0.32
Unweighted average	0.44	0.43
CIS		
Azerbaijan	0.13	0.22
Belarus	0.08	0.14
Kazakhstan	0.63	0.24
Moldova	0.24	0.22
Russia	0.10	
Tajikistan	0.10	
Ukraine	0.17	0.07
Uzbekistan	0.13	0.14
Unweighted average	0.20	0.17

Source. EBRD database on SMEs, author's calculations.

the political economies of the region seem to have settled into stable equilibria.[13]

These trends are intriguing; they are also of great normative importance. Among economists studying the region, there is now nearly universal agreement that new, that is, small, enterprises are the best engine of sustainable growth for postcommunist countries (e.g., Havrylyshyn and McGettigan,

---

[13] The one exception – the large share of small-enterprise employment in Kazakhstan – can be explained in part by the capital intensity of that country's dominant oil-and-gas sector, which has the effect of inflating the small-enterprise share of employment relative to that of turnover. That said, there has been considerable growth in the small-business sector in Kazakhstan, the possible result of aggressive reform policies pursued during the 1990s that bore fruit only later (Alam and Banerji, 2000). To the extent that this is the case, Kazakhstan represents an outlier among post-Soviet states.

2000; World Bank, 2002; Jackson, Klich, and Poznańska, 2005). It was not always this way. At the beginning of the 1990s, the overwhelming emphasis was instead on the privatization and restructuring of existing enterprises (e.g., Fischer and Gelb, 1991).[14] But time has shown that it is hard, or expensive, to teach old dogs new tricks. The question, then, is why new enterprises have taken off so unevenly across the postcommunist world. The evidence presented above suggests that the answer is not the availability of assets (storefronts, real estate, and the like) for small enterprise. Such assets were quickly transferred to private owners through small privatization in nearly every postcommunist country. Rather, something else must have discouraged the development of a small-enterprise sector in the former Soviet Union.

In the following section I explore an alternative hypothesis, one consistent with the evidence presented in the previous chapters. Privatization, especially small privatization, had the potential to tip both political support and factor allocation toward the new, small-enterprise sector wherever it was carried out. Whether it did so depended in part on the relative revenue importance of old and new firms. In Eastern Europe, as we have seen, there was little incentive to discriminate in favor of old firms for revenue reasons. In contrast, in the former Soviet Union, this incentive was paramount. Consequently, the same shock to resource allocation, carried out through privatization, could result in different equilibrium outcomes in the two halves of the postcommunist world. In Eastern Europe this shock was sufficient to realign incentives in support of new private enterprise. In the former Soviet Union it was not: politicians and factor owners were caught in a revenue trap.

5.3 "Old" and "New" Equilibria

Why was privatization insufficient in many parts of the postcommunist world to effect a shift to an economy oriented around new private enterprise? To answer this question, we must return to the model of revenue traps sketched above (and presented formally in the appendix to this chapter), in which politicians are motivated at least in part to increase tax revenue. As discussed above, this perspective differs from that of many theorists of mass privatization in postcommunist states, who explicitly or implicitly assumed that the political effect of privatization operated primarily though its direct impact on factor owners.

[14] There were exceptions, including Kornai (1990).

If we continue to view privatization as a shock to resource allocation engineered by state actors operating during a brief period when such policies could be implemented, then the question becomes the following: was the shock to resource allocation through privatization large enough for politicians to abandon the old (state-owned and formerly state-owned) enterprises on which they had been reliant for revenue and to provide collective goods to the new private sector? In posing this question, it is important to stress that the collective goods necessary for development of new firms are largely different from those required of privatized, formerly state-owned enterprises. New firms are typically small, so whatever institutional support is required of small firms in general is important for new firms in particular. Moreover, new firms typically face licensing and registration requirements not required of established firms; streamlining these requirements requires not only a change in law governing the establishment of new enterprises but adherence to that law by government bureaucrats.[15] Finally, existing firms obviously have an incentive to block new entrants, so competition policy must be both well legislated and strictly enforced.

In looking to the impact of privatization on the incentives of politicians to provide support for new enterprise, we should therefore examine that element of privatization most likely to have induced politicians to provide the collective goods necessary for new firms to flourish. Small-scale privatization provided the assets – storefronts, real estate, and so on – essential for new enterprises to take root and grow. Critically, however, in contrast to large-scale privatization, the shock to resource allocation provided by small-scale privatization was not overwhelming, involving a relatively small proportion of total assets in the economy. Consequently, privatization alone may not have been sufficient to encourage politicians to provide the collective goods necessary for truly new private economic activity to flourish.

To explain variation in outcomes, we must thus ask whether there were differences in the *resistance* of the old equilibrium in response to these moderate shocks to resource allocation. Such resistance could have taken one of two forms. First, the inherent productivity of old and new firms, independent of any productivity-enhancing effect of collective-goods provision, might have varied across countries in a systematic way. For example,

---

[15] For evidence from Russia that changes in licensing and registration requirements may not be sufficient to provoke a change in bureaucratic behavior, see CEFIR and World Bank (2002). For theoretical discussion of corruption in enterprise licensing, see Manion (1996) and Guriev (2004).

if old enterprises in the former Soviet Union were especially productive relative to those in Eastern Europe, then revenue-maximizing politicians in the eastern half of the postcommunist world would have been less inclined to abandon support for the old economy through the provision of various collective goods. However, there is little theoretical reason to suspect this to be true. If anything, intuition suggests otherwise: with a large number of Stalinist-era enterprises in the former Soviet Union, the obsolescence of the old economy there may have been greater.

Second, the old economy may have been a *relatively* important source of tax revenue in the former Soviet Union, discouraging revenue-maximizing politicians from providing the collective goods necessary for the new private economy to flourish. As we have seen in previous chapters, this appears to have been the case. The tax systems created in the former Soviet Union during the 1990s largely neglected new revenue sources such as the small-enterprise sector. As a consequence, governments in the former Soviet Union were particularly inclined to favor old enterprises in the provision of collective goods.

As a consequence, the same shock to resource allocation – small-scale privatization, carried out at the beginning of transition by policy makers who hoped to influence the political calculations of those who came later – may have produced very different effects in the two halves of the postcommunist world. In Eastern Europe, this shock seems to have been sufficient to realign the incentives of politicians in support of new private enterprise. With politicians thus promoting institutions to support new business creation, labor and capital have flowed into the new private sector. The result has been a virtuous circle of political support for new private enterprise and factor reallocation into the new private sector, much as the architects of privatization had hoped.

In contrast, in the former Soviet Union small privatization was not sufficient to overcome the reliance of politicians on the revenues provided by the old economy. Consequently, there was little investment in the institutions necessary for new businesses to flourish, and labor and capital have largely opted out of the small-business sector.[16] The result has been a vicious cycle of business as usual by politicians and factor owners. As Gerald

---

[16] Indeed, given any inherited advantages of old firms and the particular difficulty in the former Soviet Union of taxing new firms, it is possible that the "new" equilibrium did not exist. I formalize this intuition in Section 5.A.4.

144

Easter writes, referring to one of many post-Soviet countries apparently caught in a revenue trap, "while the state may be dependent on large corporations for tax revenue, Russia's corporate elite remains dependent on state patronage for wealth and status" (Easter, 2006*b*).

The example of new-business creation with which this book opened is the exception that proves the rule. Pskov authorities provided the political support necessary for a vodka sector to develop where none had previously existed. Yet this industry has little in common with the new enterprise that has been the engine of growth in Eastern Europe. Pskovpishcheprom, which emerged as the monopoly producer of vodka in Pskov oblast, is a large enterprise formed around assets seized from a preexisting food-processing sector. Competition to Pskovpishcheprom is limited, and many small retailers have suffered from the state alcohol-distribution monopoly. One is tempted to ask: with new enterprise like this, who needs old?

What are the welfare implications of these divergent trajectories? Given the presumed productivity advantages enjoyed by new enterprise in the postcommunist world, we can almost certainly conclude that the new equilibrium of Eastern Europe is better than the old of the former Soviet Union. Yet it is not necessarily the case that the new equilibrium of the former Soviet Union – if it existed – would be preferable to the old that has prevailed in practice. It is possible that the state apparatus in countries like Russia works better for old enterprises than it could reasonably be expected to work for new ones. If so, then the old equilibrium may not be best but could be what economists term *second-best*: the best that could be achieved, given the absence of incentives to support new enterprise.

Ultimately, the question is whether the moment was lost irretrievably for much of the postcommunist world during the early days of transition. If the countries of the former Soviet Union are in fact caught in a revenue trap, with politicians and factor owners mutually dependent on an old economy oriented around large and often monopolistic enterprises, then it is hard to imagine another shock on the scale of privatization that could shake them out of it. In that case, the fault lies not in the vision of privatization as a policy that could set history down a new path, but the failure to provide the institutional support that would make the new economy politically important. The decisions made as tax systems were created in the early 1990s set the stage for what was to come later. The tragedy is that the consequences of this state-building effort could not be more clearly foreseen.

5.4 Summary

With this my story comes to a close. Having shown how initial conditions drove the choice of tax systems during the 1990s, and having subsequently demonstrated the consequences of those choices for the provision of collective goods across the postcommunist world, I have suggested in this chapter the possible long-run implications of these developments. The creation of postcommunist tax systems took place contemporaneously with the shock to factor allocation brought about by mass privatization. The incentives of politicians were thus structured both by the sudden presence of labor and capital in the new private economy, and by the degree to which the new and old economy were important revenue sources. The lesser taxability of new private economic activity in the former Soviet Union – the result of decisions made in the early and mid-1990s about what revenue sources to tap – reduced the incentive for post-Soviet politicians to provide the necessary institutions for such activity to flourish. That in turn discouraged labor and capital from locating in the new private economy, producing a "revenue trap" that may be very difficult to escape. The very different outcome in Eastern Europe can be traced to the decision to develop new revenue sources, encouraging politicians in that region to behave as the architects of privatization had hoped and thus helping to bring about the expected equilibrium shift to a new political economy.

This is neither an entirely happy nor a completely unhappy ending. The reorientation of East European political economies was by no means ensured in the early 1990s. That it happened is a good thing, at least by my value system. At the same time, the failure of economic reform to fundamentally redirect politicians and factor owners away from the old economy in the former Soviet Union has real consequences for the residents of that region. Several years of strong growth notwithstanding – much of it driven by high prices for the commodities that form the base of the old economy for many countries in the region as well as by catch-up after the long "transition depression" – the long-run potential of post-Soviet economies may depend on the sort of economic activity that has yet to fully take off. Whether it does, or whether the "great divide" (Berglof and Bolton, 2002) in the postcommunist world persists, depends at this juncture on the answer to two questions: will politicians continue to provide political support to the old economy, and can the new economy grow even in the absence of a supportive government? Both my theoretical framework and a "Batesian" approach suggest that the the answer to the first question is yes:

whether for revenue reasons or because of the organization of interests, politicians seem unlikely to shift support to the entrepreneurial economy, given the current allocation of labor and capital. Hope for change therefore seems to rest on the ability of entrepreneurs to find private substitutes for public goods (e.g., Milgrom, North, and Weingast, 1990; Dixit, 2004; Greif, 2006) and so circumvent a political economy biased against them. Establishing the extent to which this is taking place is an important area of current research (e.g., Johnson, McMillan, and Woodruff, 2002; Hendley and Murrell, 2003; Frye, 2004; Pyle, 2006*b*) and should remain so.

5.A Appendix A: The Formal Logic of Revenue Traps

In this appendix I present a formal model of revenue traps. I initially describe the model and demonstrate the existence of multiple equilibria. I then present a necessary condition for privatization or a similar shock to resource allocation to result in an equilibrium shift. Following that I discuss welfare implications of the model. Finally, I illustrate the caveat that an equilibrium exists with factors of production and collective goods pooled together in a particular sector only if the strategic complementarities in that sector dominate any inherent advantages possessed by some other sector.

5.A.1 Environment and Equilibrium

Consider an economy with two economic sectors, indexed by $S \in \{O, N\}$, where O represents an "old" sector and N a "new" sector. For simplicity, assume labor to be the sole factor of production, with total labor supply perfectly inelastic and normalized to 1. Labor is completely mobile across sectors, with the (endogenous) proportion of labor in sector S equal to L_S.[17] (In what follows, I often refer to "resources" or "factors of production" rather than labor.) Labor is homogenous, and production from labor is augmented by a sector-specific productivity parameter α_S and sector-specific collective good q_S, such that total output in sector S is $Y_S = \alpha_S L_S q_S$. In the discussion below, I often focus on the case where the new sector is inherently more productive, so that $\alpha_N > \alpha_O$.

[17] Elasticity of total labor supply can be easily incorporated into the model, with no change in the main qualitative results, by assuming that there is an alternative sector R that is nonproductive (or at least nontaxable) and that provides utility to labor of $u(L_R)$, with u concave and certain boundary conditions assumed.

Simultaneously with the allocation of labor across sectors, a politician decides on the provision of collective goods. The assumption that the politician and labor move simultaneously captures the idea that the politician cannot precommit to a particular allocation of collective goods, as she is dependent on existing sources of revenue to fund both collective-goods production and any use of tax revenue for political or personal use. I assume that the politician maximizes tax revenue net of the cost of providing such goods, where an exogenous proportion τ_S of production in sector S is extracted as tax revenue, with the remainder retained by labor: the parameter τ_S reflects the taxability of the sector. Consistent with the model in Chapter 3, we can easily incorporate a decision by owners of labor to hide some portion of their production from the state, where the marginal cost of hiding production varies across sectors and τ_S is that portion of production (net of the cost of hiding) that is unhidden and taxed by the state. In the context of the model in this chapter, the parameter α_S then represents both the inherent productivity of a sector and the cost of hiding production, where for a given level of inherent productivity the parameter α_S is lower when more production is destroyed in the process of hiding revenues from the state.

In particular, I assume that the politician decides on both an allocation $\beta \in (0, 1)$ of tax revenue to collective-goods production (with the remainder retained for consumption) and a distribution (λ_O, λ_N) of the total production of collective goods q to the two sectors, with $q_S = \lambda_S q$ and $\lambda_O + \lambda_N = 1$.[18] Aggregate collective-goods production q is given by the collective-goods production function

$$q = [\beta\,(\tau_O Y_O + \tau_N Y_N)]^\gamma = [\beta\,(\tau_O \alpha_O L_O \lambda_O q + \tau_N \alpha_N L_N \lambda_N q)]^\gamma,$$

where $\gamma \in (0, 1)$ is a parameter of the model. Solving for q gives

$$q = [\beta(\tau_O \alpha_O L_O \lambda_O + \tau_N \alpha_N L_N \lambda_N)]^{\frac{\gamma}{1-\gamma}}.$$

Thus, the politician (taking L_O and L_N as given) solves

$$\max_{\lambda_O, \lambda_N, \beta} (1-\beta)\tau_O \alpha_O L_O \lambda_O q + (1-\beta)\tau_N \alpha_N L_N \lambda_N q$$
$$\text{s.t.} \quad q = [\beta(\tau_O \alpha_O\ L_O \lambda_O + \tau_N \alpha_N L_N\ \lambda_N)]^{\frac{\gamma}{1-\gamma}}$$
$$\lambda_O + \lambda_N = 1,$$

---

[18] In an extended model, we might further assume that some proportion of collective-goods production benefits both sectors. The main qualitative results of the model are more likely to hold, the smaller is that proportion.

i.e.,

$$\max_{\lambda_O,\beta} (1 - \beta)\beta^{\frac{\gamma}{1-\gamma}} [\tau_O\alpha_O L_O\lambda_O + \tau_N\alpha_N L_N(1 - \lambda_O)]^{\frac{1}{1-\gamma}} .$$

Clearly, this problem is separable in β and λ_O. The expression $(1 - \beta)\beta^{\frac{\gamma}{1-\gamma}}$ is quasiconcave in β, so the first-order condition $\beta = \gamma$ defines the politician's optimal allocation of tax revenue to collective-goods production. Intuitively, the better the collective-goods production technology (in the sense of smaller diminishing returns), the more the politician is motivated to take a small slice of a large pie rather than a large slice of a small pie. With respect to the allocation of collective goods across sectors, the politician provides collective goods only to the old sector (i.e., chooses $\lambda_O = 1$) if $\tau_O\alpha_O L_O > \tau_N\alpha_N L_N$ and only to the new sector if $\tau_O\alpha_O L_O < \tau_N\alpha_N L_N$. Similarly, given complete factor mobility and the assumption that labor retains proportion $1 - \tau_S$ of the production in sector S, labor locates entirely in the old sector if $(1 - \tau_O)\alpha_O\lambda_O > (1 - \tau_N)\alpha_N\lambda_N$ and entirely in the new sector if $(1 - \tau_O)\alpha_O\lambda_O < (1 - \tau_N)\alpha_N\lambda_N$.

Thus, labor allocation and collective-goods provision are strategic complements: both owners of labor and the politician are more likely to devote resources to a particular sector if the other does. As is typical in games of this sort, there are multiple equilibria. In particular, there are two stable equilibria: an "old" equilibrium, where labor and collective goods are allocated entirely to the old sector, and a "new" equilibrium in which they are allocated entirely to the new sector. In addition, there is an unstable intermediate equilibrium defined by the indifference conditions for collective-goods provision and labor allocation:

$$\frac{L_N}{L_O} = \frac{\tau_O\alpha_O}{\tau_N\alpha_N},$$

$$\frac{\lambda_N}{\lambda_O} = \frac{(1 - \tau_O)\alpha_O}{(1 - \tau_N)\alpha_N}.$$

The mutual dependence of the politician and labor within any sector implies that economic activity and political support stabilize around particular types of economic activity: the politician provides collective goods to an existing sector because of its revenue importance, while resources remain allocated to that sector because of collective-goods provision.

5.A.2 Resistance to Shocks

I now consider the possibility that the new sector is inherently more productive than the old (i.e., that $\alpha_N > \alpha_O$) but that the political economy remains stuck in the old equilibrium even in the presence of large shocks to resource allocation, such as that which accompanied privatization in postcommunist countries or which results from a natural disaster or war. As discussed above, for a resource shock to result in such an equilibrium shift, the politician must adjust more quickly than labor to changing circumstances, as without a corresponding change in collective-goods provision labor will flow back into the old sector. Thus, a large shock to resource allocation is a necessary, but not sufficient, condition for an equilibrium shift. (If the shock were instead to collective-goods allocation the ball would be in labor's court. However, at least in the transition context the primary shock was to resource allocation through privatization.)

Formally, assume that resources and collective goods are initially allocated to the old sector, and let δ be the proportion of labor reallocated to the new sector in response to some exogenous shock to resource allocation. Then the old equilibrium is *resistant* to this shock if the politician's best response to δ is to allocate collective goods to the old rather than to the new sector, that is, if

$$\tau_O \alpha_O (1 - \delta) \geq \tau_N \alpha_N \delta. \qquad (5.1)$$

Clearly, we can always find a δ large enough that the old equilibrium could give way to the new, but in practice there are limits to the size of exogenous shocks that may occur. As discussed above, even mass privatization in transition countries – one of the largest shocks to resource allocation in economic history – transferred a relatively small share of resources into truly new economic activity.

In particular, Condition (5.1) shows that the old equilibrium is resistant to larger shocks when the new sector is relatively difficult to tax, that is, when the ratio τ_N/τ_O is small. The politician, forced to decide whether to abandon an aging and inherently less productive sector, is less likely to do so when that sector more easily surrenders the tax revenue that she finds politically and personally valuable. Thus, revenue traps may be more likely when the old sector is more taxable than the new.

5.A.3 Welfare

I have characterized the new sector as inherently more productive than the old, but is the new equilibrium necessarily efficient? Put differently, given the constraints imposed by the political environment (including differences in taxability of the two sectors), how concerned should we be that the old equilibrium may be resistant to exogenous shocks to resource allocation?

I say that an equilibrium organized around some sector is *(constrained) socially efficient* when the value given by some social welfare function that takes as arguments the utility of all members of society – not only the politician and labor but also nonstrategic and unmodeled players who may, for example, benefit from tax revenue retained by the politician – is greater in that equilibrium than in the other stable equilibrium. To characterize this in a reduced-form way, assume that social welfare in the equilibrium where resources and collective goods are concentrated in sector S can be represented by the function

$$W_S(\tau_S, \alpha_S, \gamma, \mu) = [(1 - \tau_S) + \mu (1 - \gamma) \tau_S] (\alpha_S)^{\frac{1}{1-\gamma}} (\gamma \tau_S)^{\frac{\gamma}{1-\gamma}}, \qquad (5.2)$$

where $\mu \in [0, 1]$ is a parameter that measures the weight given to tax revenue retained by the politician and $(\alpha_S)^{\frac{1}{1-\gamma}} (\gamma \tau_S)^{\frac{\gamma}{1-\gamma}}$ is the equilibrium level of production in sector S. When $\mu = 0$, W_S is equal to labor's after-tax income, whereas when $\mu = 1$, W_S is the entirety of production retained by labor and the politician.

The new equilibrium may be socially efficient even while the old equilibrium is resistant to large shocks to resource allocation. To see this most clearly, let μ equal 1 so the new equilibrium is socially efficient if

$$(1 - \gamma \tau_N)(\alpha_N)^{\frac{1}{1-\gamma}} (\gamma \tau_N)^{\frac{\gamma}{1-\gamma}} \geq (1 - \gamma \tau_O)(\alpha_O)^{\frac{1}{1-\gamma}} (\gamma \tau_O)^{\frac{\gamma}{1-\gamma}},$$

that is, if

$$\left(\frac{1 - \gamma \tau_N}{\tau_N}\right)^{1-\gamma} \tau_N \alpha_N \geq \left(\frac{1 - \gamma \tau_O}{\tau_O}\right)^{1-\gamma} \tau_O \alpha_O.$$

Then using Condition (5.1), the condition for the new equilibrium to be socially efficient but the old equilibrium to be resistant to some exogenous shock δ can be written as

$$\left(\frac{1 - \gamma \tau_O}{1 - \gamma \tau_N} \cdot \frac{\tau_N}{\tau_O}\right)^{1-\gamma} \leq \frac{\tau_N \alpha_N}{\tau_O \alpha_O} \leq \frac{1 - \delta}{\delta}.$$

When the old sector is relatively more taxable, that is, when $\tau_N < \tau_O$, then the left-most term is less than 1, whereas for all $\delta < \frac{1}{2}$ (i.e., for all shocks to resource allocation that leave at least half of labor in the old sector) the right-most term is greater than 1. Thus, the condition holds for some parameter values and exogenous shocks to resource allocation.

Conversely, economic activity in the new sector may be inherently more productive than that in the old (i.e., $\alpha_N > \alpha_O$), but the equilibrium organized around the new sector may not be socially efficient because of differences in the taxability of the two sectors. To be more precise, the equilibrium in support of sector S is less likely to be socially efficient, the farther is τ_S from the socially optimal level of taxation (which I denote τ^e), which may be derived from the social welfare function (Equation (5.2)) as $\tau^e = \gamma/[1 - \mu(1 - \gamma)]$. Thus, for example, the old equilibrium may be preferable to the new if $\tau_N < \tau_O < \tau^e$, as in weak states that find it especially difficult to raise revenue from any source but particularly so from new economic activity, or if $\tau_N \ll \tau^e < \tau_O$, as when the economy is "cursed" by government reliance on highly taxable natural resources but alternative economic activity is very difficult to tax. Given the contribution of collective goods to production, an inability to tax a promising sector may render dependence on an inherently less productive sector second-best.

5.A.4 Necessity of Government Support

There may be environments in which it is impossible even in principle to break out of the old equilibrium. In particular, collective goods may be relatively more important to the new sector, as in postcommunist countries where private economic activity of any real scale required the active intervention of the state to create the legal and institutional infrastructure that would allow markets to function. If the old sector can continue to function even without continued investment in collective goods, then it is possible that the old equilibrium is the only equilibrium.

To see this, consider a modified production function for the old sector $Y_O = \alpha_O L_O (q_O + \bar{q}_O)$, where the parameter $\bar{q}_O > 0$ is the "inherited" collective-goods provision to the old sector. Then the new equilibrium does not exist if the marginal return to labor in the old sector is greater than that in the new sector, even when all labor is allocated to the new sector:

$$(1 - \tau_O)\alpha_O\bar{q}_O > (1 - \tau_N)(\alpha_N)^{\frac{1}{1-\gamma}}(\gamma\tau_N)^{\frac{\gamma}{1-\gamma}}. \qquad (5.3)$$

Clearly, this inequality is more likely to hold, the larger is $\alpha_O \bar{q}_O$. More interestingly, the condition may also hold if the taxability of the new sector is sufficiently low: if the new sector does not provide the resource base for collective-goods production to take place, resources may flow back into the old sector even when it is unsupported by the politician. To see this most clearly, let τ_N approach zero. Then Condition (5.3) clearly holds, as the right-hand term approaches zero.

Taxability of the new sector sufficiently high also guarantees uniqueness of the old equilibrium, as then private investment in the new sector is unattractive despite collective-goods provision to that sector. However, this is an unlikely scenario in many political-economic environments, where the state is constrained in its ability to collect revenue from all sources, but most especially from new types of economic activity.

5.B Appendix B: Progress in Privatization during First Postcommunist Decade

In the discussion above I graphically present progress with privatization in nine postcommunist countries. In the following table I give private-sector shares and EBRD privatization indexes for all postcommunist countries in Eastern Europe and the former Soviet Union but Yugoslavia, for which the EBRD provides no data.

Table 5.B.1. *Private-sector share in GDP and privatization indexes, 1999*

	1999 Private Sector Share in GDP	1999 EBRD Index of Small-Scale Privatization	1999 EBRD Index of Large-Scale Privatization
Eastern Europe and Baltics			
Albania	75	4	2
Bosnia and Herzegovina	35	2	2
Bulgaria	70	3+	3
Croatia	60	4+	3
Czech Republic	80	4+	4
Estonia	75	4+	4
Hungary	80	4+	4
Latvia	65	4	3
Lithuania	70	4+	3
Macedonia	55	4	3
Poland	65	4+	3+
Romania	60	4−	3−
Slovakia	75	4+	4
Slovenia	55	4+	3
CIS			
Armenia	60	3+	3
Azerbaijan	45	3+	2−
Belarus	20	2	1
Georgia	60	4	3+
Kazakhstan	60	4	3
Kyrgyzstan	60	4	3
Moldova	45	3+	3
Russia	70	4	3+
Tajikistan	30	3	2+
Turkmenistan	25	2	2−
Ukraine	55	3+	2+
Uzbekistan	45	3	3−

Data source. EBRD (2000).

6

Conclusions

In Chapter 1, I promised that in telling the story of representation through taxation I would provide answers to three questions. With my story now complete, it is time to revisit those questions and to summarize my answers.

What explains variation in the tax systems that evolved after communism? Variation in tax systems in Eastern Europe and the former Soviet Union is driven by variation in three initial conditions: the industrial structure inherited from communism, distance from the West, and the level of economic development at the beginning of the postcommunist transition. Countries that inherited from communism industrial structures heavily populated with large manufacturing enterprises, as reflected in highly energy-inefficient economies, displayed greater inertia, continuing to rely as in the communist era on enterprise taxation. Countries closer to the West structured their tax systems around those of the European Union, relying more on direct taxation of individuals and less on indirect taxation than their counterparts to the east. Finally, countries that were wealthier at the beginning of transition were considerably more likely to structure their tax systems around direct taxation of individuals.

Given the high correlation among these three initial conditions – relative to Eastern Europe, countries in the former Soviet Union are more heavily endowed with large manufacturing enterprises, further from the West, and poorer – two ideal types of tax systems emerged in the postcommunist world.[1] In the former Soviet Union, states continued to rely on "old" revenue sources: the enterprise taxation and indirect taxes that

[1] As in previous chapters, I follow convention by using "Eastern Europe" as shorthand for Eastern Europe and the Baltics and "former Soviet Union" to mean all post-Soviet states but Estonia, Latvia, and Lithuania.

formed the revenue base of communist economies. In contrast, in Eastern Europe, tax systems were built to capture revenue from "new" sources. This distinction was reflected in patterns of tax compliance among firms across the postcommunist world. In the former Soviet Union, officials focused especially on taxing the large monopolistic enterprises that they knew best, thus magnifying "natural" differences in the taxability of economic activity. Small firms in competitive industries, always hard to tax, found it especially easy to hide revenues from tax authorities. In contrast, in Eastern Europe the revenue net was cast more widely, such that there were fewer and smaller systematic differences in the tax compliance of firms.

Who did postcommunist politicians favor in the provision of collective goods and why? Politicians throughout the postcommunist world favored firms with greater capacity for collective action. In addition, however, politicians in the former Soviet Union – but not in Eastern Europe – were more inclined to provide collective goods to firms that were relatively easy to tax. Roughly speaking, firms in the former Soviet Union were more likely to receive collective goods from a variety of public agencies if they were large, monopolistic, and relatively tax compliant, whereas only size and monopoly status mattered for firms in Eastern Europe.

These divergent patterns of representation were a direct consequence of the different tax systems created in the two halves of the postcommunist world. The structuring of tax systems around "old" revenue sources in the former Soviet Union created perverse incentives for post-Soviet politicians to promote that which they knew how to tax. In contrast, politicians in Eastern Europe had little motivation to do so: the greater transformation of tax systems meant that systematic differences in the taxability of economic activity were fewer and smaller, and to the extent that such differences existed, they were less politically important due to the reduced reliance on enterprise taxation.

What are the consequences of variation in collective-goods provision for economic development in postcommunist states? Discriminated against in the provision of collective goods, new private economic activity in the former Soviet Union failed to take off as expected following privatization. In contrast, in Eastern Europe small-enterprise employment (roughly synonymous with new private economic activity in postcommunist countries) quickly approached levels typical for advanced market economies. In essence, new firms in the former Soviet Union had two strikes against them: not only did they find it harder to overcome their collective-action problems, but they were less important to politicians because they were poor sources of tax revenue. New firms in Eastern Europe suffered only the first of these disadvantages.

Post-Soviet countries were – and seemingly still are – caught in a "revenue trap." Politicians discriminated in the provision of collective goods in favor of sectors that were important revenue sources. Factor owners in turn chose to locate in favored sectors, thus reinforcing the incentive for politicians to discriminate in the provision of collective goods. This mutually reinforcing behavior survived the mass privatization of the 1990s, which was designed precisely to shake politicians out of their reliance on Soviet-era economic activity. The flaw in this design seems to have been the inability to foresee that postcommunist politicians would promote new private economic activity only to the extent that institutions guaranteed the political importance of the new economy. The tax systems created contemporaneously with mass privatization in the former Soviet Union provided no such guarantees.

A primary goal in telling the story of representation through taxation was to answer these questions. At the same time, I have attempted to show that the particular postcommunist experience provides a number of more general theoretical lessons. I now turn to the broader implications of those lessons, with suggestions for future research.

6.1 The Institutional Nature of State Capacity

In suggesting that taxation is central to the political economy of postcommunism, I have placed my work firmly within the Schumpeterian tradition of fiscal sociology (Schumpeter, 1991 [1918]).[2] For Schumpeter, the central fact of European history was the transition from the *demesne* state, in which revenues were derived from the ruler's own production, to the tax state, in which revenues were coerced from private economic actors. As owners of nearly all means of production, communist states were *demesne* states writ large. Revenue generation was little more than an accounting exercise, as funds were transferred from one account to another in the state monobank. This system unraveled with the economic liberalization and privatization of the early 1990s, and state actors were forced to quickly adopt means of taxation appropriate to a market economy.

---

[2] For recent reviews of work in this tradition, see Campbell (1993) and Moore (2004).

A key argument of this book is that postcommunist tax systems developed in systematic ways, assuming one form or another depending on the economic and geopolitical conditions present at the beginning of transition. Once in place, however, tax systems retained their shape. Both in the early and late 1990s, tax systems in Eastern Europe were structured around extraction of revenue from "new" revenue sources. Both in the early and late 1990s, tax systems in the former Soviet Union relied on "old" sources. As I have shown, the consequence of this difference in shape was sharply different patterns of collective-goods provision and economic development in the eastern and western halves of the postcommunist world.

Tax systems are institutions. In the long run they are endogenous, but because the cost of institutional change is high, they have an element of permanence that policy does not (Acemoglu and Robinson, 2000, 2001). A prime example is the Danegeld, a tax originally levied by Saxon kings on the population of England to fund protection against Danish tribes and that survived to form the foundation for the fiscal state inherited by the invading Normans three centuries later (e.g., Webber and Wildavsky, 1986). Given this permanence, in the short run tax systems, like other institutions, can be viewed as "humanly devised constraints" on the actions of political and economic actors (North, 1990) and so analytically may be treated as exogenous.[3]

This approach is in fact implicit in many formal models of policy choice, where policy is made subject to the constraint that taxes impose a deadweight loss or that economic actors exit to an "informal" sector if taxes are too high. In either case, the constraint can be thought to arise in part from the nature of tax systems, which provide the state with more or less fiscal capacity. Rarely, however, is the constraint the center of analysis. Rather, the important question of why governments are bigger in some countries than in others is answered by focusing on the institutions that aggregate individual preferences (e.g., Persson and Tabellini, 2000, 2005).[4] Yet intuitively it seems that differences across countries in the ability to tax different types of economic activity may be at least as large as differences in formal political institutions. A richer theory of policy choice would focus much more on this variation.[5]

---

[3] For a discussion of these complementary approaches to the study of institutions, see Shepsle (1986) and Weingast (2002).

[4] An important and recent exception is Besley and Persson (2007).

[5] This perspective has echoes in a recent literature on policy credibility in democracies, where it is argued that informal institutions that raise the cost of reneging on campaign

Conclusions

More generally, any state capacity – the ability of state actors to gather information and implement policies of their choice – is institutional in nature. Political, economic, and social constraints can discourage state actors from developing such capacity, even when greater capacity is efficient (e.g., Migdal, 1988; Geddes, 1994; Huber and McCarty, 2004). Yet the world changes, and politicians may find themselves wishing that they had invested in state capacity when they had the chance. Politicians are thus forced to react to events with the state they have rather than the one they would have preferred had they known what awaited them.

The contribution of the theoretical discussion in Chapter 3 was to show how such institutions affect bargaining over policy between politicians and organized interests. Politicians value contributions from organized interests, but they also care about the "noncontractible" behavior of both organized and unorganized groups that falls outside of the bargaining relationship. Critically, this behavior depends not only on characteristics of these groups but also on the capacity of the state to enforce compliance with policy. When the state is weak, or is weak in some areas but strong in others, then differences across groups in anticipated compliance may be large. In such environments, the most important determinant of policy choice may not be the organization of interests but variation across groups in the cost of noncompliance.

My focus in Chapter 3 was on taxation and the provision of collective goods, but the lesson is general. For example, regulators may value large over small firms not just because large firms are better organized but because it is easier to gauge their regulatory compliance (Carpenter, 2004). Depending on the context, other factors may also play a role. The public furor in early 2006 over the proposed transfer of operations at several U.S. ports to Dubai Ports World is a case in point. Not lacking for friends in Washington, Dubai Ports World nonetheless was forced to back down given the popular belief that a state-owned Arab company would be less compliant with laws and regulations governing U.S. port security than would an American or British owner. Although undoubtedly colored by prejudice, the public reaction might have been muted had concerns not already been raised about the capacity of U.S. authorities to secure port operations (e.g., General Accounting Office, 2002, 2004). The constant refrain

promises may matter at least as much as formal institutions of preference aggregation. See, for example, Robinson and Verdier (2002); Gehlbach, Sonin, and Zhuravskaya (2007); Keefer (2007); and Keefer and Vlaicu (2008).

that "our port security today and our port security tomorrow will remain exactly the same as was the case prior to any of these transactions" did little to calm the situation.[6] On the contrary, it merely highlighted that state institutions do not turn on a dime, thus focusing attention on the question of which company would be allowed to operate with a given level of oversight.

The story of Dubai Ports World illustrates that perceptions of non-compliance can trump "normal" politics – policy choice governed largely by what organized groups can credibly promise – even in countries with generally strong states. In developing countries, where states are typically weak, such bias can be extreme. State capacity may be concentrated in particular policy arenas, economic sectors, and geographic areas, such that some actors feel compelled to do what is politically valuable while others do not. In such environments, adapting policy to existing state capacity may be easier than altering the boundaries of the state.

This perspective suggests that the movement of theory between the study of developed and developing countries may have been too one-directional in recent years. With the opening of previously closed societies in the second and third worlds, many scholars of these countries have looked to the literature on policy choice in democracies for insights. That work, however, was largely developed in the study of mature democracies in wealthy countries, where the constraints of state capacity are not typically so overwhelming as they are in the developing world. As discussed above, in many developing countries policy may be determined in the short run more by these constraints than by other institutional features. At the same time, even developed countries face limits in policy implementation, especially when there is little history of intervention in some policy arena. For the analysis of such situations, the traditional emphasis on state capacity in the study of developing countries may be insightful.

6.2 The Political Consequences of Exit

The theoretical perspective in this book emphasizes a bargaining relationship between politicians and firms, where the nature of bargaining is affected by the ability of firms to "exit" from the relationship by hiding a portion of the gains from collective-goods provision. A central argument is that politicians may have fewer incentives to provide sector-specific collective

[6] Clay Lowery, Assistant Secretary of the Treasury for International Affairs, NewsHour with Jim Lehrer, February 21, 2006. Transcript available at www.pbs.org/newshour.

goods when the possibility of such exit is large. Easy exit from tax obligations implies that that the state's return on investments in collective goods is small, encouraging politicians who care about tax revenue to expend scarce resources elsewhere. As a consequence, firms may be more poorly represented, that is, may fare worse in the competition for resources, than would be the case if they found it harder to hide revenues from the state.

This argument differs sharply from many other accounts of the consequences of exit. In canonical bargaining models, bargaining power increases with the value of an outside option, that is, with the possibility of exit (e.g., Osborne and Rubinstein, 1990). This mechanism drives standard models of fiscal federalism, with the incentive of politicians to efficiently provide public goods stronger when public-goods provision is decentralized and labor and capital can easily exit to other jurisdictions (e.g., Tiebout, 1956; Brennan and Buchanan, 1980; Rubinfeld, 1987; Hoyt, 1990; Weingast, 1995). Similarly, reductions in the cost of moving labor and capital across national boundaries is argued to result in greater representation for factor owners (e.g., Bates and Lien, 1985; Milner and Keohane, 1996; Rogowski, 1998; Boix, 2003; Acemoglu and Robinson, 2006). Analogous effects appear in models of intergovernmental relations, with the utility of subnational units greater when the possibility of exit through secession is large (e.g., Treisman, 1999a; de Figuieredo and Weingast, 2005; see, however, Bednar, 2007).

How can these conflicting perspectives be reconciled? When does the possibility of exit reduce representation, and when does it increase it? Conceptually, the key distinction is between cases where one party's concessions discourage another from exiting and those where they do not. The traditional perspective emphasizes the first set of cases. Factor owners are assumed to be responsive to differences across jurisdictions in the provision of collective goods, much as subnational units are assumed to weigh concessions by the center in deciding whether to secede. In such environments, the possibility of exit improves representation.

In contrast, my primary focus in this book is on the second set of cases: the decision of firms to exit by hiding revenues from tax authorities depends little on the provision of sector-specific collective goods, as those goods are available to firms that hide as well as those that do not.[7]

---

[7] As I discuss in Chapter 4, the alternative assumption that firms that hide lose access to sector-specific collective goods is inconsistent with patterns of collective-goods provision observed in the data.

Consequently, politicians respond to exit by providing fewer collective goods: there is no point in wasting scarce resources on firms that are going to exit from their tax obligations anyway. Interestingly, as Cai and Treisman (2005) show, a similar argument may apply to interjurisdictional competition if one assumes that some jurisdictions are better endowed (e.g., with natural resources or human capital) than others. When differences in such endowments are large, investors may be inclined to exit poorly endowed jurisdictions regardless of government policy, with the consequence that governments in poorly endowed jurisdictions expend little effort encouraging them to stay.

The model of revenue traps in Chapter 5 incorporates each of the two cases. As in the traditional perspective, factor owners are responsive to differences across sectors in the provision of collective goods, reacting to relatively poor provision in one sector by exiting to the other. But as in the bargaining model of Chapter 3, factor owners can also practice a form of "internal exit," escaping their tax obligations while remaining invested in a sector. The key insight of the model of revenue traps is that large differences across sectors in the possibility of internal exit may discourage politicians from responding to exit from one sector to another. In the particular case I examine, privatization – designed to provoke an exit by factor owners from "old" to "new" economic activity and so to encourage politicians to support new private firms – did not have the desired effect, as the comparative ease with which new private firms hid revenues from the state discouraged politicians from providing the collective goods necessary for those firms to flourish.

As these examples suggest, arguments about the political consequences of exit can be quite sensitive to the particular assumptions made about the responsiveness of those with the exit option to whatever those in power can provide. A more fully elaborated theory of exit would take seriously this sensitivity, exploring the relationship between exit and representation under alternative assumptions about the determinants of exit. Given the large number of substantive areas in which arguments about exit are central, the opportunity for further theoretical insights seems large.

6.3 A Post-Olsonian Political Economy

Mancur Olson's *The Logic of Collective Action* was first published in 1965. Its initial impact on the study of politics was moderate. For the first decade after its publication, references in political science journals to

Conclusions

A. F. Bentley's *The Process of Government* (Bentley, 1908) – the seminal work of the pluralist tradition that Olson sought to destroy – rivaled those to Olson's monograph. But when it eventually caught on in the 1970s, *The Logic of Collective Action* "blew up a lot of buildings" (McLean, 2000).[8] Olson did more than show that group interest is not synonymous with group action. He created the impression, now treated as self-evident by many within the social sciences, that public policy necessarily favors those groups that manage to overcome their collective-action problems.

In this book I have attempted to chip away at this impression. True, organized interests – often small groups with concentrated benefits from collective action, as Olson described – are in a position to offer various inducements in return for favorable policy treatment. But they may not be able to credibly promise that in exchange for such treatment they will provide what politicians most desire: that members of the group will pay their taxes, comply with environmental law, or take any of a variety of other actions that must be carried out by individual members subsequent to agreement between organized groups and policy makers. As I have shown, the consequence of this lack of credibility is that unorganized groups may benefit at the expense of organized ones, not because they are more numerous (the pluralist fallacy) but because members of unorganized groups share characteristics that make it in their self-interest to do what is politically valuable. Alternatively, organized groups may benefit at the expense of unorganized ones, not because they are organized (the Olsonian fallacy) but because of what they would do regardless of whether they were organized.

I like to think that Mancur Olson would approve. After all, it is very much in the Olsonian tradition to emphasize that group members act out of individual rather than group interest. In this sense, there is more continuity between my argument and Olson's than between Olson's and the pluralist tradition he supplanted. The difference is one of perspective. Olson was interested in what happens prior to reaching the bargaining table (see also Dixit and Olson, 2000). I am more concerned with what comes after. Considered jointly, these two perspectives can contribute to a new, post-Olsonian political economy.

---

[8] In a JSTOR search of political science journals in July 2006, I found 178 articles containing the terms "Bentley" and "The Process of Government," 40 of which were published between 1966 and 1975 and 80 of which were published after 1975. In an analogous search for the terms "Olson" and "The Logic of Collective Action," I found 603 articles, 74 published between 1966 and 1975 and the remainder thereafter.

Bibliography

Acemoglu, Daron. 2005. "Politics and Economics in Weak and Strong States." *Journal of Monetary Economics* 52(7):1199–1226.

Acemoglu, Daron, and James A. Robinson. 2000. "Why Did the West Expand the Franchise? Growth, Inequality and Democracy in Historical Perspective." *Quarterly Journal of Economics* 115(4):1167–1199.

Acemoglu, Daron, and James A. Robinson. 2001. "A Theory of Political Transitions." *American Economic Review* 91(4):938–963.

Acemoglu, Daron, and James A. Robinson. 2006. *Economic Origins of Dictatorship and Democracy*. Cambridge: Cambridge University Press.

Acemoglu, Daron, Simon Johnson, and James A. Robinson. 2001. "The Colonial Origins of Comparative Development: An Empirical Investigation." *American Economic Review* 91(5):1369–1401.

Acemoglu, Daron, Simon Johnson, and James A. Robinson. 2002. "Reversal of Fortune: Geography and Institutions in the Making of the Modern World Income Distribution." *Quarterly Journal of Economics* 117(4):1231–1294.

Adolph, Christopher. 2004. "The Dilemma of Discretion: Career Ambitions and the Politics of Central Banking." Ph.D. dissertation, Harvard University.

Adolph, Christopher. 2005. "Three Simple Tests of Career Influences on Monetary Policy." Unpublished manuscript.

Aitken, Brian. 2001. "Falling Tax Compliance and the Rise of the Virtual Budget in Russia." *IMF Staff Papers* 48(Special Issue):180–208.

Alam, Asad, and Arup Banerji. 2000. "Uzbekistan and Kazakhstan: A Tale of Two Transition Paths." World Bank Policy Research Working Paper 2472.

Alexseev, Mikhail A., and Vladimir Vagin. 1999. "Russian Regions in Expanding Europe: The Pskov Connection." *Europe-Asia Studies* 51(1):43–64.

Alt, James E. 1983. "The Evolution of Tax Structures." *Public Choice* 41(1):181–222.

Alt, James E., and Michael J. Gilligan. 1994. "The Political Economy of Trading States." *Journal of Political Philosophy* 2(2):165–192.

Appel, Hilary B. 2006. "International Imperatives and Tax Reform: Lessons from Postcommunist Europe." *Comparative Politics* 39(1):43–62.

Arthur, Brian. 1994. *Increasing Returns and Path Dependence in the Economy*. Ann Arbor: University of Michigan Press.

Åslund, Anders. 1995. *How Russia Became a Market Economy*. Washington, DC: Brookings Institution.

Åslund, Anders. 2002. *Building Capitalism: The Transformation of the Soviet Bloc*. Cambridge: Cambridge University Press.

Balcerowicz, Leszek. 1994. "Understanding Postcommunist Transitions." *Journal of Democracy* 5(4):75–89.

Barbone, Luca, and Domenico Marchetti, Jr. 1995. "Transition and the Fiscal Crisis in Central Europe." *Economics of Transition* 3(1):59–74.

Bates, Robert H. 1981. *Markets and States in Tropical Africa: The Political Basis of Agricultural Policies*. Berkeley: University of California Press.

Bates, Robert H. 1989. A Political Scientist Looks at Tax Reform. In *Tax Reform in Developing Countries*, ed. Malcolm Gillis. Durham, NC: Duke University Press.

Bates, Robert H., and Da-Hsiang Lien. 1985. "A Note on Taxation, Development, and Representative Government." *Politics and Society* 14(1):53–70.

Batra, Geeta, Daniel Kaufmann, and Andrew H. W. Stone. 2003. *Investment Climate around the World: Voices of the Firms from the World Business Environment Survey*. Washington, DC: World Bank.

Baturo, Alexander, and Julia Gray. 2006. "Flatliners: The Role of Diffusion and Ideology in the Flat Tax Revolution in Eastern Europe." Paper presented at the 2006 annual meeting of the Midwest Political Science Association.

Beck, Nathaniel. 2001. "Time-Series-Cross-Section Data: What Have We Learned in the Past Few Years?" *Annual Review of Political Science* 4:271–293.

Bednar, Jenna. 2007. "Valuing Exit Options." *Publius: The Journal of Federalism* 37(2):190–208.

Bentley, Arthur F. 1908. *The Process of Government*. Chicago: University of Chicago Press.

Berenson, Marc P. 2006a. "Re-Creating the State: Governance and Power in Poland and Russia." Ph.D. dissertation, Princeton University.

Berenson, Marc P. 2006b. "Tax Messages to the State: Deciphering the Whys of Ukrainian Tax Compliance in Comparison to Poland and Russia." Paper presented at the 2006 annual meeting of the American Political Science Association.

Berglof, Erik, and Patrick Bolton. 2002. "The Great Divide and Beyond: Financial Architecture in Transition." *Journal of Economic Perspectives* 16(1):77–100.

Berkowitz, Daniel, and Wei Li. 2000. "Tax Rights in Transition Economies: A Tragedy of the Commons?" *Journal of Public Economics* 76(3):369–398.

Bernheim, Douglas B., and Michael D. Whinston. 1986. "Menu Auctions, Resource Allocation, and Economic Influence." *Quarterly Journal of Economics* 101(1):1–31.

Bernstein, Marver H. 1955. *Regulating Business by Independent Commission*. Princeton, NJ: Princeton University Press.

Besley, Timothy, and Stephen Coate. 2003. "Centralized versus Decentralized Provision of Local Public Goods: A Political Economy Approach." *Journal of Public Economics* 87(12):2611–2637.

Besley, Timothy, and Torsten Persson. 2007. "The Origins of State Capacity: Property Rights, Taxation, and Politics." NBER Working Paper No. 13028.

Bird, Richard M. 2006. VAT in Ukraine: An Interim Report. In *Taxation and Public Finance in Transition and Developing Countries*, ed. Robert W. McGee. New York: Springer.

Blanchard, Olivier, and Andrei Shleifer. 2001. "Federalism With and Without Political Centralization: China versus Russia." *IMF Staff Papers* 48(Special Issue):171–179.

Bogetic, Zeljko, and Arye L. Hillman. 1994. "The Tax Base in Transition: The Case of Bulgaria." World Bank Policy Research Working Paper 1267.

Boix, Carles. 2003. *Democracy and Redistribution*. Cambridge: Cambridge University Press.

Boycko, Maxim, Andrei Shleifer, and Robert W. Vishny. 1995. *Privatizing Russia*. Cambridge, MA: MIT Press.

Brady, Henry E., Sidney Verba, and Kay Lehman Schlozman. 1995. "Beyond SES: A Resource Model of Political Participation." *American Political Science Review* 89(2):271–294.

Brennan, Geoffrey, and James M. Buchanan. 1980. *The Power to Tax: Analytical Foundations of a Fiscal Constitution*. Cambridge: Cambridge University Press.

Brown, Annette N., Barry W. Ickes, and Randi Ryterman. 1994. "The Myth of Monopoly: A New View of Industrial Structure in Russia." World Bank Policy Research Working Paper.

Brown, J. David, and John S. Earle. 2003. "The Reallocation of Workers and Jobs in Russian Industry: New Evidence on Measures and Determinants." *Economics of Transition* 11(2):221–252.

Brown, J. David, and John S. Earle. 2006. "Job Reallocation and Productivity Growth in the Ukrainian Transition." *Comparative Economic Studies* 48(2):229–251.

Brown, J. David, John S. Earle, and Álmos Telegdy. 2004. "Does Privatization Raise Productivity? Evidence from Comprehensive Panel Data on Manufacturing Firms in Hungary, Romania, Russia, and Ukraine." Upjohn Institute Staff Working Paper 04-107.

Brown, J. David, John S. Earle, and Álmos Telegdy. 2006. "The Productivity Effects of Privatization: Longitudinal Estimates from Hungary, Romania, Russia, and Ukraine." *Journal of Political Economy* 114(1):61–99.

Bueno de Mesquita, Ethan, and Catherine Hafer. 2008. "Public Protection and Private Extortion." *Economics and Politics* 20(1):1–32.

Bunce, Valerie. 1999. *Subversive Institutions: The Design and Destruction of Socialism and the State*. Cambridge: Cambridge University Press.

Cai, Hongbin, and Daniel Treisman. 2004. "State-Corroding Federalism." *Journal of Public Economics* 88(3–4):819–843.

Cai, Hongbin, and Daniel Treisman. 2005. "Does Competition for Capital Discipline Governments? Decentralization, Globalization, and Public Policy." *American Economic Review* 95(3):817–830.

Campbell, John L. 1993. "The State and Fiscal Sociology." *Annual Review of Sociology* 19:163–185.

Carpenter, Daniel P. 2004. "Protection without Capture: Product Approval by a Politically Responsive, Learning Regulator." *American Political Science Review* 98(4):613–631.

CEFIR, and World Bank. 2002. "Monitoring of Administrative Barriers to Small Business Development in Russia." CEFIR manuscript.

Centre of Social Projecting Vozrozhdeniye. 2003. "Influence of the European Trans-Boundary Co-operation on the Regional Economic Development of Pskov Oblast." Centre of Social Projecting Vozrozhdeniye, Pskov.

Chamberlin, John. 1974. "Provision of Collective Goods as a Function of Group Size." *American Political Science Review* 68(2):707–716.

Chaudhry, Kiren Aziz. 1997. *The Price of Wealth: Economies and Institutions in the Middle East*. Ithaca, NY: Cornell University Press.

Cheasty, Adrienne. 1996. "The Revenue Decline in the Countries of the Former Soviet Union." *Finance and Development* June:32–35.

Cheibub, Joeé Antonio. 1998. "Political Regimes and the Extractive Capacity of Governments: Taxation in Democracies and Dictatorships." *World Politics* 50(3):349–376.

Clement, Cynthia, and Peter Murrell. 2001. Assessing the Value of Law in Transition Economies: An Introduction. In *Assessing the Value of Law in Transition Economies*, ed. Peter Murrell. Ann Arbor: University of Michigan Press.

Coase, Ronald. 1937. "The Nature of the Firm." *Economica* 4(16):386–405.

Coates, Dennis, and Jac C. Heckelman. 2003. "Interest Groups and Investment: A Further Test of the Olson Hypothesis." *Public Choice* 117(3–4):333–340.

Collier, Ruth Berins, and David Collier. 1991. *Shaping the Political Arena: Critical Junctures, the Labor Movement, and Regime Dynamics in Latin America*. Princeton, NJ: Princeton University Press.

Colton, Timothy J., and Stephen Holmes, eds. 2006. *The State after Communism: Governance in the New Russia*. Lanham, MD: Rowman & Littlefield.

Darden, Keith, and Anna Grzymala-Busse. 2006. "The Great Divide: Pre-communist Schooling and Post-communist Trajectories." Paper presented at the Duke Workshop on Post-Communist Political Economy and Domestic Politics.

David, Paul. 1985. "Clio and the Economics of QWERTY." *American Economic Review* 75(2):332–337.

de Figueiredo, Rui, and Barry R. Weingast. 2005. "Self-Enforcing Federalism." *Journal of Law, Economics, and Organization* 21(1):103–135.

de Melo, Martha, Cevdet Denizer, Alan Gelb, and Stoyan Tenev. 2001. "Circumstance and Choice: The Role of Initial Conditions and Policies in Transition Economies." *World Bank Economic Review* 15(1):1–31.

de Soto, Hernando. 1990. *The Other Path*. New York: Harper & Row.

Dixit, Avinash. 2004. *Lawlessness and Economics: Alternative Modes of Governance*. Princeton, NJ: Princeton University Press.

Dixit, Avinash, and Mancur Olson. 2000. "Does Voluntary Participation Undermine the Coase Theorem?" *Journal of Public Economics* 76(3):309–335.

Djankov, Simeon, and Peter Murrell. 2002. "Enterprise Restructuring in Transition: A Quantitative Survey." *Journal of Economic Literature* 40(3):739–792.

Earle, John S., and Scott Gehlbach. 2003. "A Spoonful of Sugar: Privatization and Popular Support for Reform in the Czech Republic." *Economics and Politics* 15(1):1–32.

Easter, Gerald. 2002*a*. "Politics of Revenue Extraction in Post-Communist States: Poland and Russia Compared." *Politics and Society* 30(4):599–627.

Easter, Gerald. 2002*b*. "The Russian Tax Police." *Post-Soviet Affairs* 18(4):332–362.

Easter, Gerald. 2006*a*. Building Fiscal Capacity. In *The State after Communism: Governance in the New Russia*, ed. Timothy J. Colton and Stephen Holmes. Lanham, MD: Rowman & Littlefield.

Easter, Gerald. 2006*b*. "Capital, Coercion and Post-Communist States." Unpublished book manuscript.

EBRD. 2000. *Transition Report 2000: Employment, Skills and Transition*. London: European Bank for Reconstruction and Development.

Ebrill, Liam, and Oleh Havrylyshyn. 1999. "Tax Reform in the Baltics, Russia, and Other Countries of the Former Soviet Union." IMF Occasional Paper No. 182.

Engelschalk, Michael. 2004. Creating a Favorable Tax Environment for Small Business. In *Taxing the Hard-to-Tax: Lessons from Theory and Practice*, ed. James Alm, Jorge Martinez-Vazquez, and Sally Wallace. Amsterdam: Elsevier.

Engerman, Stanley L., and Kenneth L. Sokoloff. 1997. Factor Endowments, Institutions, and Differential Paths of Growth among New World Economies: A View from Economic Historians of the United States. In *How Latin America Fell Behind*, ed. Stephen Haber. Stanford, CA: Stanford University Press.

Engerman, Stanley L., and Kenneth L. Sokoloff. 2000. "Institutions, Factor Endowments, and Paths of Development in the New World." *Journal of Economic Perspectives* 14(3):217–232.

Fearon, James D., and David D. Laitin. 2003. "Ethnicity, Insurgency, and Civil War." *American Political Science Review* 97(1):75–90.

Feld, Lars P., and Bruno S. Frey. 2002. "Trust Breeds Trust: How Taxpayers Are Treated." *Economics of Governance* 3(2):87–99.

Feld, Lars P., and Bruno S. Frey. 2007. Tax Evasion in Switzerland: The Roles of Deterrence and Tax Morale. In *Tax Evasion, Trust, and State Capacity*, ed. Nicolas Hayoz and Simon Hug. Bern, Switzerland: Peter Lang.

Fidrmuc, Jan. 2000*a*. "Economics of Voting in Post-Communist Countries." *Electoral Studies* 19(2/3):199–217.

Fidrmuc, Jan. 2000*b*. "Political Support for Reforms: Economics of Voting in Transition Countries." *European Economic Review* 44(8):1491–1513.

Fischer, Stanley, and Alan Gelb. 1991. "The Process of Socialist Economic Transformation." *Journal of Economic Perspectives* 5(4):91–105.

Fish, M. Steven. 1998. "The Determinants of Economic Reform in the Post-Communist World." *East European Politics and Societies* 12(1):31–78.

Fish, M. Steven. 2005. *Democracy Derailed in Russia: The Failure of Open Politics*. Cambridge: Cambridge University Press.

Franzese, Jr., Robert J. 2002. *Macroeconomic Policies of Developed Democracies.* Cambridge: Cambridge University Press.

Frieden, Jeffrey A. 1992. *Debt, Development, and Democracy.* Princeton, NJ: Princeton University Press.

Frohlich, Norman, and Joe A. Oppenheimer. 1970. "I Get by with a Little Help from My Friends." *World Politics* 23(1):104–120.

Frydman, Roman, and Andrzej Rapaczynski. 1994. *Privatization in Eastern Europe: Is the State Withering Away?* Budapest: CEU Press.

Frye, Timothy. 1997. Russian Privatization and the Limits of Credible Commitment. In *The Political Economy of Property Rights: Institutional Change and Credibility in the Reform of Centrally Planned Economies*, ed. David L. Weimer. Cambridge: Cambridge University Press.

Frye, Timothy. 2002*a*. "Capture or Exchange? Business Lobbying in Russia." *Europe-Asia Studies* 54(7):1017–1036.

Frye, Timothy. 2002*b*. "Private Protection in Russia and Poland." *American Journal of Political Science* 46(3):572–584.

Frye, Timothy. 2004. "Credible Commitment and Property Rights: Evidence from Russia." *American Political Science Review* 98(3):453–466.

Frye, Timothy, and Andrei Shleifer. 1997. "The Invisible Hand and the Grabbing Hand." *American Economic Review* 87(2):354–358.

Frye, Timothy, and Ekaterina Zhuravskaya. 2000. "Rackets, Regulation and the Rule of Law." *The Journal of Law, Economics, and Organization* 16(2):478–502.

Gaddy, Clifford G., and Barry W. Ickes. 1998. "Russia's Virtual Economy." *Foreign Affairs* 77(5):53–67.

Gaddy, Clifford G., and Barry W. Ickes. 2002. *Russia's Virtual Economy.* Washington, DC: Brookings Institution Press.

Gaidar, Yegor. 1999. *Days of Defeat and Victory.* Seattle: University of Washington Press.

Garrett, Geoffrey. 1998. *Partisan Politics in the Global Economy.* Cambridge: Cambridge University Press.

Geddes, Barbara. 1994. *Politician's Dilemma: Building State Capacity in Latin America.* Berkeley: University of California Press.

Gehlbach, Scott. 2003. "Taxability and State Support of Economic Activity." Ph.D. dissertation, UC Berkeley.

Gehlbach, Scott. 2007. "Electoral Institutions and the National Provision of Local Public Goods." *Quarterly Journal of Political Science* 2(1):5–25.

Gehlbach, Scott, Konstantin Sonin, and Ekaterina Zhuravskaya. 2007. "Businessman Candidates." Unpublished manuscript.

General Accounting Office. 2002. "Port Security: Nation Faces Formidable Challenges in Making New Initiatives Successful." Testimony before the Subcommittee on National Security, Veterans Affairs, and International Relations, House Committee on Government Reform, GAO-02-993T.

General Accounting Office. 2004. "Maritime Security: Substantial Work Remains to Translate New Planning Requirements into Effective Port Security." Report to Congressional Requesters, GAO-04-838.

Gordon, Roger, and Wei Li. 2005. "Puzzling Tax Structures in Developing Countries: A Comparison of Two Alternative Explanations." NBER Working Paper No. 11661.

Gould, Andrew C. 2001. "Party Size and Policy Outcomes: An Empirical Analysis of Taxation in Democracies." *Studies in Comparative International Development* 36(2):3–26.

Grafe, Clemens, and Kaspar Richter. 2001. Taxation and Public Expenditure. In *Russia's Post-Communist Economy*, ed. Brigitte Granville and Peter Oppenheimer. Oxford: Oxford University Press.

Greif, Avner. 2006. *Institutions and the Path to the Modern Economy*. Cambridge: Cambridge University Press.

Grier, Kevin B., Michael C. Munger, and Brian E. Roberts. 1994. "The Determinants of Industrial Political Activity, 1978–1986." *American Political Science Review* 88(4):911–926.

Grossman, Gene M., and Elhanan Helpman. 1994. "Protection for Sale." *American Economic Review* 84(4):833–850.

Grossman, Gene M., and Elhanan Helpman. 2001. *Special Interest Politics*. Cambridge, MA: MIT Press.

Grossman, Sanford, and Oliver Hart. 1986. "The Costs and Benefits of Ownership: A Theory of Lateral and Vertical Integration." *Journal of Political Economy* 94(4):691–719.

Grzymala-Busse, Anna, and Pauline Jones Luong. 2002. "Reconceptualizing the State: Lessons from Post-Communism." *Politics and Society* 30(4):529–554.

Guriev, Sergei. 2004. "Red Tape and Corruption." *Journal of Development Economics* 73(2):489–504.

Guriev, Sergei, and Andrei Rachinsky. 2005. "The Role of Oligarchs in Russian Capitalism." *Journal of Economic Perspectives* 19(1):131–150.

Guriev, Sergei, Igor Makarov, and Mathilde Maurel. 2002. "Debt Overhang and Barter in Russia." *Journal of Comparative Economics* 30(4):635–656.

Gustafson, Thane. 1999. *Capitalism Russian-Style*. Cambridge: Cambridge University Press.

Haber, Stephen, Armando Razo, and Noel Maurer. 2003. *The Politics of Property Rights: Political Instability, Credible Commitments, and Economic Growth in Mexico, 1876–1929*. Cambridge: Cambridge University Press.

Haggard, Stephan. 1990. *Pathways from the Periphery: The Politics of Growth in the Newly Industrialized Countries*. Ithaca, NY: Cornell University Press.

Hainsworth, Richard, and William Tompson. 2002. "Tax Policy and Tax Administration in Russia: The Case of the Banking Sector." *Post-Communist Economies* 14(3):277–300.

Hanousek, Jan, and Filip Palda. 2003. Why People Evade Taxes in the Czech and Slovak Republics: A Tale of Twins. In *The Informal Economy in the EU Accession Countries: Size, Scope, Trends and Challenges to the Process of EU Enlargement*, ed. Boyan Belev. Sofia: Center for the Study of Democracy.

Hanson, Steven E. 2001. Defining Democratic Consolidation. In *Postcommunism and the Theory of Democracy*, ed. Richard D. Anderson, Jr., M. Steven Fish,

Stephen E. Hanson, and Philip G. Roeder. Princeton, NJ: Princeton University Press.

Hardin, Russell. 1982. *Collective Action*. Baltimore, MD: Resources for the Future, Johns Hopkins University Press.

Hart, Oliver, and John Moore. 1990. "Property Rights and the Nature of the Firm." *Journal of Political Economy* 98(6):1119–1158.

Havrylyshyn, Oleh, and Donald McGettigan. 2000. "Privatization in Transition Countries." *Post-Soviet Affairs* 16(3):257–286.

Hellman, Joel S. 1998. "Winners Take All: The Politics of Partial Reform in Postcommunist Transitions." *World Politics* 50(2):203–234.

Hellman, Joel S., Geraint Jones, and Daniel Kaufmann. 2000. "'Seize the State, Seize the Day': State Capture, Corruption, and Influence in Transition." World Bank Policy Research Working Paper No. 2444.

Hellman, Joel S., Geraint Jones, Daniel Kaufmann, and Mark Schankerman. 2000. "Measuring Governance, Corruption, and State Capture: How Firms and Bureaucrats Shape the Business Environment in Transition Economies." World Bank Policy Research Working Paper No. 2312.

Hendley, Kathryn, Barry W. Ickes, and Randi Ryterman. 1998. Remonetizing the Russian Economy. In *Russian Enterprise Reform: Policies to Further the Transition*, ed. Harry Broadman. Washington, DC: World Bank.

Hendley, Kathryn, and Peter Murrell. 2003. "Which Mechanisms Support the Fulfillment of Sales Agreements? Asking Decision-Makers in Firms." *Economics Letters* 78:49–54.

Hendley, Kathryn, Peter Murrell, and Randi Ryterman. 2000. "Law, Relationships and Private Enforcement: Transactional Strategies of Russian Enterprises." *Europe-Asia Studies* 52(4):627–656.

Herlihy, Patricia. 2002. *The Alcoholic Empire: Vodka & Politics in Late Imperial Russia*. Oxford: Oxford University Press.

Herrera, Yoshiko M. 2004. "The 2002 Russian Census: Institutional Reform at Goskomstat." *Post-Soviet Affairs* 20(4):350–386.

Herrera, Yoshiko M. Forthcoming. *Transforming Bureaucracy: Conditional Norms and the International Standardization of Statistics in Russia*. Ithaca, NY: Cornell University Press.

Honaker, James, Jonathan N. Katz, and Gary King. 2002. "A Fast, Easy, and Efficient Estimator for Multiparty Electoral Data." *Political Analysis* 10(1):84–100.

Hoyt, William H. 1990. "Local Government Inefficiency and the Tiebout Hypothesis: Does Competition among Municipalities Limit Local Government Inefficiency?" *Southern Economic Journal* 57(2):481–496.

Huber, John D., and Nolan McCarty. 2004. "Bureaucratic Capacity, Delegation, and Political Reform." *American Political Science Review* 98(3):481–494.

Jackson, John E. 2002. "A Seemingly Unrelated Regression Model for Analyzing Multiparty Elections." *Political Analysis* 10(1):49–65.

Jackson, John E. 2003. A Computational Political Economy Model of Transition. In *Political Economy of Transition and Development: Institutions, Politics and Policies*, ed. Nauro F. Campos and Jan Fidrmuc. Norwell, MA: Kluwer Academic.

Jackson, John E., Jacek Klich, and Krystyna Poznańska. 2005. *The Political Economy of Poland's Transition: New Firms and Reform Governments*. Cambridge: Cambridge University Press.

Janos, Andrew. 2002. *East Central Europe in the Modern World: Political Change in the Borderlands from Pre- to Post-Communism*. Stanford: Stanford University Press.

Johnson, Simon, Daniel Kaufmann, and Andrei Shleifer. 1997. "The Unofficial Economy in Transition." *Brookings Papers on Economic Activity* 1997(2):159–221.

Johnson, Simon, Daniel Kaufmann, John McMillan, and Christopher Woodruff. 2000. "Why Do Firms Hide? Bribes and Unofficial Activity Under Communism." *Journal of Public Economics* 76(3):495–520.

Johnson, Simon, John McMillan, and Christopher Woodruff. 2000. "Entrepreneurs and the Ordering of Institutional Reform: Poland, Slovakia, Romania, Russia and Ukraine Compared." *Economics of Transition* 8(1):1–36.

Johnson, Simon, John McMillan, and Christopher Woodruff. 2002. "Courts and Relational Contracts." *Journal of Law, Economics, and Organization* 18(1):221–277.

Jones Luong, Pauline, and Erika Weinthal. 2004. "Contra Coercion: Russian Tax Reform, Exogenous Shocks, and Negotiated Institutional Change." *American Political Science Review* 98(1):139–152.

Jowitt, Ken. 1992. The Leninist Legacy. In *New World Disorder: The Leninist Extinction*. Berkeley: University of California Press.

Juurikkala, Tuuli, and Olga Lazareva. 2006. "Lobbying at the Local Level: Social Assets in Russian Firms." Bank of Finland Institute for Economies in Transition Working Paper No. 1/2006.

Karl, Terry Lynn. 1997. *The Paradox of Plenty: Oil Booms and Petro-States*. Berkeley: University of California Press.

Katz, Jonathan N., and Gary King. 1999. "A Statistical Model for Multiparty Electoral Data." *American Political Science Review* 93(1):15–32.

Keefer, Philip. 2007. "Clientelism, Credibility, and the Policy Choices of Young Democracies." *American Journal of Political Science* 51(4):804–821.

Keefer, Philip, and Razvan Vlaicu. 2008. "Democracy, Credibility, and Clientelism." *Journal of Law, Economics, and Organization*. Forthcoming.

King, Gary, Michael Tomz, and Jason Wittenberg. 2000. "Making the Most of Statistical Analysis." *American Journal of Political Science* 44(2):347–361.

Kireyev, Alexei. 2006. "The Macroeconomics of Remittances: The Case of Tajikistan." IMF Working Paper 06/2.

Kitschelt, Herbert. 2003. Accounting for Postcommunist Regime Diversity: What Counts as a Good Cause? In *Capitalism and Democracy in Central and Eastern Europe: Assessing the Legacy of Communist Rule*, ed. Grzegorz Ekiert and Stephen E. Hanson. Cambridge: Cambridge University Press.

Klaus, Václav. 1994. *Rebirth of a Country: Five Years After*. Prague: Ringier.

Klein, Benjamin, Robert Crawford, and Armen Alchian. 1978. "Vertical Integration, Appropriable Rents, and the Competitive Contracting Process." *Journal of Law, Economics, and Organization* 21(2):297–326.

Knack, Stephen, and Philip Keefer. 1995. "Institutions and Economic Performance: Cross-Country Tests Using Alternative Institutional Measures." *Economics and Politics* 7(3):207–227.

Knack, Stephen, and Philip Keefer. 1997. "Does Social Capital Have an Economic Payoff? A Cross-Country Investigation." *Quarterly Journal of Economics* 112(4):1251–1288.

Kopstein, Jeffrey. 2003. "Postcommunist Democracy: Legacies and Outcomes." *Comparative Politics* 35(2):231–250.

Kopstein, Jeffrey, and David Reilly. 2000. "Geographic Diffusion and the Transformation of the Postcommunist World." *World Politics* 53(1):1–37.

Kornai, János. 1979. "Resource-Constrained versus Demand-Constrained Systems." *Econometrica* 47(4):801–819.

Kornai, János. 1980. *Economics of Shortage*. Amsterdam: North-Holland.

Kornai, János. 1990. *The Road to a Free Economy: Shifting from a Socialist System: The Example of Hungary*. New York: W. W. Norton.

Kornai, János. 1992. *The Socialist System: The Political Economy of Communism*. Princeton, NJ: Princeton University Press.

Kryshtanovskaya, Olga. 2005. *Anatomiia Rossiiskoi Elity [Anatomy of the Russian Elite]*. Moscow: Zakharov.

Lane, David. 2001. The Political Economy of Russian Oil. In *Business and the State in Contemporary Russia*, ed. Peter Rutland. Boulder, CO: Westview Press.

Lasswell, Harold D. 1936. *Politics: Who Gets What, When, How*. New York: McGraw-Hill.

Latynina, Yuliia. 1999. *Okhota na Iziubria*. Moscow: Olma-Press.

Ledeneva, Alena V. 1998. *Russia's Economy of Favors: Blat, Networking and Informal Exchange*. Cambridge: Cambridge University Press.

Levi, Margaret. 1988. *Of Rule and Revenue*. Berkeley: University of California Press.

Lieberman, Evan S. 2002. "Taxation Data as Indicators of State–Society Relations: Possibilities and Pitfalls in Cross-National Research." *Studies in Comparative International Development* 36(4):89–115.

Lipset, Seymour Martin, and Stein Rokkan. 1967. Cleavage Structures, Party Systems, and Voter Alignments: An Introduction. In *Party Systems and Voter Alignments*, ed. Seymour Martin Lipset and Stein Rokkan. New York: Free Press.

Lipton, David, and Jeffrey Sachs. 1990. "Privatization in Eastern Europe: The Case of Poland." *Brookings Papers on Economic Activity* 1990(2):293–333.

Lopez-Claros, Augusto, and Sergei V. Alexashenko. 1998. "Fiscal Policy Issues during the Transition in Russia." IMF Occasional Paper No. 155.

Łoś, Maria, and Andrzej Zybertowicz. 2000. *Privatizing the Police-State: The Case of Poland*. New York: Palgrave Macmillan.

MacFarquhar, Rory. 1997. "Taxes in Russia." *Russian Economic Trends Monthly Update* December.

Malesky, Edmund. 2006. "Straight Ahead on Red: The Mutually Reinforcing Impact of Foreign Direct Investment and Local Autonomy in Vietnam." Unpublished manuscript.

Manion, Melanie. 1996. "Corruption by Design: Bribery in Chinese Enterprise Licensing." *Journal of Law, Economics, and Organization* 12(1):167–195.

Martin, Cathie Jo. 1991. *Shifting the Burden: The Struggle over Growth and Corporate Taxation*. Chicago: University of Chicago Press.

Martin, Cathie Jo, and Duane Swank. 2004. "Does the Organization of Capital Matter? Employers and Active Labor Market Policy at the National and Firm Levels." *American Political Science Review* 98(4):593–611.

Martinez-Vazquez, Jorge, and Robert McNab. 2000. "The Tax Reform Experiment in Transitional Countries." Andrew Young School of Policy Studies Working Paper 00-1.

McFaul, Michael. 1995. "State Power, Institutional Change, and the Politics of Privatization in Russia." *World Politics* 47(2):210–243.

McKinnon, Ronald. 1997. Market-Preserving Federalism in the American Monetary Union. In *Macroeconomic Dimensions of Public Finance: Essays in Honor of Vito Tanzi*, ed. Mario I. Blejer and Teresa Ter-Minassian. London: Routledge.

McLean, Iain. 2000. "The Divided Legacy of Mancur Olson." *British Journal of Political Science* 30(4):651–668.

Megginson, William L., and Jeffrey M. Netter. 2001. "From State to Market: A Survey of Empirical Studies on Privatization." *Journal of Economic Literature* 39(2):321–389.

Meltzer, Allan H., and Scott F. Richard. 1983. "Tests of a Rational Theory of the Size of Government." *Public Choice* 41(3):403–418.

Mertens, Jo Beth, and Jean Tesche. 2002. "VAT Revenues in the Russian Federation: The Role of Tax Administration in Their Decline." *Public Budgeting and Finance* 22(2):87–113.

Migdal, Joel S. 1988. *Strong Societies and Weak States*. Princeton, NJ: Princeton University Press.

Mikhailov, Nikolai, Richard G. Niemi, and David W. Weimer. 2002. "Application of Theil Group Logit Methods to District-Level Vote Shares: Tests of Prospective and Retrospective Voting in the 1991, 1993, and 1997 Polish Elections." *Electoral Studies* 21(4):631–648.

Milgrom, Paul, Douglass C. North, and Barry R. Weingast. 1990. "The Role of Institutions in the Revival of Trade: The Law Merchant, Private Judges, and the Champagne Fairs." *Economics and Politics* 2(1):1–23.

Milner, Helen V., and Robert O. Keohane. 1996. Internationalization and Domestic Politics: An Introduction. In *Internationalization and Domestic Politics*, ed. Robert O. Keohane and Helen V. Milner. Cambridge: Cambridge University Press.

Mitra, Pradeep, and Nicholas Stern. 2003. "Tax Systems in Transition." World Bank Policy Research Working Paper No. 2947.

Moore, Mick. 2004. "Revenues, State Formation, and the Quality of Governance in Developing Countries." *International Political Science Review* 25(3):297–319.

Morozov, Alexander. 1996. "Tax Administration in Russia." *East European Constitutional Review* 5(2/3):39–47.

Murphy, Kevin M., Andrei Shleifer, and Robert W. Vishny. 1989. "Industrialization and the Big Push." *Journal of Political Economy* 97(5):1003–1026.

Newbery, David M. 1995. "Tax and Benefit Reform in Central and Eastern Europe." CEPR Discussion Paper 1167.

Newcity, Michael A. 1986. *Taxation in the Soviet Union*. New York: Praeger.

North, Douglass C. 1990. *Institutions, Institutional Change and Economic Performance.* Cambridge: Cambridge University Press.

Nye, John V. C. 2007. *War, Wine, and Taxes: The Political Economy of Anglo-French Trade, 1689–1900.* Princeton, NJ: Princeton University Press.

O'Dwyer, Conor. 2004. "Runaway State Building: How Political Parties Shape States in Postcommunist Eastern Europe." *World Politics* 56(4):520–553.

O'Dwyer, Conor. 2006. *Runaway State-Building.* Baltimore, MD: Johns Hopkins University Press.

O'Dwyer, Conor, and Branislav Kovalčík. 2007. "And the Last Shall Be First: Party System Institutionalization and Second-Generation Economic Reform in Post-communist Europe." *Studies in Comparative International Development* 41(4):3–26.

Olson, Mancur. 1965. *The Logic of Collective Action: Public Goods and the Theory of Groups.* Cambridge, MA: Harvard University Press.

Olson, Mancur. 1982. *The Rise and Decline of Nations: Economic Growth, Stagflation, and Social Rigidities.* New Haven, CT: Yale University Press.

Osborne, Martin J., and Ariel Rubinstein. 1990. *Bargaining and Markets.* San Diego: Academic Press.

Pacek, Alexander, Grigore Pop-Eleches, and Joshua A. Tucker. 2007. "Disenchanted or Discerning? Voter Turnout in Post-Communist Countries." Unpublished manuscript.

Page, Scott E. 2006. "Path Dependence." *Quarterly Journal of Political Science* 1(1):87–115.

Papke, Leslie E., and Jeffrey M. Wooldridge. 1996. "Econometric Methods for Fractional Response Variables with an Application to 401 (K) Plan Participation Rates." *Journal of Applied Econometrics* 11(6):619–632.

Peltzman, Sam. 1976. "Toward a More General Theory of Regulation." *Journal of Law and Economics* 19(2):211–240.

Persson, Torsten, and Guido Tabellini. 2000. *Political Economics: Explaining Economic Policy.* Cambridge, MA: MIT Press.

Persson, Torsten, and Guido Tabellini. 2005. *The Economic Effects of Constitutions.* Cambridge, MA: MIT Press.

Pevehouse, Jon C. 2005. *Democracy from Above: Regional Organizations and Democratization.* Cambridge: Cambridge University Press.

Pierson, Paul. 2004. *Politics in Time: History, Institutions, and Social Analysis.* Princeton, NJ: Princeton University Press.

Ponomareva, Maria, and Ekaterina Zhuravskaya. 2004. "Federal Tax Arrears in Russia: Liquidity Problems, Federal Redistribution, or Regional Protection?" *Economics of Transition* 12(3):373–398.

Pop-Eleches, Grigore. 2007. "Historical Legacies and Post-Communist Regime Change." *Journal of Politics* 69(4):908–926.

Przeworski, Adam. 1991. *Democracy and the Market: Political and Economic Reforms in Eastern Europe and Latin America.* Cambridge: Cambridge University Press.

Putnam, Robert D. 1993. *Making Democracy Work: Civic Traditions in Modern Italy.* Princeton, NJ: Princeton University Press.

Pyle, William. 2006*a*. "Collective Action and Post-Communist Enterprise: The Economic Logic of Russia's Business Associations." *Europe-Asia Studies* 58(4):491–521.

Pyle, William. 2006*b*. "Resolutions, Recoveries and Relationships: The Evolution of Payment Disputes in Central and Eastern Europe." *Journal of Comparative Economics* 34(2):317–337.

Qian, Yingyi, and Barry R. Weingast. 1996. "China's Transition to Markets: Market-Preserving Federalism, Chinese Style." *Journal of Policy Reform* 1(2):149–185.

Rabin, Matthew. 1993. "Incorporating Fairness into Game Theory and Economics." *American Economic Review* 83(5):1281–1302.

Radaev, Vadim. 2002. "Entrepreneurial Strategies and the Structure of Transaction Costs in Russian Business." *Problems of Economic Transition* 44(12):57–84.

Robinson, James A., and Thierry Verdier. 2002. "The Political Economy of Clientelism." CEPR Working Paper 3205.

Roeder, Philip G. 2001. The Rejection of Authoritarianism. In *Postcommunism and the Theory of Democracy*, ed. Richard D. Anderson, Jr., M. Steven Fish, Stephen E. Hanson, and Philip G. Roeder. Princeton, NJ: Princeton University Press.

Rogowski, Ronald. 1998. Democracy, Capital, Skill, and Country Size: Effects of Asset Mobility and Regime Monopoly on the Odds of Democratic Rule. In *The Origins of Liberty*, ed. Paul W. Drake and Mathew D. McCubbins. Princeton, NJ: Princeton University Press.

Roland, Gérard. 2000. *Transition and Economics: Politics, Markets, and Firms*. Cambridge, MA: MIT Press.

Roland, Gérard, and Thierry Verdier. 1994. "Privatization in Eastern Europe: Irreversibility and Critical Mass Effects." *Journal of Public Economics* 54(2):161–183.

Roland, Gérard, and Thierry Verdier. 2003. "Law Enforcement and Transition." *European Economic Review* 47(4):669–685.

Rosenstein-Rodan, Paul N. 1943. "Problems of Industrialisation of Eastern and South-Eastern Europe." *Economic Journal* 53(210/211):202–211.

Rubinfeld, Daniel. 1987. Economics of the Local Public Sector. In *Handbook of Public Economics*, ed. Alan J. Auerbach and Martin Feldstein. Amsterdam: North-Holland.

Rutland, Peter. 2001. Introduction: Business and the State in Russia. In *Business and the State in Contemporary Russia*, ed. Peter Rutland. Boulder, CO: Westview Press.

Rutland, Peter. 2004. Putin and the Oligarchs. In *Putin's Russia: Past Imperfect, Future Uncertain (Second Edition)*, ed. Dale R. Herspring. Lanham, MD: Rowman & Littlefield.

Sachs, Jeffrey. 1994. *Poland's Jump to the Market Economy*. Cambridge, MA: MIT Press.

Sandler, Todd. 1992. *Collective Action: Theory and Applications*. Ann Arbor: University of Michigan Press.

Schaffer, Mark E., and Gerard Turley. 2002. Effective vs. Statutory Taxation: Measuring Effective Tax Administration in Transition Economies. In *Institutional Change in Transition Economies*, ed. Michael Cuddy and Ruvin Gekker. Aldershot, UK: Ashgate.

Schmidt, Klaus. 2000. "The Political Economy of Mass Privatization and the Threat of Expropriation." *European Economic Review* 44(2):817–868.

Schrad, Mark L. 2001. "The Liquor Question in the Russian Federation: Monopoly and Excise-Tax Control Regimes in a Historical Perspective." M.A. thesis, Georgetown University.

Schumpeter, Joseph A. 1991 [1918]. The Crisis of the Tax State. In *Joseph A. Schumpeter: The Economics and Sociology of Capitalism*, ed. Richard A. Swedberg. Princeton, NJ: Princeton University Press.

Seabright, Paul. 1996. "Accountability and Decentralisation in Government: An Incomplete Contracts Model." *European Economic Review* 40(1):61–89.

Shafer, D. Michael. 1994. *Winners and Losers: How Sectors Shape the Developmental Prospects of States*. Ithaca, NY: Cornell University Press.

Shepsle, Kenneth A. 1986. Institutional Equilibrium and Equilibrium Institutions. In *Political Science: The Science of Politics*, ed. Herbert Weisberg. New York: Agathon.

Shleifer, Andrei, and Daniel Treisman. 2000. *Without a Map: Political Tactics and Economic Reform in Russia*. Cambridge, MA: MIT Press.

Shleifer, Andrei, and Robert W. Vishny. 1994. "Politicians and Firms." *Quarterly Journal of Economics* 109(4):995–1025.

Sigelman, Lee, and Langche Zeng. 1999. "Analyzing Censored and Sample-Selected Data with Tobit and Heckit Models." *Political Analysis* 8(2):167–182.

Sinha, Aseema. 2005. "Understanding the Rise and Transformation of Business Collective Action in India." *Business and Politics* 7(2):Article 2.

Slider, Darrell. 1999. "Pskov under the LDPR: Elections and Dysfunctional Federalism in One Region." *Europe-Asia Studies* 51(5):755–767.

Slinko, Irina, Evgeny Yakovlev, and Ekaterina Zhuravskaya. 2005. "Laws for Sale: Evidence from Russian Regions." *American Law and Economics Review* 7(1):284–318.

Sonin, Konstantin. 2005. "Provincial Protectionism." Unpublished manuscript.

Steinmo, Sven. 1993. *Taxation and Democracy*. New Haven, CT: Yale University Press.

Steinmo, Sven, and Caroline Tolbert. 1998. "Do Institutions Really Matter? Taxation in Industrialized Democracies." *Comparative Political Studies* 31(2):165–187.

Stepanyan, Vahram. 2003. "Reforming Tax Systems: Experience of the Baltics, Russia, and Other Countries of the Former Soviet Union." IMF Working Paper 03/173.

Stewart, Mark B. 1983. "On Least Squares Estimation When the Dependent Variable Is Grouped." *Review of Economic Studies* 50(4):737–753.

Stigler, George J. 1971. "The Theory of Economic Regulation." *Bell Journal of Economics* 2(1):3–21.

Svejnar, Jan. 2002. "Transition Economies: Performance and Challenges." *Journal of Economic Perspectives* 16(1):3–28.

Swank, Duane, and Sven Steinmo. 2002. "The New Political Economy of Taxation in Advanced Capitalist Democracies." *American Journal of Political Science* 46(3):642–655.

Tanzi, Vito. 2001. Creating Effective Tax Administrations: The Experience of Russia and Georgia. In *Reforming the State: Fiscal and Welfare Reform in Post-Socialist Countries*, ed. János Kornai, Stephan Haggard and Robert R. Kaufman. Cambridge: Cambridge University Press.

Tanzi, Vito, and George Tsibouris. 2000. "Fiscal Reform over Ten Years of Transition." IMF Working Paper 00/113.

Tarrow, Sidney. 1998. *Power in Movement: Social Movements and Contentious Politics (Second Edition)*. Cambridge: Cambridge University Press.

Tarschys, Daniel. 1998. "Tributes, Tariffs, Taxes and Trade: The Changing Sources of Government Revenue." *British Journal of Political Science* 18(1):1–20.

Tedds, Lindsay M. 2007. "Keeping It off the Books: An Empirical Investigation into the Characteristics of Firms That Engage in Tax Noncompliance." Unpublished manuscript.

Thelen, Kathleen. 1999. "Historical Institutionalism in Comparative Politics." *Annual Review of Political Science* 2:369–404.

Tiebout, Charles M. 1956. "A Pure Theory of Local Expenditures." *Journal of Political Economy* 64(5):416–424.

Tilly, Charles. 1992. *Coercion, Capital, and European States, AD 990–1990*. Cambridge, MA: Blackwell.

Tompson, William. 2005. "Putting Yukos in Perspective." *Post-Soviet Affairs* 21(2):159–181.

Tomz, Michael, Jason Wittenberg, and Gary King. 2003. "CLARIFY: Software for Interpreting and Presenting Statistical Results, Version 2.1." Stanford University, University of Wisconsin, and Harvard University. Available at http://gking.harvard.edu.

Tomz, Michael, Joshua A. Tucker, and Jason Wittenberg. 2002. "An Easy and Accurate Regression Model for Multiparty Electoral Data." *Political Analysis* 10(1):66–83.

Treisman, Daniel. 1999*a*. "Political Decentralization and Economic Reform: A Game-Theoretic Analysis." *American Journal of Political Science* 43(2):488–517.

Treisman, Daniel. 1999*b*. "Russia's Tax Crisis: Explaining Falling Tax Revenues in a Transitional Economy." *Economics and Politics* 11(2):145–169.

Treisman, Daniel. 2006. "Fiscal Decentralization, Governance, and Economic Performance: A Reconsideration." *Economics and Politics* 18(2):219–235.

Tucker, Joshua A. 2006. *Regional Economic Voting: Russia, Poland, Hungary, Slovakia and the Czech Republic, 1990–1999*. Cambridge: Cambridge University Press.

Verba, Sidney, Kay Lehman Schlozman, and Henry E. Brady. 1995. *Voice and Equality: Civic Voluntarism in American Politics*. Cambridge, MA: Harvard University Press.

Volkov, Vadim. 2002. *Violent Entrepreneurs: The Use of Force in the Making of Russian Capitalism*. Ithaca, NY: Cornell University Press.

Way, Lucan. 2002. "The Dilemmas of Reform in Weak States: The Case of Post-Soviet Fiscal Decentralization." *Politics and Society* 30(4):579–598.

Way, Lucan, and Stephen Collier. 2004. "Beyond the Deficit Model: Social Welfare in Post-Soviet Georgia." *Post-Soviet Affairs* 20(3):258–284.

Webber, Carolyn, and Aaron Wildavsky. 1986. *A History of Taxation and Expenditure in the Western World*. New York: Simon & Schuster.

Weingast, Barry R. 1995. "The Economic Role of Political Institutions: Market-Preserving Federalism and Economic Development." *Journal of Law, Economics, and Organization* 11(1):1–31.

Weingast, Barry R. 2002. Rational-Choice Institutionalism. In *Political Science: State of the Discipline*, ed. Ira Katznelson and Helen V. Milner. New York: W. W. Norton.

Weinthal, Erika, and Pauline Jones Luong. 2002. "Energy Wealth and Tax Reform in Russia and Kazakhstan." *Resources Policy* 27(4):1–9.

Western, Bruce. 1998. "Causal Heterogeneity in Comparative Research: A Bayesian Hierarchical Modelling Approach." *American Journal of Political Science* 42(4):1233–1259.

Weyland, Kurt. 1998. "From Leviathan to Gulliver? The Decline of the Developmental State in Brazil." *Governance: An International Journal of Policy and Administration* 11(1):51–75.

White, Stephen. 1995. *Russia Goes Dry*. Cambridge: Cambridge University Press.

Williamson, Oliver. 1975. *Markets and Hierarchies*. New York: Free Press.

Williamson, Oliver. 1985. *The Economic Institutions of Capitalism*. New York: Free Press.

Wittenberg, Jason. 2006. *Crucibles of Political Loyalty: Church Institutions and Electoral Continuity in Hungary*. Cambridge: Cambridge University Press.

Woodruff, David. 2000. *Money Unmade: Barter and the Fate of Russian Capitalism*. Ithaca, NY: Cornell University Press.

World Bank. 2002. *Transition: The First Ten Years*. Washington, DC: World Bank.

Yakovlev, Andrei. 2001. "'Black Cash' Tax Evasion in Russia: Its Forms, Incentives and Consequences at Firm Level." *Europe-Asia Studies* 53(1):33–55.

Zellner, Arnold. 1962. "An Efficient Method of Estimating Seemingly Unrelated Regressions and Tests for Aggregation Bias." *Journal of the American Statistical Association* 57(298):348–368.

Zhuravskaya, Ekaterina. 2000. "Incentives to Provide Local Public Goods: Fiscal Federalism, Russian Style." *Journal of Public Economics* 76(3):337–368.

Author Index

Acemoglu, Daron, 28, 62, 158, 161
Adolph, Christopher, 109
Aitken, Brian, 49
Alam, Asad, 141
Alchian, Armen, 62
Alexashenko, Sergei V., 25, 45
Alexseev, Mikhail A., 2
Alt, James E., 30, 93
Appel, Hilary B., 22, 29
Arthur, Brian, 128
Åslund, Anders, 133

Balcerowicz, Leszek, 13, 133
Banerji, Arup, 141
Barbone, Luca, 22, 31
Bates, Robert H., 4, 61, 130, 161
Batra, Geeta, 43
Baturo, Alexander, 28
Beck, Nathaniel, 109
Bednar, Jenna, 161
Bentley, Arthur F., 163
Berenson, Marc P., 36, 41, 113
Berglof, Erik, 146
Berkowitz, Daniel, 50
Bernheim, Douglas B., 62, 79
Bernstein, Marver H., 71
Besley, Timothy, 38, 72, 158
Bird, Richard M., 26
Blanchard, Olivier, 7

Bogetic, Zeljko, 30
Boix, Carles, 28, 161
Bolton, Patrick, 146
Boycko, Maxim, 133
Brady, Henry E., 61
Brennan, Geoffrey, 161
Brown, Annette N., 21, 30
Brown, J. David, 138–140
Buchanan, James M., 161
Bueno de Mesquita, Ethan, 114
Bunce, Valerie, 128

Cai, Hongbin, 50, 162
Campbell, John L., 157
Carpenter, Daniel P., 71, 159
CEFIR, 143
Centre of Social Projecting Vozrozhdeniye, 2
Chamberlin, John, 61
Chaudhry, Kiren Aziz, 30
Cheasty, Adrienne, 22, 24
Cheibub, Joeé Antonio, 28, 61
Clement, Cynthia, 134
Coase, Ronald, 62
Coate, Stephen, 72
Coates, Dennis, 130
Collier, David, 132
Collier, Ruth Berins, 132
Collier, Stephen, 92
Colton, Timothy J., 39
Crawford, Robert, 62

181

Author Index

Wooldridge, Jeffrey M., 44
World Bank, 139, 140, 142, 143

Yakovlev, Andrei, 66
Yakovlev, Evgeny, 69

Zellner, Arnold, 33
Zeng, Langche, 44
Zhuravskaya, Ekaterina, 7, 50, 69, 114, 159
Zybertowicz, Andrzej, 72, 91

Subject Index

Africa, 13
Albania, 31, 41
Armenia, 29

Baltic states, 1, 5
  see also individual countries
barter, 2
  see also under tax compliance
Belarus, 1, 39
Britain, 16
Bulgaria, 30
Business Environment and Enterprise
  Performance Survey (BEEPS), 18,
  42, 68, 88–93, 130

capture, 39, 71
  compared to exchange, 69
casual heterogeneity, 75, 88, 102–103,
  117
Colbert, Jean Baptiste, 5
collective action, 14
  determinants of, 60, 92–94
  limits to conventional
    understanding, 70–72, 82, 163
  problem, 2, 10, 13, 16, 60–61
  see also under representation through
    taxation
collective good, definition, 11
collective-goods provision
  ability to discriminate in, 72–73,
    83–84, 89–92, 97, 99, 105

and collective action, 94–98
measurement of, 89
and tax compliance, general,
  98–101
variation across countries, 12, 16, 18,
  87–88, 101–113, 156
  see also representation through
    taxation: model of
Commonwealth of Independent States
  (CIS), 20, 26
  see also Soviet Union, former
competition policy, 143
compositional data, 32, 108–110
contracts
  noncontractible provisions, 61, 64,
    65, 71, 159
  social, 61
corruption, 14, 89, 143
critical junctures, 132
Czech Republic, 135

Danegeld, 158
demand, inelastic, 3
developing countries, 63, 160
Dubai Ports World, 159–160

Eastern Europe
  definition, 5
  see also individual countries
economic activity, new vs. old, 6, 16,
  18–19, 129, 156–157

190

Yoshiko Herrera, *Imagined Economies: The Sources of Russian Regionalism*

J. Rogers Hollingsworth and Robert Boyer, eds., *Contemporary Capitalism: The Embeddedness of Institutions*

John D. Huber and Charles R. Shipan, *Deliberate Discretion? The Institutional Foundations of Bureaucratic Autonomy*

Ellen Immergut, *Health Politics: Interests and Institutions in Western Europe*

Torben Iversen, *Capitalism, Democracy, and Welfare*

Torben Iversen, *Contested Economic Institutions*

Torben Iversen, Jonas Pontussen, and David Soskice, eds., *Union, Employers, and Central Banks: Macroeconomic Coordination and Institutional Change in Social Market Economics*

Thomas Janoski and Alexander M. Hicks, eds., *The Comparative Political Economy of the Welfare State*

Joseph Jupille, *Procedural Politics: Issues, Influence, and Institutional Choice in the European Union*

Stathis Kalyvas, *The Logic of Violence in Civil War*

David C. Kang, *Crony Capitalism: Corruption and Capitalism in South Korea and the Philippines*

Junko Kato, *Regressive Taxation and the Welfare State*

Robert O. Keohane and Helen B. Milner, eds., *Internationalization and Domestic Politics*

Herbert Kitschelt, *The Transformation of European Social Democracy*

Herbert Kitschelt, Peter Lange, Gary Marks, and John D. Stephens, eds., *Continuity and Change in Contemporary Capitalism*

Herbert Kitschelt, Zdenka Mansfeldova, Radek Markowski, and Gabor Toka, *Post-Communist Party Systems*

David Knoke, Franz Urban Pappi, Jeffrey Broadbent, and Yutaka Tsujinaka, eds., *Comparing Policy Networks*

Allan Kornberg and Harold D. Clarke, *Citizens and Community: Political Support in a Representative Democracy*

Amie Kreppel, *The European Parliament and the Supranational Party System*

David D. Laitin, *Language Repertoires and State Construction in Africa*

Fabrice E. Lehoucq and Ivan Molina, *Stuffing the Ballot Box: Fraud, Electoral Reform, and Democratization in Costa Rica*

Mark Irving Lichbach and Alan S. Zuckerman, eds., *Comparative Politics: Rationality, Culture, and Structure*

Evan Lieberman, *Race and Regionalism in the Politics of Taxation in Brazil and South Africa*

Marino Regini, *Uncertain Boundaries: The Social and Political Construction of European Economies*

Marc Howard Ross, *Cultural Contestation in Ethnic Conflict*

Lyle Scruggs, *Sustaining Abundance: Environmental Performance in Industrial Democracies*

Jefferey M. Sellers, *Governing from Below: Urban Regions and the Global Economy*

Yossi Shain and Juan Linz, eds., *Interim Governments and Democratic Transitions*

Beverly Silver, *Forces of Labor: Workers' Movements and Globalization since 1870*

Theda Skocpol, *Social Revolutions in the Modern World*

Regina Smyth, *Candidate Strategies and Electoral Competition in the Russian Federation: Democracy Without Foundation*

Richard Snyder, *Politics after Neoliberalism: Reregulation in Mexico*

David Stark and László Bruszt, *Postsocialist Pathways: Transforming Politics and Property in East Central Europe*

Sven Steinmo, Kathleen Thelen, and Frank Longstreth, eds., *Structuring Politics: Historical Institutionalism in Comparative Analysis*

Susan C. Stokes, *Mandates and Democracy: Neoliberalism by Surprise in Latin America*

Susan C. Stokes, ed., *Public Support for Market Reforms in New Democracies*

Duane Swank, *Global Capital, Political Institutions, and Policy Change in Developed Welfare States*

Sidney Tarrow, *Power in Movement: Social Movements and Contentious Politics*

Kathleen Thelen, *How Institutions Evolve: The Political Economy of Skills in Germany, Britain, the United States, and Japan*

Charles Tilly, *Trust and Rule*

Daniel Treisman, *The Architecture of Government: Rethinking Political Decentralization*

Lily Lee Tsai, *Accountability without Democracy: How Solidary Groups Provide Public Goods in Rural China*

Joshua Tucker, *Regional Economic Voting: Russia, Poland, Hungary, Slovakia and the Czech Republic, 1990–1999*

Ashutosh Varshney, *Democracy, Development, and the Countryside*

Jeremy M. Weinstein, *Inside Rebellion: The Politics of Insurgent Violence*

Stephen I. Wilkinson, *Votes and Violence: Electoral Competition and Ethnic Riots in India*

Jason Wittenberg, *Crucibles of Political Loyalty: Church Institutions and Electoral Continuity in Hungary*

Elisabeth J. Wood, *Forging Democracy from Below: Insurgent Transitions in South Africa and El Salvador*

Elisabeth J. Wood, *Insurgent Collective Action and Civil War in El Salvador*